RESEARCH METHODOLOGY

Research Methodology

Dr Suman Kalyan Chaudhury
Dr Santanu Kumar Das

KALPAZ

ISBN : 978-93-5128-205-1
Price : ₹ 1150

First Published, 2016

Published by

Kalpaz Publications
C-30, Satyawati Nagar,
Delhi-110052
Ph. : 9212142040
E-mail: kalpaz@hotmail.com

Printed at : G. Print Process, Delhi

Cataloging in Publication Data—DK

Courtesy: D.K. Agencies (P) Ltd. <docinfo@dkagencies.com>

Chaudhury, Suman Kalyan, 1972- **author.**

Research methodology / Dr. Suman Kalyan Chaudhury, Dr. Sanatnau Kumar Das.

pages cm

Includes bibliographical references and index.

1. Research—Methodology. I. Das, Sanatnau Kumar, author. II. Title.

LB2369.C43 2016 DDC 001.42 23

Contents

Frequently Used Terms in Research Studies

APA : American Psychological Association
CATI : Computer-assisted telephone interviewing
CBA : Cost-benefit analysis
CEA : Cost-effectiveness analysis
CER : Control event rate
CoE : Code of ethics
DSM : Diagnostic and Statistical Manual of Mental Disorders
DV : Dependent variable
EBP : Evidence-based practice
EER : Experimental event rate
exp : Experiment or experimental study
H : Hypothesis
Ha : Alternate hypothesis
H0 : Null hypothesis
HSO : Human service organisation
ILL : Interlibrary loan
IRB : Institutional review board
IT : Information technology
IV : Independent variable
IVR : Interactive voice response
MIS : Management information system
NGO : Nongovernmental organisation
NNH : Number needed to harm
NNT : Number needed to treat
NPO : Nonprofit organisation
NS : Not statistically significant
O/B ratio : Odds-to-benefit ratio

OE	:	Observed effect or outcome variable (also known as DV)
PE	:	Programme evaluation
PI	:	Principal investigator
PIN	:	Personal identification number
QL	:	Qualitative research
QN	:	Quantitative research
QoL	:	Quality of life
Ques.	:	Question
R or **(R)**	:	Randomisation
RBI	:	Relative benefit increase
RCT	:	Randomised controlled trial
Rel.	:	Reliability
RRI	:	Relative risk increase
RRR	:	Relative risk reduction
S	:	Statistically significant
SSR	:	Single-system research
ToC	:	Table of contents
Val.	:	Validity
X	:	Main treatment effect (also known as IV)
X-axis	:	Horizontal line on a graph
Y-axis	:	Vertical line on a graph

Commonly Used Abbreviations in Research Studies

Abbreviation	Explanation
Anon	anonymous (it is used where the author is not known)
art	'article'
aug	'augmented'
bk	'book'
( )	'Brackets' (used around word (s) inserted with in quotes
bull	'bulletin'
c.	'copyright' (it is used when the date of publication is not given)
c.ca,	cira; about or approximately (it is used to refer dates)
cf-	'confer'; compare
Chap(s).	chapter, chapters
Col; cols,	'column(s)'
ed.(s)	'editor(s); edited, 'edition'
e.g.	'for example'
enl.	'enlarged'
et.al	'et al' and others (it is used to refer co-authors when there are three or more authors)
et. alibi	and elsewhere.
et.seq	'et sequens' and the following
etc.	'el centra'.
f.,ff-	'the page, pages following'
fac.	facsimile
Fig(s)	figure; figures
ibid	ibidem'; in the same place or work (used when two or more successive foot notes refer to the

same work; if reference is to different page(s), page numbers are specified)

idem. 'the same' (used when a footnote refers to the same work and the same page as the previous foot note)

i.e. 'id esf; that is

infra 'below'

l.ll. 'line, lines'

loc.cit 'loco citaco', in the place cited (it is used when reference is made to the same place, that is same page, as a preceding but not immediately preceding reference; used with last names of author only)

MS.,MSS 'manuscript, manuscripts'

n.nn. 'note or foot note, notes for footnotes'

N.B. 'nota bene', note well.

n.d 'no date of publication given'

No(s). 'number(s)'

n.p. 'no place of publication given'

op.cit. 'opere citato'; in the work cited (used when reference is made to the same work as a preceding but not immediately preceding references; abbreviation follows authors name but precedes page reference)

p.,pp. 'page, pages' (e.g., p. 50; pp. 5-10)

par(s) 'paragraph(s) (e.g., par.56)

passim 'here and there' (it is generally used to refer to opinions, attitudes etc. on a number of different pages)

pt(S) 'part(s)' (e.g., pt IV)

q.v. 'quod vide'; which see.

rev. 'revised or revision'

Sec(s) 'section (s)'

[sic] 'thus' (it is used to call attention to the fact that an error in spelling, grammar, was in the original; enclosed by square brackets and placed immediately after the word or phrase in question)

sig. signature

St.	stanza
sups.	supplements.
supra.	above,
trans.	'translator, translated,
vide	translation'
v.vv.	see
viz,	verse, verses 'videlicet; namely.
Vol(s)	'volumes'
Vs.	'versus'; against
(...)	(omission in quoted matter up to one paragraph in length)

1

Introduction to Research

Introduction

Human beings are interested to acquire information from different sources. They are always eager to know more. It is never ending. This urge of acquiring information is ever present in every individual. Human beings are always asking questions and try to find out answers for that. This urge has contributed to the development of human beings in all sphere of life such as economic, social, commercial, scientific and cultural aspects.

They have adopted different ways to gather information. They acquired knowledge through enquires, analysis, and interpretations. The methods used are also changing when there is development in thoughts and views. One method which is treated as best one for conducting enquiry at one time may become outdated when there is advancement of tools and technologies. It also changes when there is changes in the problems faced by the society.

Man used different methods for acquiring knowledge. The basic methods adopted for acquiring knowledge are through natural or evolutionary changes, trial and error and generalising from experiences or facts. Today men acquire knowledge through a systematic method which is generally known as research.

Meaning and Definition

Research can be generally defined as a systematic method of finding solutions to problems. In common, research refers to a search for knowledge. It is a systematic enquiry seeking facts through objective verifiable methods in order to discover the relationship among them and to presume broad principles or laws from them. In other words it refers to the systematic method consisting of enunciating the problems, formulating hypothesis, collecting the facts or data, analysing the facts and reaching certain conclusions either in the form of solution or certain generalisations for some theoretical formulation.

Several authors have defined research in a number of ways. The Webster's International Dictionary defines research as, "a careful critical enquiry or examination in seeking facts or principles; diligent investigation in order to ascertain something."

According to Robert Ross, "research is essentially an investigation, a recording and an analysis of evidence for the purpose of gaining knowledge."

According to John W Best, "research may be defined as the systematic and objective analysis and recording of controlled observations that may lead to the developments of generalisations, principles or theories, resulting in prediction and possible ultimate control of events."

According to Clifford Woody, "research comprises defining and redefining problems, formulating hypothesis or suggested solutions; collecting, organising and evaluating data, making deductions and reaching conclusions and at last carefully testing the conclusions to determine whether they fit in formulating hypothesis."

A broad definition of research is given by Martyn Shuttleworth - "In the broadest sense of the word, the definition of research includes any gathering of data, information and facts for the advancement of knowledge."

Another definition of research is given by Creswell who states that - "Research is a process of steps used to collect and analyse information to increase our understanding of a topic or issue". It consists of three steps: Pose a question, Collect data to answer the question, and Present an answer to the question.

All these definitions indicate that research is only a systematic enquiry into the existing system of knowledge to disapprove or approve or to arrive at new conclusions for the betterment of the existing system.

The systematic approach relating to generalisation and the formulation of theory is called research. In this sense research is a systematic method consisting of enunciating the problem, formulating hypothesis, collecting the facts or data, analysing the facts and reaching certain conclusions either in the form of solutions towards the concerned problem or in certain generalisations for some theoretical formulation.

Characteristics of Research

From the above definitions we can assess the characteristics of research as follows:

- Research means the discovery of new knowledge.
- Research is essentially an investigation.
- Research is related with the solution of a problem.
- It gives prominence on the development to generalisation of theories or principles that will help in predicting the future occurrences.
- It is based on observation or experimental evidences.
- It demands accurate observation or experimentation.
- It involves collection of new data from first hand sources and secondary sources.
- The collected data is used for a new purpose.
- Expertise is required in research because skill is required to enquire and gather data, and to understand and analyse data.
- In research, the researchers try to find out answers for unsolved questions.
- It should be carefully recorded and reported.
- Patience is required for conducting research.

In short, Research is an exciting opportunity to learn about a particular area for which we have a defined interest.

Objectives of Research

The most important objectives of research are to discover the truth or facts by applying scientific procedures or methods. Even though each research study has its specific objectives, in general, Research in any discipline has the following objectives:

1. To find out new techniques or generalisations with old data.
2. To find out generalisations or conclusions with new data.

3. To attempt to arrive at more conclusions from the same set of data.
4. To find or resolve the contradictions existing in the area of study.
5. To gain familiarity with a phenomena or to achieve a new insight into it.
6. To test a hypothesis of a casual relationship between variables.

Sri, Young, Pauline describes the main objectives of research. They are given below:

1. To explore and understand human behaviour and social life.
2. To explore, analyse and conceptualise social life.
3. To extent, correct or verify knowledge.
4. To find explanation for unexplained social phenomena.
5. To clarify the doubtful and correct the misconceived facts of social life.
6. To provide new insights into organised society and its social structures.

Importance of Research

The importance of research is enhancing day by day. Complexity of the society, growth of business, structural changes in the society, government policies etc have increased the importance of the research. Thus, the importance of research is outlined below:

1. Helps in solving societal problems: Social science research study the problems of the society and also suggest remedial measures.

2. Useful to different sections of the society: Research is useful to students, politicians, academicians, literary men and other intellectuals. It provides knowledge and new information to these sections.

3. It is helpful to industrial concerns: Different types of research are conducted by business concerns such as marketing research, operation research, motivation research etc. all these researches helps the management to take suitable decisions at correct time.

4. It acts as a basis for government policies: Research is conducted before introducing the policies of the government. For example, economic survey is conducted before preparing the annual budget. The problems of businessmen, farmers, artisans, teachers and various sections of the society can be studied with the help of research. It will help the governments chalk out proper policies and programmes.

Qualities of a Good Research

Research is related with acquisition of knowledge. It is the process of a methodical study of any particular issue or topic or area of investigation with an attempt to discover or to find out precious facts for further application. So a good research should possess certain qualities which are given below.

1. Systematic: A good research must be always systematic. It should be preceded in a specified manner with the well-defined rules. If a systematic research is followed it will avoid guessing for arriving decisions and conclusions.

2. Logical: If must be logical. It must be guided with logical rules of reasoning. Both deduction and induction must be adopted to arrive at generalisations. Induction is the process of reasoning from an individual to the general. The deductions are the process of reasoning from general to the individual.

3. Empirical: A good research should be empirical. That means a research should always be supported by empirical facts or data.

4. Replicable: It should be able to verify the results obtained from research by replicating the study.

Qualities of a Good Researcher

The quality of the research work depends upon the good qualities of researcher. He should possess the following qualities.

1. Scientific approach: A researcher should have a scientific approach. He/she should not have personal likes and dislikes related with the research work. That means the research work conducted by him/her should not be influenced by the researchers personnel prejudices and pride.

2. Hunter of truth and knowledge: An excellent researcher should always seek truth and knowledge. He/she should be always eager to get truthful knowledge from his/her study.

3. Alert: A good researcher should be alert to recognise, be grateful for, and analyse all changes including even the smallest changes in the situation of study.

4. Power to understand: He should be able to grasp even minute details of study quickly.

5. Well educated: A good researcher should be well educated and trained personnel. He should be well versed with the area of study.

6. Patience: The research is a combination of success or failure. So the researcher should be patient and courageous. He should be able to complete the work.

Research Methods

These are the methods or techniques that are used for conducting research. Research methods can be classified into three groups.

- Methods concerned with collection of data.
- Statistical techniques which are used for establishing relationship between data and the unknown.
- Methods which are used to evaluate the accuracy of the results obtained.

Research Methodology

It is the systematic way to solve problems. Research is a process through which we attempt to achieve systematically and with the support of data the answer to a question, the resolution of a problem, or a greater understanding of a phenomenon. It is the systematic way to solve problems. This process, which is frequently called research methodology.

According to Dickinson Mc Graw and George Watson, the procedure by which researcher goes about their work of describing, explaining, and predicting phenomena are called methodology. Methodoloy is the study of methods. Thus, research methodology describes the logic behind a particular method for the refferred research study.

The core concept underlying all research is its methodology. It is not enough to follow the research procedures without an intimate understanding that research methodology directs the whole effort -Where critical decisions are made and where organising, planning, and directing the whole project take place. The methodology controls the study, dictates the acquisition of the data, and arranges them in logical relationships, sets up a means of refining the raw data, contrives an approach so that the meanings that lie below the surface of those data become manifest, and finally issues a conclusion or series of conclusions that lead to an expansion of knowledge. The entire process is an integrated effort as well as an appreciation of its component parts. Thus, research methodology has two primary functions:

1. To control and dictate the acquisition of data.
2. To enclose the data after acquisition and extract meaningfulness from them.

Research methodology is the description, explanation and justification of various methods of conducting research. The researchers should know how to develop certain indices or tests, how to calculate the mean, the mode, the median, or the standard deviation or chi square, and how to apply the particular research techniques. He should also need to know of these methods or techniques which are relevant and which are not, and what would they mean and indicate and why? We should consider research methods and the logic behind the method we use in the context of our research study. We should also explain why we are using a particular method or technique and why we are not using others.

Research Process or Steps in Research

Research process consists of a series of actions or steps necessary to carry out research effectively. There are a number of well recognised steps or procedure for doing research. But one should remember that the various steps involved in a research process are not mutually exclusive; nor they are separate and distinct. The following are the well recognised steps or procedure in a typical social sciences research study.

1. Tentative or temporary selection of the research problem.
2. Initial survey of literature.
3. Finalising the research problem.
4. Extensive literature survey.
5. Developing the hypotheses.
6. Preparation of the research design.
7. Determination of the sample design.
8. Collecting the data.
9. Execution of the project.
10. Analysis of data.
11. Testing of hypothesis.
12. Arriving at generalisations and interpretations.
13. Preparation of the reports or presentation of the results.

TYPES OF RESEARCH

The following are the different types of research:

1. Pure Research

Pure or basic or fundamental or theoretical research is an original type of research. It is mainly concerned with generalisations and with the formulation of a theory. It is a search for broad principles and synthesis without any immediate utilisation of objectives. Generally it is an intellectual exploration arising from voracious intellectual curiosity through which universal laws and theories are established.

According to Pauline V. Young, "gathering knowledge for knowledge's sake is termed as pure or basic research." E.g.; research relating to pure mathematics and some natural phenomena. Research studies conducted related with human behaviour for making generalisation about human behaviour is also a fundamental research.

The pure research is not related with solving problems any practical problems. The pure research leads to discovery of new theories and development of existing theories. Basic research is more unanticipated the results are only seen in the long term. It lays the foundation for applied research.

Features of pure research

Following are the features of pure research:

- Pure research is the basic research related with principles or laws or rules.
- The aim of this research is to attainment of the knowledge and truth.
- It is concerned with the theoretical aspect of a science.
- It tries to find out cause and effect relationship in social phenomina.
- It verifies the old established principles and laws.
- It is mainly concerned with generalisations and with the formulation of a theory.
- It is undertaken for the sake of the knowledge without any intension to apply it in practice.
- It lays the foundation for applied research.

2. Applied Research or Action Research

It is also known as action research because it is related with a particular project and problem. It may relate current activity or immediate practical situations. This type of research is conducted on the basis of application of theories or models for finding a solution for an immediate problem faced by the society. It suggests ways for the solution of social problems. In other words it is conducted to test the basic assumptions and the validity of theory under a given situation. For example, Research conducted to identify social, economic and political trends of a particular situation or marketing research. Research in the field of social planning, social legislation, social hygiene, religion etc are known applied research.

Some view action research as a philosophy of research rather than a method of research. They reject the attempted separation of the investigator and the problem, and instead embrace research that has the specific goal of social change, where the research is participatory and emancipatory.

Features of Applied Research

Following are the features of applied research

- It is carried out to find a solution to real life problem requiring an action or policy decision.
- It is conducted on the basis of application of theories or models for finding a solution for an immediate problem faced by the society.
- It may incidentally contribute to the development of theoretical knowledge by testing the theory.

Difference Between Basic Research and Applied Research

Pure Research	*Applied Research*
1. It is concerned with generalisations and with the formulation of a theory.	1. It is related with application of theories or models for finding a solution for an immediate problem faced by the society.
2. It studies any problems.	2. It studies problems with immediate social consequences.

(Contd.)

(Contd. Table)

Pure Research	*Applied Research*
3. It aims to publish research report.	3. It aims at bringing out actionable points quickly.
4. Reports prepared in technical language.	4. Reports are prepared in common knowledge.
5. It tries to explain why things happen.	5. It tries to explain how things can be changed.
6. It is free-form and Basic research is more serendipitous - the results are only seen in the long term.	6. It is goal-oriented.
7. Investigators look into problems that they find professionally interesting.	7. The researchers have a specific goal in mind, and must produce it in a fixed amount of time.
8. Success is measured by how interesting the discoveries are.	8. Success is measured by how well the goal is achieved.

3. Social Science Research

Scientific research used by physical scientists has a long history. The social scientists used scientific method in researches only in the late eighteenth century. It was developed further in present century. A social research deals scientific investigations conducted in the field of social sciences and also in behavioural sciences. According to Pauline V Young, social research is, "The systematic method of discovering new facts or verifying old facts, their sequences, their interrelationship, casual explanations and natural laws which govern them."

In the words of Herring, "Scientific research is a cumulative process; it is also a rejected process, especially in the social sciences, the understanding can be (advanced) not only by gains in knowledge but also by discovering outworn assumptions".

In the words of Slessinger and Stevenson, Social science research aims to, "Extend, correct or verify knowledge, whether that knowledge aids in the Construction of a theory or in the practice of an art".

Social research involves the application of scientific method for the understanding, studying and analysing of social life in order to modify, correct or verify the existing knowledge as a system. It deals with human behaviour and social problems. Thus, social science research studies the social values, beliefs, traditions, events etc. It also tries to find out new facts and verifies old facts on the basis of applying certain tests on old facts.

Objectives of social research

The following are the important objectives of social research.

- It facilitates to acquire new knowledge in order to gain insight into existing problems.
- It also helps to acquire scientific knowledge about the social phenomenon and social facts.
- It assists to understand the human behaviour and its interaction with the social institutions.
- It will help to develop tools of analysis and to test it against the complex human behaviour and social institutions.
- It is helpful for promoting social welfare and to diagnose social problems. It also helps to suggest effective treatments to rinse out society of its inhibitions and weakness.
- It is useful in guiding social policies and planning.
- It can help to identify the causes of social evils and problems.

Motives of Social Research

According to Pauline V Young, there are four main motives for social research. They are given below:

(a) Desire to understand the cause effect relationship of some social phenomena.

(b) Desire to discover new theories, concepts, and techniques in older to gain knowledge more efficiently. In these contexts quantitative techniques are applied to social research for more hale and precise results.

(c) Both curiosity and necessity may be motivating factors for social research. The human minds always want to know the unknown and explore unexploited areas. Social research is a means by which unknown factors may be explored to explain social phenomena.

(d) The explanation, analysis and understanding of social phenomena are sometimes the motivating factors for social research.

Assumptions of Social Research

Social research is based on certain assumptions which are explained below:

(a) It is assumed that a social researcher is able to conduct a neutral or unbiased study. It requires non-interference, earnestness, honesty and impartiality.

(b) It is assumed that there is some kind of natural law or norm in the society and all social events are based on it.

(c) It is presumed that there is a cause and effect relationship between social behaviour and events. It is presumed that similar causes produce similar effects under similar conditions.

(d) It is assumed that there is a possibility of drawing representative samples from the whole population. It is also assumed that study is possible with the representative sample and the result represents the whole population from which samples are drawn.

(e) It is also assumed society consist of fairly homogeneous groups. These groups are known as ideal groups. The behaviour of the ideal group is same as that of other groups.

(f) The other assumption is that social events are changeable to scientific study and the human behaviour follows the same trend.

Importance of Social Research

Research is done to know unknown facts or acquire new knowledge. It has significance in the society. As there is new knowledge it will affect the society also.

(a) Acts as a Guide to social planning: Social research has an important role to play in guiding social planning. The success of the social planning depends upon the available knowledge of societal resources of the people, their liabilities, their culture, their needs and problems. Social research provides sufficient knowledge and information about the problems and resources of the people.

(b) Provide knowledge to control: Social research provides first-hand information about the working of society, organisation, and other institutions. It gives more power to control the society as a whole.

(c) Suggests suitable remedial measures: Social research tries to provide remedial measures necessary to solve the societal problems.

(d) Works as sound base for prediction: In social research prediction of social facts are possible. It helps as a guide to social growth on proper ways and leads to achieve the objectives.

(e) Identification of social evils: Social research can disclose and identify the social evils faced by the society. On the basis of such information necessary action can be taken to eradicate such problems.

4. Descriptive research

Descriptive research is research of fact finding. It is simplest type of research. Descriptive study is designed to gather descriptive information. It provides information for formulating complex studies. The data needed for study are collected through observation, interview and mailed questionnaire. It does not deal with testing of hypothesis.

It is generally used in physical, natural sciences, and social sciences. The major use of descriptive research is explanation of the state of affairs as it exists at present. It portrays accurately the characteristics of a particular individual situation or group and to determine the frequency of occurrence of such events. It includes surveys and fact finding enquires of different kinds. Descriptive research is applications to problems which satisfy certain criteria such as:

- The problem must be describable.
- The data should be amenable for reliability and significance.
- It is possible to develop valid standards of comparison.
- It should provide itself to verifiable procedures of collection and analysis of data.

It aims at identifying the various features of a commodity or problem under study. But it does deal with testing of proposition or hypothesis. According to Black James A. and Dean J. Champion, it can reveal potential relationship between variables, thus setting the stage for more elaborate investigation later. Information obtained through descriptive research can be used for prediction about areas of social life. It provides information, which is needed for planning social action programmes.

5. Analytical research

In analytical research the available information or data are analysed and critical evaluations are made to solve the problems. Analytical study is primarily concerned with testing of hypothesis and specifying and interpreting relationships. In this study mathematical models and advanced statistical techniques like correlation, multivariate analysis is employed. It concentrates on analysing data in depth and examines relationship from various angles. This method is widely used in business and other fields in which quantitative numerical data are produced. It is primarily used to measure variables, to compare groups, and to verify association between variables. Necessary data required for analysis are collected from primary sources and secondary sources.

Difference between descriptive research and analytical research

I. In descriptive study, the researcher identifies relevant variables but does not aim at testing hypothesis. Analytical study is primarily concerned with testing hypothesis and specifying and interpreting the relationship.

II. Simple statistical tools like average, percentages etc. are used in descriptive study. In analytical study, advanced statistical tools like correlation, multivariate analyses etc. are widely used.

6. Quantitative research and Qualitative research

Quantitative research is based on the measurement of a quantity or amount. It is concerned with qualitative phenomena. Motivation research is a qualitative research. This type of research is specifically important in behavioural sciences where the aim is to discover the underlying motives of human behaviour. Attitude or opinion research is a qualitative research because it is designed to find out the feeling or thought of people about a particular subject.

7. Empirical research

It relies on experience or observation alone. It is a data based research. The conclusions derived are capable of being verified by observation or on experience. It is suitable when poof is sought to verify certain variables affects the other variables in some way. In this study the researcher should provide himself with a working hypothesis or guess as to the possible results. Then he collects necessary data to prove or disprove the hypothesis.

8. Conceptual research

This type of research is conducted by philosophers and thinkers to develop new concepts. It is related with theory or conceptual idea.

9. Experimental research

The cornerstones of science are experimental and creative research. Experimental research is primarily concerned with cause and effect. That means it is helpful to know the cause and effect relationships under controlled experiments. Researchers identify the variables of interest, and try to determine if changes in one variable (called the independent variable, or cause) result in changes in another (called the dependent variable, or effect). Experimental research might be used to determine if a certain material is fire-resistant or if a new teaching method achieves better results.

In this study the researcher selects two indistinguishable or identical groups which exist in physical and natural sciences. Experimental research has limited application in social science. Both groups should be identical in terms of the characteristics of the fact under study. One of the groups is experimental groups and other is controlled group. Experimental group depicts experimental variables. The difference between the experimental and control groups outcome is attributed to the effect of the experimental value. For example, a person wants to study the impact of the use of chemical fertiliser. He selects two identical plots for study. The plots are identical in relation with fertility of soil, climate, irrigation used and techniques used etc. he applies chemical fertiliser in experimental plot. The difference in the yield of plots indicates the effect of chemical fertiliser.

Some variables might be present that are neither the independent nor the dependent variable, but still need to be considered. Experimental research has limited application in social science. It is carried out in different stages such as the trial and error approach, and through the controlled experimental by precise definition of terms, concepts etc.

10. Exploratory research

There are certain studies for which comprehensive or in-depth analysis or investigation is required to derive solutions for problems. This method is adopted when the results are not obtained on observation basis. In this connection certain hypothesis are formulated and it is tested through exploratory research. It also helps to classify the concepts, establishing priorities for further research arrangement of problems priority wise etc.

In other words exploratory research is a preliminary study of a new problem about which the researcher has little or no knowledge. For example, a doctor conducts an initial investigation on patient who is suffering from a new ill for getting some clue about the illness. It usually takes the form of a pilot study. It does not attempt to test hypotheses. But it lays the foundation for the formulation of different hypothesis of research problem.

The main objectives of exploratory research is

(a) To generate new ideas.
(b) To make an exact formulation of the problem.
(c) To gather information for elucidation of concepts.
(d) To decide whether it is feasible to attempt the study.

The following are the different types of exploratory researches:

I. Literature survey: Literature survey is a study, which involves collection of literature in the selected area of research in which the researcher has little experience. It will help to provide further clue for advanced research. Example, review of wholesale price index, periodic stock exchange reports etc.

II. Experience survey: Experience survey is related with conducting informal interviews with experienced persons in the area of study. It will help the researcher to secure an insight into the subject and its various particulars, which is helpful to carry out further research. This survey may yield a new hypothesis. Examples, technology forecasting, portfolio management, investment decisions etc.

III. Study of insight stimulating cases: An intensive study of selected cases is conducted in an unexplored area. It will help to get stimulating insights about the topic.

11. Creative Research

Creative research involves the development of new theories, new procedures and new inventions. For example, a computer scientist might apply new algorithms for managing a computer system, an economist might develop a new model of the world economic system, or an electronic engineer might design a new radio. Creative research is used to some extent in all fields. Unlike experimental research, creative research is much less structured and cannot always be preplanned.

Creative research includes both practical and theoretical research. Practical creative research is about the design of physical things and the development of real-world processes. Theoretical creative research is about the discovery or creation of new models, theorems, algorithms, etc. Practical research mainly proceeds by trial and error.

12. Historical Research

Studies of the past to find cause-effect patterns are known as historical research. It is often geared towards using past events to examine a current situation and to predict future situations (e.g. stock-market forecasting). The research does not directly study current causes or effects. Data is gathered from primary sources (i.e. records made when the past events took place) and secondary sources (i.e. records made after the events took place).

The objective of historical research is to find out explanations generalisations from the past trends in order to understand the present and to foresee the future. The success of historical research depends upon the relevance, completeness, reliability, ingenuity and adequacy of the collected data.

The following steps are to be followed while conducting an historical research:

- Examine the feasibility of the study.
- Formulate the selected problem for study. Design the plan of study.
- Locate the sources of data.
- Test the genuineness of the source of data and examine the validity of data.
- Collect the relevant data from the correct sources.
- Check and cross check the relevant data.

- Arrange the collected data in a logical manner.
- Meaningful interpretations and generalisation should be made by adopting induction process.

13. Expository Research

This research is based purely on existing information, and normally results in 'review'-type reports. By reading widely on a field, and then comparing, contrasting, analysing and synthesising all points of view on a particular subject, a researcher can often develop important new insights. An analysis of the works of a prominent author or a comparison of the tax structures in developed and developing countries are both examples of this type of research.

14. Ex-Post Facto Research

Ex *post facto* means "from after the fact", and this type of research typically occurs when data are available that could not be generated by experimental research. It is important to note that for *ex post facto* research to be valid, the researcher must eliminate all other possible causes. It is a systematic empirical enquiry in which the scientists do not have direct control of independent variables because their manifestations have already occurred or because they are inherently not manipulated.

15. Diagnostic Research

It is similar to descriptive research. It aims to identify the causes of a problem and finds possible solution for solving the problems. It is directed towards discovering what is happening and what can be done about.

16. Evaluation Research

Evaluation research is done to access the effectiveness of implemented social or economic programmes. It is a type of applied research. It is done to asses or appraises the quality and quantity of an activity and its performance, and to specify its attributes and conditions required for its success. There are three types of evaluations.

(a) Simultaneous evaluation: It is a social audit on an ongoing programme. It is a continuous process. The objective of this evaluation is to evaluate the quality of implementation. It also serves as feed-back for improving the performances.

(b) Periodic evaluation: This type of evaluation is done after the completion of one phase or a project.

(c) Terminal evaluation: It is conducted after the completion of the entire project.

17. Case Study

Case study is a method or technique or an approach of exploring or analysing the life of a social unit. The social unit may be a person or a family or institution or an organisation or a community.

In the words of Pauline V Young, "a comprehensive study of a social unit -be that unit a person, a group, a social institution, a district or community is called a case study".

Researcher Robert K. Yin defines the case study research method as an empirical inquiry that investigates a contemporary phenomenon within its real-life context; when the boundaries between phenomenon and context are not clearly evident; and in which multiple sources of evidence are used.

A case study is best defined as an in-depth study of a single unit (a relatively bounded phenomenon). It is a comprehensive study through which one can know precisely the factors and causes of a particular phenomenon. It is also a very good method for collecting data about an individual, a family or a group of persons. Case study research shines at bringing us to an understanding of a complex issue or object and can extend experience or add strength to what is already known through previous research. Case studies emphasise detailed contextual analysis of a limited number of events or conditions and their relationships.

As the business is concerned a case study describes typical administrative issues or problems confronting a manager in an organisation. Ideally it is taken from real life. It is usually presented from the standpoint of the decision-maker involved. Researchers have used the case study research method for many years across a variety of disciplines. Social scientists, in particular, have made wide use of this qualitative research method to examine contemporary real-life situations and provide the basis for the application of ideas and extension of methods.

Critics of the case study method believe that the study of a small number of cases can offer no grounds for establishing reliability or generality of findings. Others feel that the intense exposure to study of the case biases the findings. Some dismiss case study research as useful only as an exploratory tool. Yet researchers continue to use the case study research method with success in carefully planned and crafted studies of real-life situations, issues, and problems. Reports on case studies from many disciplines are widely available in the literature.

Many renowned case study researchers such as *Robert E. Stake, Helen Simons, and Robert K. Yin* have written about case study research and suggested techniques for organising and conducting the research successfully. The case study involves the following steps:

(a) Determine and define the research problem
(b) Select the cases and determine data gathering and analysis techniques
(c) Prepare to collect the data
(d) Collect data in the field
(e) Evaluate and analyse the data
(f) Prepare the report

(a) Determine and Define the Research Problem

The first step in case study research is to establish a firm research focus. The researcher ascertains the centre of the study by forming problem or questions to be studied and determining a purpose for the study. The research object in a case study is often a programme, an entity, a person, or a group of people. Each object is likely to be intricately connected to political, social, historical, and personal issues, providing wide ranging possibilities for questions and adding complexity to the case study. The researcher investigates the object of the case study in depth using a variety of data gathering methods to produce evidence that leads to understanding of the case and answers the research questions.

Case study research generally answers one or more questions which begin with "how" or "why." The questions are targeted to a limited number of events or conditions and their inter-relationships. To assist in targeting and formulating the questions, researchers conduct a literature review. This review establishes what research has been previously conducted and leads to refined, insightful questions about the problem.

Careful definition of the questions or problem at the beginning locates where to look for evidence and helps determine the methods of analysis to be used in the study. The literature review, definition of the purpose of the case study, and early determination of the potential audience for the final report guide how the study will be designed, conducted, and publicly reported.

(b) Select the Cases and Determine Data Gathering and Analysis Techniques

During the design stage of case study research:

- The researcher decides the approaches to be used to select a single or multiple real-life cases for examining it in depth.
- He also determines which instruments and data gathering approaches are to be used for study. When multiple cases are used, each case is treated as a single case. Conclusions derived from each case can then be used as information contributing to the whole study but each case remains a single case.
- Excellent case studies carefully select cases and carefully examine the choices available from among many research tools available in order to increase the validity of the study. Careful discrimination at the point of selection also helps erect boundaries around the case.

The researcher must determine whether to study cases which are unique in some way or cases which are considered typical and may also select cases to represent a variety of geographic regions, a variety of size parameters, or other parameters. A useful step in the selection process is to repeatedly refer back to the purpose of the study in order to focus attention on where to look for cases and evidence that will satisfy the purpose of the study and answer the research questions posed. Selecting multiple or single cases is a key element, but a case study can include more than one unit of embedded analysis. For example, a case study may involve study of a single industry and a firm participating in that industry. This type of case study involves two levels of analysis and increases the complexity and amount of data to be gathered and analysed.

A key strength of the case study method involves using multiple sources and techniques in the data gathering process. The researcher determines in advance what evidence is to sillier and what analysis techniques are to use with the data to answer the research questions. Data gathered is normally largely qualitative, but it may also be quantitative. Tools to collect data can include surveys, interviews, documentation review, observation, and even the collection of physical artifacts.

The researcher must use the designated data gathering tools systematically and properly in collecting the evidence. Throughout the design phase, researchers must ensure that the study is well constructed to ensure construct validity, internal validity, external validity, and reliability.

I. Construct validity requires the researcher to use the correct measures for the concepts being studied.

II. Internal validity (especially important with explanatory or causal studies) demonstrates that certain conditions lead to other conditions and requires the use of multiple pieces of evidence from multiple sources to uncover convergent lines of inquiry. The researcher strives to establish a chain of evidence forward and backward.

III. External validity reflects whether or not findings are generalise beyond the immediate case or cases; the more variations in places, people, and procedures a case study can withstand and still yield the same findings, the more external validity. Techniques such as cross-case examination and within-case examination along with literature review help to ensure external validity.

IV. Reliability refers to the stability, accuracy, mill precision of measurement. Exemplary case study design ensures that the procedures used are well documented and can be repeated with the same results over and over again.

(c) Prepare to Collect the Data

A case study research generates a large amount of data from multiple sources. So a systematic organisation of the data is important to prevent the researcher from becoming overwhelmed by the amount of data and to prevent the researcher from losing sight of the original research purpose and questions. Advance preparation assists in handling large amounts of data in a documented and systematic fashion. Researchers prepare databases to assist with categorising, sorting, storing, and retrieving data for analysis.

Exemplary case studies

Exemplary case studies prepare

I. Good training programmes for investigators.
II. Establish clear protocols and procedures in advance of investigator field work.
III. Conduct a pilot study in advance of moving into the field in order to remove obvious barriers and problems.

I. The investigator training programme

The investigator training program covers the basic concepts of the study, terminology, processes, and methods, and teaches investigators how to properly apply the techniques being used in the study. The programme also trains investigators to understand how the gathering of data using multiple techniques strengthens the study by providing opportunities for triangulation during the analysis phase of the study. The programme covers protocols for case study research, including time deadlines, formats for narrative reporting and field notes, guidelines for collection of documents, and guidelines for field procedures to be used. Investigators need to be good listeners who can hear exactly the words being used by those interviewed.

II. Qualifications for investigators

Qualifications for investigators also include being able to ask good questions and interpret answers. Good investigators review documents looking for facts, but also read between the lines and pursue collaborative evidence elsewhere when that seems appropriate. Investigators need to be flexible in real-life situations and not feel threatened by unexpected change missed appointments, or lack of office space. Investigators need to understand the purpose of the study and grasp the issues and must be open to contrary findings. Investigator must also be aware that they are going into the world of real human beings who may be threatened or unsure of what the case study will bring.

III. Conduct a pilot test

After investigators are trained, the final advance preparation step is to select a pilot site and conduct a pilot test using each method so that problematic areas can be uncovered and corrected. Researchers need to anticipate key emblems and events, identify key people, prepare letters of Introduction, establish rules for confidentiality, and actively opportunities to revisit and revise the research design in to address and add to the original set of Research Questions.

(d) Collect Data in the Field

The researcher must collect and store multiple sources of evidence comprehensively and systematically, in formats that in the referenced and sorted so that converging lines of inquiry and patterns can be uncovered. Researchers carefully observe the object of the case study and identify causal factors associated with the observed phenomenon. Re-negotiation of arrangements with the objects of the study or addition of questions to interviews may be necessary as the study progress. Case study research is flexible, but when changes made, they are documented systematically.

Use field notes

Exemplary case studies use field notes and databases to categories and reference data so that it is readily available for subsequent reinterpretation. Field notes record feelings and instinctive guess, pose questions, and document the work in progress. They record testimonies, stories, and illustrations Which Inch can be used in later reports. They may warn of impending bias because of the detailed exposure of the client to special attention, or give an early signal that a pattern is emerging. They assist in determining whether or not the inquiry needs to be reformulated or redefined based on what is being observed. Field notes should be kept separate from the data being collected and stored for analysis.

Maintaining the relationship between the issue and the evidence is mandatory. The researcher may enter some data into a database and physically store other data, but the researcher documents, classifies, and cross-references all evidence so that it can be efficiently recalled for sorting and examination over the course of the study.

(e) Evaluate and Analyse the Data

The researcher examines raw data using many interpretations in order to find linkages between the research object and the outcomes with reference to the original research questions. Throughout the evaluation and analysis process, the researcher remains open to new opportunities and insights. The case study method, with its use of multiple data collection methods and analysts techniques, provides researchers with opportunities to triangulate data in order to strengthen the research findings and conclusions.

The tactics used in analysis force researchers to move beyond initial impressions to improve the likelihood of accurate and reliable findings.

Sort the Data

Exemplary case studies will deliberately sort the data in many different ways to expose or create new insights and will deliberately look for conflicting data to disconfirm the analysis. Researchers categorise, tabulate, and recombine data to address the initial propositions or purpose of the study, and conduct cross-checks of facts and discrepancies in accounts. Focused, short, repeat interviews may be necessary to gather additional data to verify key observations or check a fact.

Specific Techniques

Specific techniques include placing information into arrays creating matrices of categories, creating flow charts or other displays, and tabulating frequency of events. Researchers use the quantitative data that has been collected to corroborate and support the qualitative data which is most useful for understanding the rationale or theory underlying relationships. Another technique is to use multiple investigators to gain the advantage provided when a variety of perspectives and insights examine the data and the patterns. When the multiple observations converge, confidence in the findings increases. Conflicting perceptions, on the other hand, cause the searchers to pry more deeply.

Another technique, the cross-case search for patterns, keeps investigators from reaching premature conclusions by requiring that investigators look at the data in many different ways. Cross-case analysis divides the data by type across all cases investigated. One researcher then examines the data of that type thoroughly. When a pattern from one data type is corroborated by the evidence from another, the finding is stronger. When evidence conflicts, deeper probing of the differences is necessary to identify the cause or source of conflict. In all cases, the researcher treats the evidence fairly to produce analytic conclusions answering the original "how" mid "why" research questions.

(f) Prepare the Report

Exemplary case studies report the data in a way that transforms a complex issue into one that can be understood, allowing the reader to question and examine the study and reach an understanding independent of the researcher. The goal of the written report is to portray a complex problem in a way that conveys a vicarious experience to the reader. Case studies present data in very publicly accessible ways and may lend the reader to apply the experience in his or her own real-life- situation. Researchers pay particular attention to displaying sufficient evidence to gain the reader's confidence that all avenues have been explored, clearly communicating the boundaries of the case, and giving special attention to conflicting propositions.

Techniques for composing the report can include handling each case as a separate chapter or treating the case as a chronological recounting. Some researchers report the case study as a story. During the report preparation process, researchers critically examine the document looking for ways the report is incomplete. The researcher uses representative audience groups to review and comment on the draft document. Based on the comments, the researcher rewrites and makes revisions. Some case study researchers suggest that the document review audience include a journalist and some suggest that the documents should be reviewed by the participants in the study.

Review of Literature

A literature review is an account of what has been published on a topic by accredited scholars and researchers. The literature review is a critical look at the existing research that is significant to the work that the researcher is carried out. Some people think that it is a summary: this is not true. Although the researcher need to summarise relevant research, it is also vital that to evaluate the work, shows the relationship between different works, and show how it relates to work of researchers. So researchers should go through the available literature relating to the field of study to keep himself update in his field and related areas.

A review of literature is not a mere reading. It is focused and directed towards specific purpose. A researcher should selected literatures, which are very much related with his study.

Literature to be reviewed, related with study includes

(a) **Books** (Encyclopedias, Year books, Text books, Reference books)

(b) **Journals** (International and National journal of different subject)

(c) **Reports** (Committee Reports, Commissions Reports, Seminar Reports, Conference Proceedings)

(d) Research Dissertations and Thesis

(e) Newspapers

(f) Micro forms such as audio and video tapes, internet

Objective of the review of literature

Review of literature is needed due to the following reasons.

(a) To attain a background knowledge of the research topic.

(b) To identify the concepts related with the topic.

(c) To formulate research hypotheses.

(d) To recognise suitable methodology, research design, measurement methods and techniques of analysis.

(e) To find out data sources used by other researchers.

(f) To study how other researchers structured their reports.

Review Questions

1. What is research? What are its features?
2. Define research? Explain the importance of research?
3. What are the important objectives of research?
4. What is a Pure or basic or fundamental or theoretical research?
5. Write short notes on
   (i) Action research
   (ii) Descriptive research
   (iii) Empirical research
   (iv) Conceptual research
   (v) Experimental research
   (vi) Expository Research
   (vii) Historical Research
   (viii) Exploratory research
   (ix) Creative Research
   (x) Diagnostic Research

6. Explain case study? What are the steps required in a case study?
7. Distinguish between basic research and applied research?
8. What is research methodology? What are the important steps in research?
9. What is the need for reviewing literature?
10. What is social research? What are its importance's and objectives?

2

Survey, Sample Design and Sampling

Introduction

The survey is a non-experimental, descriptive research method. Survey method is a device for collecting data or factual information of certain desired characteristics of universe. Surveys can be useful when a researcher wants to collect data on phenomena that cannot be directly observed.

Data are usually collected through the use of questionnaires, although sometimes researchers directly interview subjects. Surveys can use qualitative (e.g. ask open-ended questions) or quantitative (e.g. use forced-choice questions) measures.

Features of the survey method

Following are the features of survey method:

1. Survey method is a field study.
2. It seeks responses directly from the respondents.
3. It can cover a very huge population.
4. It an extensive as well as intensive study.
5. A survey covers a definite geographical area.

Objectives of survey

The survey is conducted for the following purposes:

1. To provide information to government or planners or business enterprises.
2. It is used to explain a phenomenon.
3. Surveys are designed to make comparison of demographic groups. For example, to compare group behaviour of low paid workers and highly paid workers.

4. Surveys conducted to know cause and effect relationship is useful for making predictions.

Types of Surveys

There are two basic types of surveys: cross-sectional surveys and longitudinal surveys.

Cross-sectional Surveys

Cross-sectional surveys are used to gather information on a population at a single point in time. An example of a cross-sectional survey would be a questionnaire that collects data on how parents feel about Internet filtering, as of March of 2004. A different cross-sectional survey questionnaire might try to determine the relationship between two factors, like religiousness of parents and views on Internet filtering.

Longitudinal Surveys

Longitudinal surveys gather data over a period of time. The researchers may then analyse changes in the population and attempt to describe and/or explain them. The three main types of longitudinal surveys are trend studies, cohort studies, and panel studies.

(a) Trend Studies

Trend studies focus on a particular population, which is sampled and scrutinised repeatedly. While samples are of the same population, they are typically not composed of the same people. Trend studies, since they may be conducted over a long period of time, do not have to be conducted by just one researcher or research project. A researcher may combine data from several studies of the same population in order to show a trend. An example of a trend study would be a yearly survey of librarians asking about the percentage of reference questions answered using the Internet.

(b) Cohort Studies

Cohort studies also focus on a particular population, sampled and studied more than once. But the focus of the cohort studies may be different. For example, a sample of 2002 graduates of government college Chatrapur at the Berhampur University could be questioned regarding their attitudes toward paraprofessionals in libraries. Five years later, the researcher could question another sample of 2002 graduates, and study any changes in attitude. A cohort study would sample the same class, every time. If the researcher studied the class of 2007 five years later, it would be a trend study, not a cohort study.

(c) Panel Studies

The researcher tries to find out why changes in the population are occurring by using the same sample of people every time. That sample is called a panel. It is known as panel studies. A researcher could, for example, select a sample of B Com graduate students, and ask them questions on their library usage. Every year thereafter, the researcher would contact the Mime people, and ask them similar questions, and ask them the reasons for any changes in their habits. Panel studies, while they can yield extremely specific and useful explanations, can be difficult to conduct. They tend to be expensive, they take a lot of time, and they suffer from high attrition rates. Attrition is what occurs when people drop out of the study.

The difference between cohort study and panel study is that, in case of cohort study different subgroups of the same class every time is used while in case of panel study same group and same member elements are used. Moreover, panel study is more of longitudinal in nature and cohort studies are usually based on two or more cross sectional studies.

Methods of Survey

There are two methods of survey

(a) Census method

(b) Sample method

(a) Census survey

The census method involves a complete enumeration of all mills of the population or universe. All things in any field of inquiry constitute a "Universe" or Population It is the aggregate of all units possessing certain specified characteristics on which the sample seeks to draw inferences. Census method enables to yield correct factual data. This type of enquiry involves great deal of time, money and energy. Although the census method gives correct factual information. It may be incomplete, inadequate and inaccurate. When the universe is small it is better to adopt census method for collection of information.

Complete enquiry or survey is impossible in practice in all. So sample technique is used in all spheres of life, in sample method the enumeration of only a sample part of the population or universe is done.

Merits of Census Survey

The following are the merits of complete enumeration survey.

- The data are collected from each and every item of the population.
- The results are more accurate and reliable.
- Intensive study is possible.
- Collected data can be used for various surveys and analysis.

Demerits of Census Survey

The following are the demerits of complete enumeration survey.

- It requires more time, efforts and money.
- Large number of enumerators is needed to collect data.
- If the universe is infinite, it is not possible to conduct complete enumeration survey.

(b) Sample Survey

A sample is a smaller representation of a large unit or value. So a sample is that part of universe or population which select for the purpose of investigation. The selected respondents constitute sample and the selection process is called sampling and the survey so conducted is called sample survey. Sampling may be defined as, "the selection of part of an aggregate or totality on the basis of which a judgment inference about the aggregate or totality is made".

Merits of Sample Survey

The merits of sample survey are as follows:

- It helps to collect a lot of information from different types of individuals such as their personal characteristics, attitudes, opinions etc.
- It facilitates drawing generalisations about large population on the basis of study of their representative sample.
- In survey method various methods can be adopted to collect data.
- It is useful to verify theories.

Demerits of Sample Survey

The Demerits of sample survey are as follows:

- The feasibility of survey method depends upon the willingness and cooperation of the respondents.
- Sampling survey is subject to sampling error.
- The results of the survey are subject to respondent errors. If the respondent's respondent is not true, it will give misleading results.
- There is a chance of measurement errors.
- There is limit in the collection of information in a particular survey.
- It is not suited for studies related to historical development.
- It is expensive.

Sample Design

A sample design is a definite plan for obtaining a sample for a given population. It refers to the technique or the procedure the researcher would adopt in selecting items for sample. According to Gerald Hursh, "A sample design is the theoretical basis and the practical means by which we infer the characteristics of some population by generalising from the characteristics of relatively few of the units comprising the population".

In many research projects, the opinions of a small number of individuals (a "sample") are used to estimate the beliefs among a much larger population. If the sample is well-designed and selected, the sample's opinions mirror the incidences of the larger population in general and decision-makers can use this information with confidence. If the samples are faulty, however, the information is worthless. Too often firms gather information from whoever can be easily recruited without regard to how well they represent the larger population.

Sample design is determined before data are collected. There are many sample designs from which a researcher can choose one. Some of the designs are easier to apply and certain others are not. The researcher should select an appropriate sample design which is suitable for his study.

Steps in Sampling Design

The sampling process consists of the following steps:

1. Define the population or universe
2. State sampling frame
3. Identify the sampling unit

4. State sampling method.
5. Determine the sample size
6. Spell out the sampling plan
7. Select the sample

1. Define the Population or Universe

It is the first step in developing any sample design. The set of objects technically called universe is clearly defined. The universe can be finite or infinite. In finite universe the number of items is limited. In the case of infinite universe the number of items is infinite. That means we can't measure the number of units. For example, number of stars in the sky.

2. State the sampling frame

After defining the population the sampling frame is to be stated. It is the source list from samples is draw. It contains the names of all items of the universe. It is the means on representing the elements of the population. For example, telephone book, directory etc. If sampling frame is not available the researcher should prepare it.

The Problems relating to sampling frame are as follows:

(a) The first problem is related with non-converge and incompleteness. For example, voters list in a constituency is incomplete due to non-inclusion of voters who works in gulf countries. Such incomplete frames cannot yield representative samples.

(b) Appearance of Clusters of elements is the other problem. For example, list collected from municipality shows the house numbers of the houses situated in a locality. But it does not give the name of the persons living in those households.

(c) Inclusion of foreign element in the list. For example, the voters list includes the name of persons who have already died.

(d) Another problem is duplication. Some items are appearing in the list more than once.

3. Identify the sampling unit

A decision related to sampling unit is to be taken before selecting sample for study. Sampling unit (e.g. state, village etc) may be geographical one or a construction of unit (E.g., construction of a shop) or a social unit (e.g., a school or club). The researcher should select one or more of the sampling unit.

4. State sampling method

There a number of methods used for selecting samples. It includes probability sampling methods, non-probability sampling methods. Out of this the researcher should select one method by which sampling units are to be selected.

5. Determine the sample size

This refers to the number of items to be selected from the universe. The researcher should determine the sample size beforehand. It is a very crucial problem concerned with the researcher. The sample size should not be large or small. It should be optimum. That means the sample size selected is one which fulfills the requirement of consistency, competence, flexibility and representativeness. While selecting the sample size the researcher should consider what amount of precision is required in his work. He should also decide the confidence level for estimate. Budgetary constraints should be considered while selecting the sample size. Apart from the parameters of interest in research study is taken into account while deciding the sample size. For example, a researcher is interested in knowing some average or other measure concerning the population.

6. Spell out the sampling plan

In this stage the researcher should state the operational procedures for selection of the sample. That means he should decide the techniques which are used in selecting the item of sample. In fact it is the sample design.

7. Select the sample

It is the last step. The needed samples are to be selected. The office and field work required to carry out for the selection of the sample.

Features of a Good Sample Design

A flood sample design should have the following characteristics.

- The outcome of a good sample design must be a truly sample.
- The selected sample design should not cause more errors.
- Sample design should be viable on the basis of budget constraints.

- A good sample design is able to control systematic bias effectively.
- The researcher should be able to apply the results of the study conducted on the basis of the sample selected.
- If the sample is well-designed and selected, the sample's opinions mirror the preferences of the larger population in general and decision-makers can use this information with confidence.

Types of Sample Design or Methods or Techniques of Sampling

There are different types of samples designs or techniques, general sampling methods are classified into two.

I. Probability sampling or random sampling

II. Non-probability sampling on non-random sampling.

Probability Sampling

Random sampling is the purest form of probability sampling Probability sampling is also known as chance sampling, probability sample is one in which each member of the population has an equal chance of being selected. This is most simple procedure for drawing a sample from a given population or universe. The sample units are drawn without showing any regard to the character of the population. It is the blind chance that determines whether an item or the other selected. So in probability samples, each member of the population has a known non-zero probability of being selected. The advantage of probability sampling is that sampling error can be calculated.

Features of probability sampling method

(a) Every population has a chance of being selected.

(b) Such chance is known as probability.

(c) Probability sampling helps to select representative samples.

(d) Through randomisation, the danger of unknown sampling bias or errors can be minimised.

(e) It is generally used when a greater degree of accuracy is required for study.

Classification of random sampling:

The random samples can be classified in to two types.

(A) Simple or unrestricted sample.

(B) Restricted random sample.

The choice of these depends on nature of research problem, the non-availability of a good sampling frame, money, and time, desired level of accuracy in the sample and data collection methods. Each of these has its advantages and disadvantages.

A. Simple or Unrestricted Samples

It refers to the method in which each and every item of population or universe has an equal and independent chance of being included in the sample. The underlying feature of random sample is that the personal factor is eliminated in the selection of the sample. The investigator is not exercising his for selecting the items.

Random sampling ensures the law of statistical regularity. The law states that if on an average, the sample chosen is random one; the sample will have the same composition and characteristics as in the universe. This is the reason why random sampling is considered as the best technique for selecting a representative sample. The following are the main features of simple random sampling.

Features of simple or unrestricted samples

1. Each person has same chance as any other of being selected.
2. Standard against which other methods are sometimes evaluated.
3. Suitable where population is relatively small and where sampling frame is complete and up-to-date.

The simple or unrestricted samples are usually obtained by using two methods namely, lottery method and random numbers method.

Lottery method

It is the process of drawing lot from the population or universe. In this method all the items of universe are represented in small chits of paper of same size. Then the chits are folded in the same manner and mixed together. All the chits are deposited in a basket. All samples are picked from these chits with help of a blind folded person.

Random Number Method

Under this method we use random number tables to select samples from the universe. Three such table numbers are noteworthy. They are

(i) Tippet's table of random numbers.
(ii) Kendall and Babington Smith numbers.
(iii) Fisher and Yates numbers.

From these, Tippets number is more popular. It is very simple to select the required random sample with the help of these number tables.

Procedure for selection of sample

1. Obtain a complete sampling frame or source list.
2. Give each case a unique number, starting at one.
3. Decide on the required sample size.
4. Select that many numbers from a table of random numbers or using computer.

Table of random numbers (usually found at back of statistics textbooks) e.g.

92941 04999	77422	25992	27372
94157 43252	83266	47196	94045
48135 34237	46293	46178	50 110
78907 37586	50940	88094	28209
82843 43383	32561	62108	46076

Decide on a pattern of movement through table and stick to it, i.g. numbers from every second column and every row. If a number comes up twice or a number is selected which is larger than population number, discard it.

Merits of simple unrestricted sample

Following are the merits of simple unrestricted sample:

- The items are selected at random in simple random method. So there will be no possibility of personal bias.
- It presents the population in a better way.
- Probability theory can be used to measure the precision of sample results because sample errors follow the principles of chance.

Demerits of simple unrestricted sample

Following are the demerits of simple unrestricted sample:

- It all is expensive.
- The process is time consuming.
- Random sampling may produce the most non-random looking results.

B. Restricted Random Samples

Unrestricted random sampling is a time consuming process and it involves cost and time. It cannot be adopted when the sample size is large. So to increase the efficiency of sampling technique restricted random sampling method is used. It includes

1. Stratified sampling
2. Cluster sampling
3. Multi-stages Cluster sampling
4. Systematic sampling
5. Random Route Sampling

1. Stratified Sampling

Under this method, all people in sampling frame are divided into "strata". Each of these small individual units are called stratum; in plural strata means groups or categories. Here the entire population is divided or subdivided into groups on the basis of homogeny. Within each stratum, a simple random sample or systematic sample is selected.

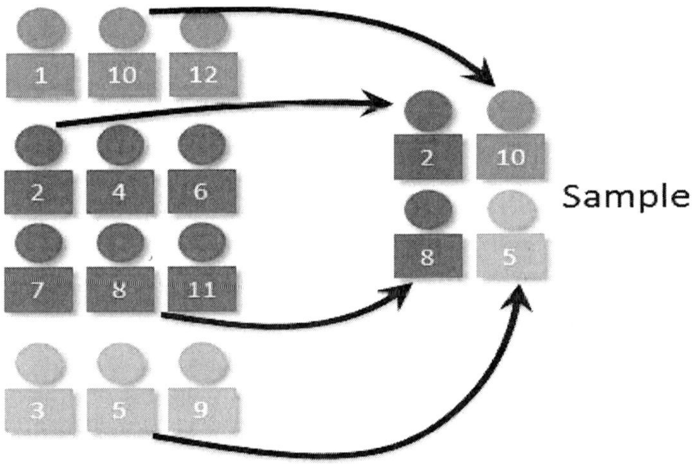

This technique enhances the efficiency of the sampling by dividing the whole universe into homogenous groups or strata on the basis of certain common characteristics. Geographical, sociological and economic characters are used for classifying the universe into strata.

After stratifying universe, the next step is to take decision with regard to the number of sample to be drawn from each stratum. The process employed in determining the number of items to be drawn from each stratum is called allocation. The allocation may be proportionate or disproportionate. In the case of proportionate stratified random sampling plan, the number of items to be drawn from stratum may be proportional to the total number of universe. But in disproportionate random sampling plan, the number of samples to be drawn from stratum may be not proportion to the universe. This method is useful for large heterogeneous population. It is a good method to use when-you are concerned that certain groups within your research population may not be sufficiently represented in your simple random sample.

Stratified samples are well worth pursuing if resources of researcher will allow this because such samples tend to have lower sampling errors when compared with simple random samples. It is easy to see why, when you think about it. In Stratified Sampling, additional key information about the population has been used to inform the selection. In a simple random sample, only the number corresponding to the individual in the sampling frame is used.

Example of stratified sampling -we want to ensure that a sample of five students from a group of 50 contains both male and female students are to be selected in same proportions as in the full population (i.e. the group of 50). First we divide that population into male and female. In this case, suppose there are 22 male students and 28 females.

To work out the number of males and females in the sample

No. of males in sample = (5 / 50) x 22 = 2.2

No. of females in sample = (5 / 50) x 28 = 2.8

We obviously can't interview .2 of a person or .8 of a person, we have to "round" the numbers. Therefore, we choose two males and three females in the sample. These would be selected using simple random or systematic sample methods.

Merits

Following are the merits of stratified sampling :

- It is more representative. In this method the population is first divided into various strata and then a sample is drawn from each stratum. So all groups are represented by samples.
- Stratified sampling ensures greater accuracy.
- Stratified Samples can be more concentrated geographically.
- It is easy to carry out.

Limitations

Following are the demerits of stratified sampling :

- Classifying population into strata is a difficult task.
- The items from each stratum should be randomly selected. It requires the service of experts.
- This method is expensive.

2. Cluster Sampling

This method is often used when there is no satisfactory sampling frame available and a list has to be constructed. This happens, for example in areas where adequate population lists are lacking. Under this method the population or universe is divided into number of clusters or large groups which will form the basis for primary sampling units. These clusters may be village wards, geographical units, social units etc. After forming clusters, a few sample clusters are selected by using unrestricted sampling method. These selected clusters are called primary sampling units. (PSU)

An important consideration in this type of sampling is how many clusters to use. Cluster samples tend to have less precision

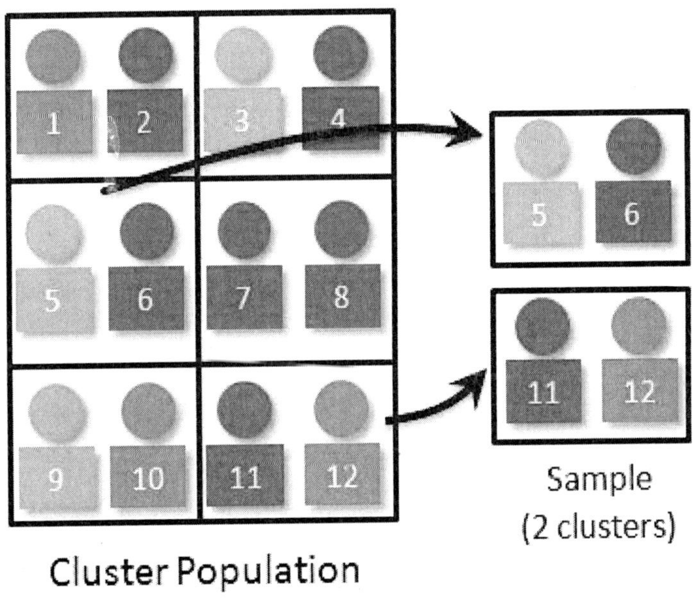

than other forms of sampling and using a small number of clusters may reduce costs, but will not decrease the sampling error. Increasing the number of clusters can improve precision- but of course, will increase the cost and time duration of data collection.

3. Multistage Cluster Sampling

Multistage sampling is a modification of cluster sampling in which a sample rather than a 100 per cent sample of the whole cluster is used at the second stage. This type of sampling is often used in national surveys run. In the first stage the initial flusters are randomly selected. These initial clusters are called the In-Primary Sampling Units PSUs. Then in a second stage, a random sample is set up within the selected PSUs. It is known as multistage cluster sampling.

Difference between Cluster Sampling and Stratified Sampling

The main difference between cluster sampling and stratified sampling lies with the inclusion of the cluster or strata. In stratified sampling the group or strata are divided in such a way that there is much homogeneity within each group and there is marked difference between various groups and strata. But in cluster sampling the universe is divided into groups of clusters in such a way that there is much heterogeneity within each cluster and there is small difference between the clusters.

Merits of cluster sampling

Following are the merits of cluster sampling:

- Multi stage sampling introduces flexibility in sampling method which is lacking in other methods.
- Another advantage of this method is that sub-division into second stage unit need to be carried out only for first stage units. So it is particularly valuable in survey of underdeveloped areas where no source list is available.
- The cost of this method is much less when compared with other sampling methods.
- Sampling under this method does not require much time.
- This method is much easier compared with other methods.
- This method promotes the convenience of fieldwork as it could be done in solid places.

Demerits of Cluster sampling

Following are the demerits of cluster sampling

- From all the different type of probability sampling, this technique is the least representative of the population. The tendency of individuals within a cluster is to have similar characteristics and with a cluster sample, there is a chance that the researcher can have an overrepresented or underrepresented cluster which can skew the results of the study.
- This is also a probability sampling technique with a possibility of high sampling error. This is brought by the limited clusters included in the sample leaving off a significant proportion of the population un-sampled.
- This method is statically less efficient than other probability sampling methods.

Area sampling

Area sampling is a form of cluster sampling. As per this method, clusters consisting of specific geographical areas like districts, talukas etc. are randomly drawn. Such a sampling is called area sampling. It is not a separate method of sampling.

4. Systematic Sampling or Quasi Random Sampling

The systematic sampling method involves ordering of the universe. The ordering may be in alphabetical, numerical, geographical, and any other basis. A particular problem that; can arise with systematic sampling is called periodicity. This occurs when there is some systematic arrangement of people

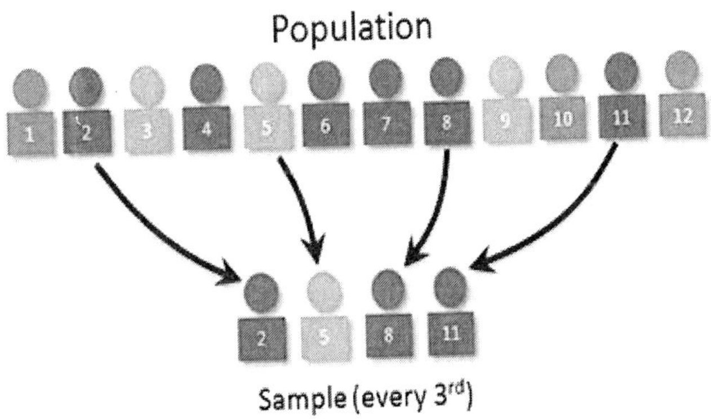

in the sampling frame and can lead to an unrepresentative sample.

It is similar to simple random sampling, but instead of selecting random numbers from tables, we move through list (sample frame) picking every nth name. The method is to select every nth item from the list. I_n refers to the sampling interval.

Sampling interval (I_n) = *Sample Size (n) ÷ Population Size (N)*

The first item between the first and *n* the item is selected at random. The procedure for drawing a systematic sample is actually simpler than a simple random sample. Again, an accurate sampling frame is needed. Then the number of items to be included in sample is to be decided. Dividing the number in the population by the number in the sample gives you the sampling fraction. For example, suppose you have a population of 1000 people and you want to take a sample of 100. The sampling fraction is 100/1000 = 1/10 (or 10 per cent if you prefer to think in percentage terms). We would select every tenth person to be in the sample. However, it is important to select the starting point randomly. Suppose you choose to stall at number 6. The person corresponding to the number 6 in the sampling frame will be in your sample, then person number 16, then 26 and so on until you have your sample of 100.

For example, we have a complete list of 1000 students in our college. We want to draw a sample of 200 out of this population. In this case, *n* the item is to be selected. Here *k* the item is 5 (1000/200). The first item of the sample is selected at random. The item is selected in between one and five. To find out other samples five is to be added with first randomly selected item. If the selected first item is four then the second item will be nine. Then third item is 14, 4th item is 19 and so on.

Merits Systematic Sampling

Following are the merits of systematic sampling.

- Systematic sampling is relatively simple compared with random sampling method.
- The time and work involved in sampling by this method are relatively smaller.

- If population is large, the samples obtained by using this method yield results similar to those obtained by proportional stratified sampling.
- This method is economical than that of the simple random sampling.
- Sample is spread evenly over the population.

Demerits of Systematic Sampling

Following are the demerits of systematic sampling:

- The selection may be affected by bias of the drawer if all the chits which are designed to draw samples are not of identical size, shape and colour.
- It is not suitable for a large sized universe for that it will be very difficult to write down the names or particulars of a large number of units on the chits of paper.
- It consumes lot of time and energy.

5. Random Route Sampling

This method is used in market research surveys - mainly for sampling households, shops, garages and other premises in urban areas. Address is selected at random from sampling frame (usually electoral register) as a starting point. Interviewer then give instructions to identify further addresses by taking alternate left- and right-hand turns at road junctions and calling at every nth address (shop, garage etc.)

Morits

Following are the merits of Random route sampling:

- May be saving in time.
- Bias may be reduced because interviewer has to call at clearly defined addresses - not able to choose.

Demerits

Following are the demerits of Random route sampling:

- Characteristics of particular areas (e.g., poor/ rich) may mean that sample is not representative.
- Open to abuse by interviewer because difficult to check that instructions fully carried out.

Non-Probability Sampling

It is not always possible to undertake a probability method of sampling, such as in random sampling. For example, there is not a complete sampling frame available for certain groups of the population e.g. the elderly; people who are attending a football match; people who shop in a particular part of town. Another factor to bear in mind is that many of the probability sampling methods described above may mean that researchers would have to undertake a postal or telephone survey delivery or might be expected to go from house to house. Some of the problems are low response rate. In a non-probability sample, some people have a greater, but unknown, chance than others of selection. In non-probability sampling, the degree to which the sample differs from the population remains unknown.

This type of sampling technique does not give any assurance whether every element has chance of being included in sample. In non-probability samples, there is no way of calculating the margin of error and the confidence level. The important non-probability methods are as follows:

1. Accidental sampling
2. Quota sampling
3. Purposive or judgment sampling
4. Convenience sampling
5. Snowball sampling
6. Self-selection

The Advantages of non-probability sampling methods are as follows:

- It is a cheaper method.
- It is used when sampling frame is not available.
- It is useful when population is so widely dispersed that cluster sampling would not be efficient.
- It is often used in exploratory studies, e.g. for hypothesis generation.
- Some research is not interested in working out what proportion of population gives a particular response but rather in obtaining an idea of the range of responses on ideas that people have.

1. Accidental Sampling

In this method the researcher simply contacts and picks up a case which he come across and thus continuing the process till the total sample reaches a designated size. For instance, the researcher may take the first 100 persons he meets any one of the area or avenue who are willing to be interviewed or to provide the information required.

The Merits of accidental sampling are as follows

- It is economical and convenient.
- It can also afford a basis for stimulating insights and hypothesis.
- It is also useful in those cases where too much accuracy is not needed.

2. Quota Sampling

It is a type of judgment sampling. In this method quotas are set up according to some specified characteristics. For example, On the basis of income groups. Each interviewer is then asked to interview a certain number of persons which constitutes his quota. Quota sampling is often used in market research. Interviewers are required to find cases with particular characteristics. They are given quota of particular types of people to interview and the quotas are organised in such a way that the final sample should be representative of population. The quota sampling has three stages of selection.

- Classify the population in terms of same characteristics of which sample is to be represented. For examplo, Age.
- Determination of the proportion of the population falling into each group or class on the basis of known assumed or estimated composition of the population.
- Assign quota of respondents to various interviewers.

In another variant of quota sampling, the number of people selected does not necessarily match the proportion in tho research population. Interviewers may be told to recruit a minimum number of people in each particular group. This non-proportionate quota sampling is often used to ensure that all groups are represented in the sample, even if they make up only a very small percentage of the research population.

Disadvantage of Quota Sampling

Interviewers choose who they like (within above criteria) and limy therefore select those who are easiest to interview, so bias can result. It is also impossible to estimate accuracy of the sample selected because it is not random sample.

3. Purposive Sampling

A purposive sample is one which is selected by the researcher subjectively. The researcher attempts to obtain sample that appears to him/her to be representative of the population and will usually try to ensure that a range from one extreme to the other is included. In other words in purposive sampling people/ units/ elements/ in the sample are selected because they are regarded as having similar characteristics to the people in the designated research population. So, for example, in research investigating the management skills of owner/managers of small enterprises, the researcher might select some typical owner managers to take part in the study. They will not be selected randomly. One advantage of this kind of sample is that it is usually possible to get a targeted sample together very quickly - and hence cheaply.

It is often used in political polling - districts chosen because their pattern has in the past provided good idea of outcomes for whole electorate.

4. Convenience Sampling

A convenience sample is used when we simply stop anybody in the street who is prepared to stop, or when we wander round a business, a shop, a restaurant, a theatre or whatever, asking people we meet whether they will answer our questions. In other words, the sample comprises subjects who are simply available in a convenient way to the researcher. There is no randomness and the likelihood of bias is high. We can't draw any meaningful conclusions from the results. The results obtained by this method can hardly be representative of the population.

However, this method is often the only feasible one, particularly for students or others with restricted time and resources, and can legitimately be used provided its limitations are clearly understood and stated.

Because it is an extremely haphasard approach, students are often tempted to use the word "random" when describing their sample where they have stopped people in the street, as they see it "at random".

5. Snowball Sampling

It is yet another form of purposive sampling which is often used to reach research populations that are difficult to find. It has been used for studies of deviant behaviour. For example, studies of the homeless, where no sampling frame exists. Having decided on the characteristics of the people to be included in the sample, we find one- and ask that one person if they know of others like themselves-and so on.

In other words, we initially contact a few potential respondents and then ask them whether they know of anybody with the same characteristics that we are looking for in our research...

6. Self-Selection

Self-selection is perhaps self-explanatory. Respondents themselves decide that they would like to take part in our survey.

Comparison between Probability Sampling & Non-Probability Sampling

In probability sampling every element in the population has a known non-zero probability of selection. The simple random is the best known probability sample, in which each member of the population has an equal probability of being selected. Probability sampling designs are used when the representativeness of the sample is of importance in the interest of wider generalisability. When time or other factors, rather than generalisability, become critical, non-probability sampling is generally used.

In non-probability sampling the probability of any particular element of the population being chosen is unknown. The selection of units in non-probability sampling is quite arbitrary, as researchers rely heavily on personal judgment. It should be noted that there are no appropriate statistical techniques for measuring random sampling error from a non probability sample. Thus projecting the data beyond the sample is statistically inappropriate. Nevertheless, there are occasions when non-probability samples are best suited for the researcher's purpose.

In non-probability sampling designs, the elements in the population do not have any probabilities attached to their being chosen as sample subjects. This means that the findings from the study of the sample cannot be confidently generalized to the population. However the researchers may at times be less concerned about generalisability than obtaining some preliminary information in a quick and inexpensive way. Sometimes non- probability could be the only way to collect the data.

SAMPLE SIZE

It is difficult to decide the size of the sample. It is one of the problems confronted by the researcher. If sample is larger than what is required, it will increase cost and time of the researcher. If a small sample is selected, the results obtained may be relatively less accurate. So the size of the sample may be optimum size. An optimum sample may be defined as that size of sample which fulfills the requirements of efficiency, representativeness, reliability, flexibility. A lot of factors have to be considered while deciding the size of the sample. Practical issues such as time and other resources will be very influential but there are other more theoretical considerations. The following points are considered while deciding the size of the sample.

1. Nature of the population

If the composition of the survey population is more homogeneous, fewer cases will yield better results. But if the population is more heterogeneous in nature number of cases may be required to constitute a reliable sample size.

2. Complexity of tabulation

The size of the sample determines how the findings are grouped, classified and tabulated. If these groups are greater in number large size of the sample may be needed to yield dependable statistical results. The size of sample chosen should be large enough to give an adequate and reliable measure of the smallest important categories of data or Information.

3. Problems related with collection of data

Time and money available for research is considered while collecting data. The volume of data collected depends upon length of the questionnaire, the number of field workers, likely response rate (which itself will depend on sampling method selected), type of sampling method in use and the method of data collection. So methodology selected for the purpose of research is an important factor.

4. Type of sampling

The size of the sample is also determined by the type sampling method adopted. If stratified sampling method is adopted, smaller sample will be sufficient.

5. Basic information

Before determining the size of the sample for study, it is better to secure some basic information about the population. Such information may be got through pilot study, past surveys, experience of the experts etc.

6. Degree of accuracy required for the study

It depends upon the size of the 'acceptable' *sampling error.* (How much error can be tolerated?) Simple random samples tend to have larger sampling error that stratified samples. If we are using the latter, the sample size could perhaps be reduced, the researcher may tolerate the margin of error to five per cent or two per cent depending upon the degree of accuracy required in the study. So for the purpose of study the researcher should decide:

(a) The desired level of confidence.
(b) Extent to which there is variation in the population with regard to key characteristics of the study.

Principles of Sampling

There are two important principles upon which the theory of sampling is based.

1. The Law of Statistical Regularity

A reasonably large sample selected at random from a large population will be, on average, representative of the characteristics of that population. This law is derived from the mathematical theory of probability.

2. The Law of the Inertia of Large Numbers

Large groups of data show a higher degree of stability than smaller ones; there is a tendency for variations in the data to be cancelled out by each other.

Criteria for Selecting Sampling Procedure

The quality of the research, the validity of its findings, among other things depends upon the suitability of the sampling design selected for study. The researcher considers a number of factors while selecting a sampling plan. They are:

(a) The nature of the problem
(b) The goal of the researcher
(c) The geographical area covered by the survey
(d) The size of the population under study
(e) The extent of facts available about the population
(f) Availability of funds
(g) The available time for study
(h) Desired reliability of the results

Selection of a sampling technique or procedure is a difficult task. The following criteria can be used for selecting the sampling technique:

- The purpose of the survey
- Measurability
- Degree of precision
- Information about population
- The nature of the population
- The geographical area covered by the survey
- Fund availability
- Time
- Economy

(a) The purpose of the survey

Selection of the suitable sampling method depends upon the purpose of the survey conducted by the researcher. If the researcher intends to generalise his findings it is better to adopt probability-sampling method. Further the selection of a particular probability sampling depends upon the geographical area of the survey and the size and nature of the population under study.

(b) Measurability

All probability-sampling methods do not permit measurable e.g. a systematic sampling from a population with periodic variation. If research objective requires statistical inference, then the samples are drawn by applying simple random sampling method or stratified sampling method. Probability samples only allow the computation of sampling error and its computation is required in the application of statistical inference theory.

(c) Degree of Precision

The degree of precision required is one of the criteria for selection of a sampling method. If a high degree of precision is required, then it is better to adopt random sampling method. In other cases where no precise results are required, use convenient random sampling method.

(d) Information about the population

If sufficient information about population is not available it is difficult to apply probability-sampling methods. Under this circumstances, an exploratory stuffy is conducted to gather required information, and then apply probability sampling method.

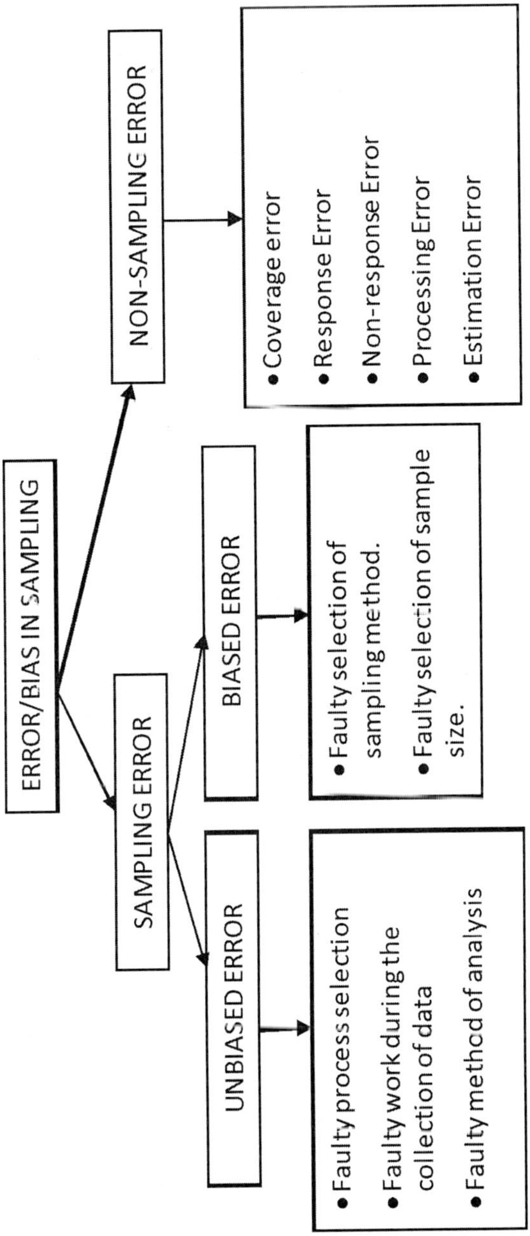
ERROR/BIAS IN SAMPLING
SAMPLING ERROR
NON-SAMPLING ERROR
• Coverage error
• Response Error
• Non-response Error
• Processing Error
• Estimation Error
BIASED ERROR
• Faulty selection of sampling method.
• Faulty selection of sample size.
UNBIASED ERROR
• Faulty process selection
• Faulty work during the collection of data
• Faulty method of analysis

(e) Nature of the population

If the variable under study is homogenous in nature it is better to adopt even simple random sampling method. If the population is hydrogenous, stratified random sampling is appropriate.

(f) Geographical area of the study

If the area covered is very large and the size of the population is also very large, it is suitable to adopt multistage cluster sampling.

(g) Availability of fund

It is one of the limiting factors. If the availability of the fund is limited it is better to choose a less costly sampling plan like multistage cluster sampling. But if precision is to be attained it is better to collect the required fund or to give up the study.

(h) Time

The availability of time for the completion of the study is the other criteria for selecting the sampling method. If time is limited it is better to select simple random sampling method instead of multistage sampling.

(i) Economy

A sample is economical if the precision per unit cost is higher and variance cost is low. That means the economy can be achieved if the desired level of precision per unit is achieved at minimum cost.

Sampling Bias

Sampling analysis involve two types of costs namely, the cost of collecting data and cost of an incorrect inference resulting from the data. There are two causes for incorrect inference resulting from data. They are *(1) systematic Bias (2) sampling error.* Systematic bias occurs from the errors in the sampling procedure. It cannot be reduced or eliminated by increasing the size of the samples. The following are the main causes of systematic bias.

(a) **Unsuitable sample frame or source list:** If the sampling frame is a biased representative of population, it will result in systematic bias.

(b) **Faulty measuring device:** If the measuring device is continually in error it will be a cause for systematic bias.

For example, if the questionnaire is a biased one, it will result in systematic bias.

(c) **Non- respondents:** If we are unable to sample all individuals included in the sample, there may be the chance of occurring systematic bias.

(d) **Indeterminacy principle:** Indeterminacy principle is a cause of systematic bias. It is seen that individuals act differently when kept under observation than when they do when kept in non-observed situation.

(e) **Usual bias in reporting data:** There are usual biases while reporting of data by respondents. It is also cause of cresting systematic bias. The people will not reveal their true feeling in psychological surveys.

2. SAMPLING ERROR

The errors which arise due to the use of sampling surveys are known as sampling errors. These are random variations in the sample estimates around the true population parameters. *Sampling errors* occur when estimates are derived from a sample rather than a census of the population. The sample used for a particular survey is only one of a large number of possible samples of the same size and design that could have been selected. Even if the same questionnaire and instructions were used, the estimates from each sample would differ from the others. This difference, termed sampling error, occurs by chance, and its variability is measured by the standard error associated with a particular survey.

Sampling error can be measured for a given sample design and size. It decreases when the size of the sample increases. That means the sampling error can be controlled.

Types of Sampling Errors

There are two types of sampling errors:

(a) Biased errors.

(b) Unbiased errors.

Biased Errors

These are the errors which are occurring due to the faulty selection of the sampling method due to the prejudice of the researcher. As a result of such selection certain errors may occur. These errors are known as biased error or cumulative errors or non-compensating errors. Such type of error does not increase when the sample size is increased. The size of the error will increase when the size of the sample is enhanced.

Unbiased Errors

This type of bias is occurring due to chance differences between the items included in the sample and items not included in the sample. It is known as random sampling errors. It can be decreased by increasing the size of the sample. So it is known as non-cumulative error.

Causes of bias

Bias may arise due to

(i) Faulty process selection.
(ii) Faulty work during the collection of information.
(iii) Faulty methods of analysis.

(i) Faulty process selection

Faulty selection of sample may arise due to the following ways:

(a) Deliberate selection of the sample by the researcher.
(b) Possibility of conscious or unconscious bias in the selection of the random sample. The researcher or investigator claims that the sample is selected randomly even though it is not selected randomly.
(c) If an item chosen through random sampling is substituted by another item, it will be a source for bias.
(d) If all items which are selected randomly are not covered for study it will be a cause for bias.
(e) If the respondents are not filling the entire questionnaire and return it the researcher, it will be a reason for creating bias.

(ii) Faulty work during the collection of information

The regular error in measurement will be a reason for bias. If the error in measurement is occurred in samples, it will create much bigger errors. Bias may arise due to wrong definition of population, improper formulation of decision, securing inadequate source list etc. Improper design on questionnaires, interview schedule, ill-trained interviewer, etc. will also make bias.

(iii) Faulty methods of analysis

If proper methods of analysis are not adopted, it will be reasons for bias.

3. NON-SAMPLING ERRORS

Non-sampling errors can be occurred in any survey whether a complete enumeration or sampling. It includes mistakes and biases. Mistakes may be committed at the time of tabulation. It can occur at every stage of planning and execution of the census or survey. It can be attributed to many sources, such as response differences, definitional difficulties, differing respondent interpretations, and respondent inability to recall information. Non-sampling error tends to increase when the sample size is increasing.

Non-sampling errors may occur from one or more of the following factors:

1. Inappropriate statistical unit.
2. Inadequacy of data specification.
3. Inaccurate or unsuitable methods of interview or observation or measurement with inadequate or vague schedule.
4. Lack of trained and experienced investigators.
5. Error caused due to non-response of respondents.
6. Error occurring in data processing operations.

Likewise there are number of errors which are occurring. Some examples of non-sampling errors are:

- The sampling process is such that a specific group is excluded or under-represented in the sample, deliberately or inadvertently. If the excluded or under-represented group is different, with respect to survey issues, then bias will occur.
- The sampling process allows individuals to select themselves. Individuals with strong opinions about the survey issues or those with substantial knowledge will tend to be over-represented, creating bias.
- If people who refuse to answer are different, with respect to survey issues, from those who respond then bias will occur. This can also happen with people who are never contacted and people who have yet to make up their mind about the answers.
- If the response rate (the *proportion* of the sample that takes part in a survey) is low, bias can occur because respondents may tend consistently to have views that are more extreme than those of the *population* in general.
- The wording of questions, the order in which they are asked and the number and type of options offered can influence survey results.

- Answers given by respondents do not always reflect their true beliefs because they may feel under social pressure not to give an unpopular or socially undesirable answer.
- Answers given by respondents may be influenced by the desire to impress an interviewer.

Characteristics of Non-sampling errors

- can occur in all aspects of the survey process other than sampling.
- exist in both sample surveys and censuses.
- are difficult to measure.

Non-sampling errors can occur because of problems in coverage, response, non-response, data processing, estimation and analysis. Each of these types of errors is explained below.

Coverage errors

An error in coverage occurs when units are omitted, duplicated or wrongly included in the population or sample. Omissions are referred to as "under-coverage", while duplication and wrongful inclusions are called "over-coverage". Coverage errors are caused by defects in the survey frame, such as inaccuracy, incompleteness, duplications, inadequacy or obsolescence. Coverage errors may also occur in field procedures (e.g., while a survey is conducted, the interviewer misses several households or persons).

Response errors

Response errors result when data is incorrectly requested, provided, received or recorded. These errors may occur because of inefficiencies with the questionnaire, the interviewer, the respondent or the survey process.

- **Poor questionnaire design**

It is essential that sample survey or census questions are worded carefully in order to avoid introducing bias. If questions are misleading or confusing, then the responses may end up being distorted.

* For more information, refer to the section on Questionnaire design.

- **Interview bias**

An interviewer can influence how a respondent answers the survey questions. This may occur when the interviewer is too friendly or aloof or prompts the respondent. To prevent this, interviewers must be trained to remain neutral throughout the interview. They must also pay close attention to the way they ask each question. If an interviewer changes the way a question is worded, it may impact the respondent's answer.

- **Respondent errors**

  Respondents can also provide incorrect answers. Faulty recollections, tendencies to exaggerate or underplay events, and inclinations to give answers that appear more 'socially desirable' are several reasons why a respondent may provide a false answer.

- **Problems with the survey process**

  Errors can also occur because of a problem with the actual survey process. Using proxy responses (taking answers from someone other than the respondent); or lacking control over the survey procedures are just a few ways of increasing the possibility for response errors.

Non-response errors

Non-response errors are the result of not having obtained sufficient answers to survey questions. There are two types of non-response errors: complete and partial.

- **Complete non-response errors**

  These errors occur when the results fail to include the responses of certain units in the selected sample. Reasons for this type of error may be that the respondent is unavailable or temporarily absent, the respondent is unable or refuses to participate in the survey, or the dwelling is vacant. If a significant number of people do not respond to a survey, then the results may be biased since the characteristics of the non-respondents may differ from those who have participated.

- **Partial non-response errors**

  This type of error occurs when respondent provide incomplete information. For certain people, some questions may be difficult to understand. To reduce this form of bias, care should be taken in designing and testing questionnaires. Appropriate edit and imputation strategies will also help minimise this bias. More information on editing and imputation can be found in the chapter entitled Data Processing.

Processing errors

Processing errors sometimes emerge during the preparation of the final data files. For example, errors can occur while data are being coded, captured, edited or imputed. Coder bias is usually a result of poor training or incomplete instructions, variance in coder performance (i.e., tiredness, illness), data entry errors, or machine malfunction (some processing errors are caused by errors in the computer programmes). The same thing can be said about captured errors. Sometimes, errors are incorrectly identified during the editing phase. Even when errors are discovered, they can be corrected improperly because of poor imputation procedures.

Estimation errors

Statistics Canada and other data-collecting agencies devote much effort to designing and monitoring surveys in order to make them as error-free as possible. If an inappropriate estimation method is used, then bias can still be introduced, regardless of how errorless the survey had been before estimation.

Here is an example of a potentially inappropriate estimation. We know that global warming is an issue where there is a lot of debate. To accurately measure this phenomenon, one should know how to come up with an acceptable "average global temperature".

Review Questions

1. What is survey? What are its basic types?
2. What are the methods of survey?
3. What is Sample Survey?
4. Define a sample design and explain the Steps in Sampling Design.
5. What are the important Features of a Good Sample Design?
6. What are the different types of sample design or methods or techniques of sampling?
7. What is Probability Sampling?
8. Write notes on Simple or Unrestricted Sample are restricted random samples.

9. Explain the Random Number Method.
10. What is the different Non-Probability Sampling methods used for survey?
11. What are Advantages of non-probability methods.
12. What are the points to be considered while deciding the size of the sample?
13. What is systematic Bias and sampling errors?
14. What are the Types of Sampling Errors?
15. What are non-sampling errors?
16. Write short notes on:
    (a) Stratified sampling
    (b) Cluster sampling
    (c) 3 Multi-stages Cluster sampling
    (d) Systematic sampling
    (e) Random Route Sampling
    (f) Accidental sampling
    (g) Quota sampling
    (h) Purposive or judgment sampling
    (i) Convenience sampling
    (j) Snowball sampling
    (k) Self-selection

3

Research Problem and Design

Introduction

In every field, our knowledge is incomplete and problems are waiting to be solved. We try to resolve these unanswered problems by asking relevant questions and seeking answers to them. Research is not an excursion into happy expectation, of loudly hoping that the data necessary to solve the problem will somehow unexpectedly turn up. The overall research effort must be implicitly planned and logically designed. Researchers plan their overall research design and specific research methods in purposeful way. That is, to yield data relevant to their particular research problem. Depending on the specific research question, different designs and methods will be more or less appropriate.

The role of research is to provide a method for obtaining those answers by inquiringly studying the evidence within the parameters of the scientific method. Research is a process through which we attempt to achieve systematically and with the support of data the answer to a question, the resolution of a problem, or a greater understanding of a phenomenon. So research is a systematic process which involves a number of steps. They are explained below.

1. Tentative selection of the topic or research problem

The first and foremost task of a researcher is single out or identifies the areas of research or problem he wants to study.

In the case of government organisations the areas of research is suggested by administrators or policy makers. As students of research are concerned they can get the help guides or researchers in the universities and research institutions to identify the area of study. He should discuss the problem with his friends or with his colleagues or with the experts in the field. It is essential to understand the problem of study well. He should go through professional journals dissertations, research reports etc to discover the unanswered questions. He can also conduct the survey of literature discover unanswered questions.

The general topic selected is then converted into a specific problem. It constitutes the first step of scientific enquiry. There are two types of research problem:

- Problem related to state of nature.
- Problem related to relationship between variables.

At the time of selecting the tentative research problem or topic a quick scanning of existing literature is essential so as to avoid duplication of studies. He should also consider the time and availability of resources for the successful completion of the project.

Sources of problem

To identify the research problem the following sources can be used:

- **Reading:** When we study certain reports or books certain question may arise in our mind. Likewise when we go through certain research reports, the area of research report may strike in our mind.
- **Academic experience:** Research problems can also be found out through discussion with colleagues, or from out of class discussions, or from classroom discussions or from classroom lectures.
- **Daily experience:** We will get problems for research from our daily experiences.
- **Exposure to field situations:** Field works, extension work etc will help to trace out the research problems.
- **Discussion:** Discussions with experts, researchers, administrators, and business executives will help the researcher to identify new research problems.

2. Initial survey of literature

After the tentative selection of the problem the researcher is required to go through the relevant literature, a general overview of the literature should be done. At this stage the researcher should review two types of literature:

- The conceptual literature relating to the concepts and theories.
- The empirical literature consisting of studies made earlier which are similar to proposed for study.

The ultimate objective of initial review of literature is to bring out of a frame of reference for the research. It will help to develop an understanding of the basic facts, major issues or controversies, underlying theories relating to his studies. The frame of reference made will help the researcher to specify the research problem in a meaningful manner.

3. Finalisation or selection of research problem

After the initial survey, the researcher should select the problem and it should rephrase into analytical or operational lines. That means the problem should be finalised and it should put into specific terms. While selecting the problem the following points are also considered.

- The subject of the research should not be too wide and non-reliable in nature.
- The topic should not be too narrow.
- The problem or topic selected should suit to his academic background, research talent, knowledge and experience of the researcher.
- The limitations such as time and availability of money are also considered while selecting the problem.

After selecting the problem, a brief summary of the topic should be written. It is known as synopsis. The synopsis indicates what is to be included for study. It should also indicate the importance of the study and methods of research.

4. Formulation of a problem

Now the next step is formulating the research problem. That means the selected problem should be translated and transformed into a scientific research question. It provides the following benefits:

- Correct formulation of a research problem gives a sense of direction to the research.
- It identifies the scope of the research.
- The formulation of problem helps to point out the limitations of the research.
- It also elucidates the problem.
- It establishes the major assumptions.
- It states the context of the problem.
- It affords economy in research.

Steps in Formulation of Research Problem

The following steps are to be followed to formulate a research problem:

(a) **Specify the Research Objectives:** A clear statement of objectives will help you develop effective research. It will help the decision-makers evaluate your project. It's critical that you have manageable objectives. (Two or three clear goals will help to keep your research project focused and relevant.)

(b) **Review the Environment or Context of the Research Problem:** As a researcher, you must closely observe the environment. This will help you determine whether the findings of your project will produce enough information to be worth the cost. In order to do this, you have to identify the environmental variables that will affect the research project.

(c) **Explore the Nature of the Problem:** Research problems range from simple to complex, depending on the number of variables and the nature of their relationship. If you understand the nature of the problem as a researcher, you will be able to better develop a solution for the problem. To help you understand all dimensions, you might want to consider focus groups of consumers, sales people, managers, or professionals to provide what is sometimes much needed insight.

(d) **The Consequences of Alternative Courses of Action:** There are always consequences to any course of action. Anticipating and communicating the possible outcomes of various courses of action is a primary responsibility in the research process.

(e) **Extensive literature survey:** Conducting an extensive survey is the next job of the researcher. The final objective of the extensive survey of literature is to prepare bibliography of woks for study and consultation. The researcher can also use the abstraction and indexing of journals, published and unpublished bibliographies. He should tap academic journals, conference proceedings, government reports, books etc depending upon the nature of the problem. When the researcher searches in one source it may lead to another source. The earlier studies conducted in the relevant topics and related topics are also to be gone thoroughly. Review of the previous related research topics will help the research to formulate a satisfactory structure for his project. He can depend upon a good librarian mid a library for this purpose.

5. Formulation of hypothesis

After conducting an extensive survey of literature the next step in research is state the working hypothesis or hypothesis in clear terms. A hypothesis is a tentative assumption made in order to draw out and test its logical or empirical consequences. It is the crucial point of research. There may be one or more or several hypothesis for the same study. All these hypothesis are predictions. It will serve as a guide for research. The hypothesis should be formulated before collecting data. It should be very specific and limited to the concerned problem. The hypotheses are never proved. It is to be tested. It also affects the manner in which tests must be conducted in the analysis of data and indirectly the quality of data which is required for the analysis.

The hypothesis should show the relationship among different variables of study. It leads the researcher to right path. It sharpens the thinking process. It helps to attention on more important aspects of the research problem.

Some type of research does not need hypothesis. But as general rule hypothesis is very useful in research.

Working hypothesis is developed:

- by conducting discussion with colleagues and experts about the problem.
- by examining data and records related with the problem.
- by reviewing similar studies in this area or of the similar problems.

- by exploratory personal investigation. It involves original field interviews on a limited scale with interested parties' and individuals.

6. Definition of concepts

The next in the formation process is to define the concepts involved in the title, objectives, investigative questions and hypothesis. The operational definitions specify the measurement parameters of the variables.

7. Preparation of the research design

The researcher will have to state the conceptual structure with in which the research should be conducted. It is the design. Tho function of the research design is to provide: the collection of relevant evidence with minimal expenditure of effort, time and money. It depends upon the purpose research. The purpose of research can be grouped into following categories, (i) Exploration, (ii) Description, (iii) Diagnosis and (iv) Experimentation.

In the case of exploration a flexible research design is relevant. A flexible research design provides opportunity for considering many different aspects of a problem which is considered suitable.

But the purpose of research is to provide an accurate description of a situation or of an association between variables, and then the suitable design will be one which minimises bias and maximises reliability of the data collected and analysed.

The following points are considered while preparing a search design suitable for a particular research problem:

- The way of obtaining information.
- The skill possessed by the researcher and his staff members.
- The time available for research.
- The finance available for research.

8. Determination of the sample design

The researcher must decide the sample design to be used for the research purposes by considering the nature of enquiry and other related factors. Sample design indicates the way of selecting sample required for study. In other words, a sample design is a definite plan determined before any data are actually collected obtaining a sample from a population.

9. Collection of data

All kinds of research work require data. The data can be collected in different ways. The secondary data or information may be collected both from published and unpublished sources. Certain agencies provide numerous data which are useful for research. The agencies include the Reserve Bank of India, Mumbai, Planning Commission, New Delhi, Registrar of Census Operations, New Delhi, Central Statistical Organisation, New Delhi, Directorate of Economic and Statistics, New Delhi etc. Primary data can be collected through survey or experiment.

(A) *Survey:*

That means if data are not readily available, we want to collect data through survey method. Survey method is a device used for collecting desired data or information from universe. Under this method data can be collected through observation, personal interview, by mailing questionnaire, through schedules and through telephone interviews.

(B) Experiment:

If experiment is adopted for collection of data, the researcher observes some quantitative measurements of the data. With the help of such experiment, he examines the truth contained) in the hypothesis.

The researcher should select any one of the method for data collection after considering the nature of investigation, objective and the scope of enquiry, financial resources available time and the desired degree of accuracy.

10. Execution of the project

It is a very important step in research process. If the execution of the project proceeds on correct lines, the data collected would be adequate, dependable and sufficient. The researcher should see that the project is executed in proper way. If data is collected through interview, then proper training should be given to interviewers. But if survey is conducted through the structured questionnaire, it should be machining processed one.

11. Analysis of data

After data collection the next step is analysis of data. For the purpose of analysis of data, a number of operations are to be done. It includes establishment of categories, the application of these categories to raw data through coding, tabulation and making inferences. Researcher should classify the raw data into some purposeful and usable categories. Coding operation is done at this stage through which the categories of data are transferred in to symbols that may be tabulated and counted. The next process is tabulation. Large volume of data collected is condensed to few groups and tables for further analysis. Computers can be used for this purpose.

After tabulation, analysis of data is to be done on the basis of various percentages, coefficients etc. For this purpose the researcher can use various statistical techniques.

There are several methods for analysis of data. The researcher should choose the appropriate methods suitable for research. It can be decided even before the collection of data. Statistics plays an important role for analysing the data.

12. Testing of hypothesis

After analysing the data, the next job of the researcher is to test the hypothesis which is formulated by him earlier. He wants to see whether the analysed data supports hypothesis or not. There are various tests which can be applied for testing hypothesis. They are Chi square test, F test, t test etc. the technique to be chosen depends upon the convenience, availability of data, exposure of various methods etc.

The hypothesis performs three functions:

- To test theories
- To suggest theories
- To describe social phenomena.

13. Arriving at generalisations

When a hypothesis is tested and upheld several times, it may be elevated to generalisations. That means a theory can build. But if there is no hypothesis, the findings of the research should be explained on the basis of certain theory, is known as interpretation.

14. Preparation of the report or thesis

The last step of the research is to state the results of research or write the conclusions derived from the study. Then researcher prepares a report and it indicates what he has done to study the concerned problem. The purpose of report or thesis is to communicate others the nature of the problem studied, the design and methodology used and the results conclusions arrived. The report or theses can be divided in different sections and chapters. By doing so the researcher is able to present data in a systematical manner. The thesis can be divided into the following sections.

A. Preliminary pages. It shows the title and date followed acknowledgment and forward. Then it is followed by table contents. After that page, there is list of tables, list of graphs and charts.

B. Text of thesis: The text of thesis indicates the following:

(i) Introduction
(ii) Review of literature
(iii) Hypothesis
(iv) Methodology
(v) Presentation of results
(vi) Conclusions

C. End matter

The end matter consists of the following:

(I) Bibliography -List of books, journals, reports etc.
(II) Appendices- it should be enlisted in support of technical data.
(III) Index.

Research Design or Plan

A researcher should think about the way in which he should proceed in attaining his objective in his research work. He has to make a plan of action before starting the research. This plan of study of a researcher is called the research design. It is essential for the success of the research. Without this the research become futile and results in waste of time. This will enable the researcher to save time and resources. Research design is a comprehensive plan of the series of operations that a researcher intends to carry out to accomplish the research objectives. It is the blueprint for the study.

According to Claire Sellitz, "A research design is the arrangement of conditions for collection and analysis of data in a manner that aims to combine relevance to the research purpose with economy in procedure."

In the words of Bernard S. Philips, "the research design constitutes the blueprint for the collection, measurement and analysis of data. It aids the scientist in the allocation of his limited resources by posing crucial choices".

Research design is systematic planning of research, usually including the formulation of a strategy to resolve a particular question; the collection and recording of the evidence; the processing and analysis of these data and their interpretation; and the publication of results.

A research design is the plan, structure and strategy of investigation conceived so as to obtain answers to research questions and to control variance. A good research design must possess the important features of objectivity, reliability, validity and generalisation. In the words of Miller, "designed research is the planned sequence of the entire process involved in conducting a research study."

The researcher should prepare a well-designed plan or design in advance for all research operations. It will facilitate smooth working of the research. All the research designs have to answer to the following questions:

1. What is the study about?
2. For what purpose the study is carried on?
3. Types of data required.
4. Where the data can be found?
5. Where or in what areas the study will be carried on?
6. What period of time the study will include?
7. How much material or how many samples will be needed?
8. On what basis of sample will be used?
9. What method of gathering data will be used?
10. How will the data be analysed?
11. What will be the style of report preparation?

Thus, the thoughtfulness which enters into the decisions relating to what, where, when, how much, by what means, make up a plan of study or a research design.

Features of Research Design

From the above definitions we can state the important features of the research design.

- It is a plan that denotes the sources and types of information relevant to the research problem.

- It is a strategy which specifies the approach used for gathering and analysing data.
- It comprises the time and cost budgets since most studies are done under these limitations.
- The research design depends upon the purpose of the research.

Need for Research Design

A research design facilitates the smooth conduct of research operations. It helps to get maximum quantity of information at minimum cost, time and effort. To conduct the research study we want to collect data and analyse it. For this purpose, a research plan or design is to be worked out. A research design stands for advance planning of the methods to be adopted for collecting the relevant data and the techniques to be used in the analysis by considering the time, number of staff, and money. The research design should be prepared with great care because any error will upset the entire project. It is the firm foundation of a research study.

Before starting a project, an efficient and appropriate design must be prepared. The design helps the researcher to organise the ideas in a form whereby he can look the inadequacies.

Essential Concepts Concerning to a Research Design

There are various concepts related with research design. They are explained below :

1. Dependent and independent variables

If one variable depends upon another variable is termed as dependent variable. The variable that is forerunner to the dependent variable is termed as independent variable. For example height depends upon age. Here height is a dependent variable and age is the independent variable.

2. Extraneous variable

These are the independent variables which are not related for the study, but at the same time it affects the dependent variable. The effect noticed on dependent variable as a result of unrelated variable is technically described as experimental error. For example, the researcher wants to study the relationship between student's gain in social studies success and self-concepts. Here self-concept is an independent variable and social studies success is a dependent variable. The social studies success is also influenced by the intelligence of the students. But it is not related with the researchers study. So it is an extraneous variable. The researcher should design his research in such a way that the study should be related to the effect of independent variable on dependent variable and not to extraneous variable.

3. Control

The effect of extraneous variable should be minimised as far as possible. The term control is used when we design the study by minimising the effects of extraneous variables.

4. Confounded relationship

If the dependent variable is not free from the influence of extraneous variable such a relationship is known as confounded relationship.

5. Research hypothesis

A hypothesis is a logical supposition, a reasonable guess, an educated conjecture. It may direct our thinking to the possible source of information that will aid in resolving the research problem through the resolution of each attendant sub-problem. The research hypothesis is a predictive statement that relates to an independent variable to the dependent variable. Generally the research hypothesis must contain at least one independent variable and one dependent variable.

6. Experimental and non-experimental hypothesis testing research

When the purpose of research is to test a hypothesis, then it is termed as research hypothesis. It may be experimental design or non-experimental design. When an independent variable is manipulated in a research such a research is termed as experimental hypothesis testing research. If the independent variable is not manipulated, is called non-experimental hypothesis testing research. For example, a researcher wants to study whether the intelligence affects the mark scoring ability of a group of student. For this purpose he selects 60 students randomly and test as their brain power and mark scoring ability by calculating the coefficient of correlation between the two set of scores. This case is an example of non-experimental hypothesis testing research. In this example brain power is the independent variable that is not manipulated. Suppose the researcher selects 60 students who are doing a course in computer accounting. He wants to study the effectiveness of the training programme on the students' performance level. For this purpose the researcher divides 60 students into two groups such as 30 in group X and other 30 in group Y. Group X is going on usual study programme and group Y is indulged in special studies programmes. This is an example of experimental hypothesis test research because the independent variable - the type of training programme is manipulated.

7. Experimental and control groups

When a group is exposed to some special condition in an experimental research it is termed as experimental group anew if the group is exposed of usual conditions it is termed control group. In the above example Group X is the controlled group and group Y is the experimental group.

8. Treatments

Treatments are the different conditions under which groups are put. In the above example there are two treatments such as special studies programme and usual study programme.

9. Experiment

An experiment is process of examining the truth of a statistical hypothesis relating to some research problem.

10. Experimental unit

These are the predetermined plots where different treatments are applied.

Stages of Research Design

The following are the important steps or components on research plan. They are not mutually exclusive but interdependent in nature.

1. Selection of a problem

In the initial stage of research the researcher wants to formulate a research problem. Research problem must rise from the minds of the researcher. The formulation of research problem is the basic and most important step in research because it is a systematic effort to gain new knowledge. The research problem may be generated from different sources. The sources of research idea include individual experience, guess, written material, persona conversation, day-to-day practical experience, research findings, etc. The research problem formulation depends upon the purposes. It also depends on the way in which the problem is formulated.

- Explanatory design is followed if the problem is an explanatory one.
- If the problem is to depict distinctiveness of groups or situations, a descriptive design is necessary.
- If the study intend to get a solution of a particular problem a diagnostic design is necessary.
- A historical design is adopted if the problem involves historical analysis.
- If the researcher wants to test a hypothesis of casual, relationship between variables, the experimental design is the best choice.

The selection of the problem must be preceded by a pilot study. The researcher can ensure the practicability of the study with the help of pilot study.

2. Review of the existing literature

It is the preliminary step before attempting the plan of study. All the relevant materials connected with the selected problem are to be reviewed. It is necessary to indicate how the problem under study is related with the existing literature. After review of the existing literature, the researcher will get an insight to the problem under study. It will enable him to formulate a correct plan for his future investigation.

3. Sources of the information to be utilised

The type of study depends upon the sources of information. There are mainly three sources of data namely, documentary sources of both official and unofficial nature, personal sources and library sources. The Documentary sources of information: include published and unpublished documents, reports, statistics, manuscripts; letters etc. Documentary sources may be primary or secondary. The primary sources are the sources from which the researcher collects information first hand.

4. Nature of study

The next step in research study is to ascertain the nature of study. He wants to ascertain whether the study is a statistical study or a comparative study or experimental study or a combination of all.

5. Objectives of study

The researcher should state the objectives of the study in clear terms. The objective of study differs from the nature of studies and goal to be achieved. It may be to gather descriptive data or explanatory data or data from which theoretical constructs should be inferred etc. in certain times the researcher is required to formulate and test hypothesis.

6. Geographical area to be covered

The physical boundaries of the area to be covered for study should be specifically mentioned in the research design.

7. Socio-cultural context of study

If the problem is related with human beings, then the socio-cultural pattern of people is to be ascertained.

8. Period of study

The period of study or time dimensions of study is to be ascertained in the case of historical studies. It will help to implore the problem easily.

9. Dimension of the study

It is essential to make clear the number of cases to be studied. The limitation of the proposed study should be mentioned very clearly in the research design.

10. Basis for selecting the data

The basis of data selection depends upon time and cost factors especially in social research. It is more economical and efficient if study is done on the basis of sample rather than universe. But the selected sample must be the representative of the universe. The size of the sample does not give any guarantee to its representativeness of the universe. In general small samples which are selected scientifically is more than large samples.

11. Technique of study

Necessary data are to be collected for study. A suitable technique is to be decided for collecting data. The technique may be observation, interview schedules and questionnaire or in combination of all. The technique of study normally is upon the nature of study.

12. The control of error

It is applied in experimental studies. In the laboratory is usually possible to control all variables or source of error experimentation should consider the variables which all operating in a given situation.

Research design for exploratory studies

It is also known as formulative research studies. The main object of such studies is that to formulate a problem foil precise investigation or developing hypothesis. The important emphasis in this study is the discovery of ideas and insights. The exploratory study is always adopted in those problems for which only little knowledge or information are available. Generally, the following methods are adopted for this type of study.

1. The survey of the concerned literature.
2. A survey of people who have practical experience with the problem to be studied.
3. An analysis of insight stimulating examples.

1. Survey of the literature

It is the important method to formulate a problem. For this purpose the work already done in relation to the problem be others is to be reviewed. All the literature related to that problem selected is to be reviewed thoroughly. It is done mainly to show how the problem under study relates the previous research studies. Apart from this, it is required to show how the existing problem differs from the existing literature. Hypothesis stated in previous studies are also to be reviewed and their usefulness should be evaluated as a basis of new research. Sometimes the hypothesis may have been explicitly stated by previous researchers. In the light of their usefulness, it is also to consider whether that suggests new hypothesis for our problem under study. In some cases hypothesis has not formulated so far. In such cases the important task is to review the literature for deriving the relevant hypothesis from it.

2. The experience survey

It is seen that a small proportion of the existing knowledge and experience of the people is published in written form. So it survey is to be conducted among the people who have had practical experience with the problem to be studied. The main object of such a survey is to obtain new sights to the problem. The experienced people can contribute new ideas. Such reservoirs of experience could be tremendous value in helping social scientists to be aware of the important influences updating in any situation that may be called upon for study. The experience survey helps the researcher to define the problem consciously and helps in formulation of research Hypothesis.

3. The analysis of insight stimulating examples

It is only an intensive study for suggesting hypothesis for research. It is particularly useful in the areas where practical science is lacking to serve as a guide. Under this method, Intensive study of the selected phenomenon is done. No Simple rule can be established for the selection of the instances to be studied. The experience indicates that certain types are more appropriate than others. The researcher's attitude, the intensity of the study, ability of the investigator to draw together diverse information into a unified interpretation are the main features which make this method appropriate.

Research Design for Descriptive Studies

The main aim of descriptive studies is to portray accurately the characteristics of a particular group or situation. Studies related specific predictions with narration of facts and characteristics related with an individual, group or situation are some of the examples of descriptive studies. Most of the social research comes under this category. It may relate to study of the people of the community, their age and distribution, their national or social background, educational status etc. The study may also be related with the health to the factory employees, their safety etc. the following steps are involved in descriptive studies.

- Formulation of the objectives of study.
- Define the population or universe.
- Select the sample.
- Design the method of data collection.
- Analyse data and results.

Research Design for Diagnostic Studies

A diagnostic study determines the frequency with which something occurs or its association with something else. The study related with where a particular variable is associated with other variables is a diagnostic study. For example, to discover the problems of farmers or college teachers. The diagnostic study involves the same steps as in the case of descriptive studies.

Research Design for Experimental Studies

The purpose of experimental studies is to test the hypothesis of casual relationship between variables. In this study two groups are compared in terms of the assured effect of the experimental variable. The validity of the experiment depends upon the equivalence between the control group and the experimental group chosen.

Merits of Research Design

The research design has the following benefits:

- It helps to save researchers time, money and energy.
- It helps to prepare and execute the various activities related to study systematically.
- It helps the researcher to document the research activities.
- It ensures proper time schedule for the implementation of the project.
- It provides confident to the researcher for completing the larch work.
- It provides a sense of success at every stage of work.

Review Questions

1. "Research is a systematic process which involves a number of steps." Explain.
2. What are the important Features of Research Design.
3. Explain the Need for Research Design in research.
4. There are various concepts related with research design, explain.
5. What are the stages of Research Design Research Design Exploratory Studies?
6. Write notes on
   (a) Research design for descriptive studies
   (b) Research design for diagnostic studies
   (c) Research design for diagnostic studies
7. Explain the Merits of research design.

4

Collection of Data

Introduction

All types of research require data. So the basic problem of every enquiry is to collect facts and figures relating to particular phenomenon under study. The collection of data is the primary step in statistical investigation. Collection of data is a process of enumeration together with the proper recoiling of results. The success of the enquiry depends upon proper collection of data.

Data

Data are facts, figures and other relevant materials, past and present serving as basis for study and analysis. For example, sex, age, social class, religion, income level of respondents in consumer behaviour study.

Importance of Data

- The data serves as a bases or raw material for analysis.
- To draw specific inferences analysis of factual data is required. Inferences based on mere images do not provide correct answers for the research problems.
- The quality of the findings of the study is determined by the relevance, adequacy and the reliability of the collected data.
- It forms the basis for the testing of hypotheses, which is formulated for the purpose of study.
- It provides the facts and figures required for the constructions of measurement scales and tables, which are analysed, with the help of quantitative techniques.

Classification of Data

Data collected by the researcher come; under two broad categories, (i) Primary data (ii) secondary data.

Primary Data

Primary data are those data which are collected for the first time. In other words the primary data are original in character. These data is collected by the researcher or through investigators or enumerators for the first time. Census survey of population, automobiles, livestock, and court records, personal diaries, personal documents etc are coming under this category. Primary data is considered as the raw material to which statistical methods are applied for the purposes of analysis and interpretation. In other words, primary data is the information generated to meet the specific requirements of the investigation at hand.

Secondary data

The secondary data are those data which have already been collected, tabulated and presented in some form by someone else for some other purpose. It means data that are already available. Economic surveys of the Government of India, economic reviews published by various state governments, Census data, and data relating to agriculture, industry, forestry, education etc. by the government are the examples of secondary data. The secondary data are in the form of finished products. Researcher has to modify such data for their individual requirements. The secondary sources may be both internal and external in character.

(a) Internal Secondary Data

Internal secondary data refers the information that already exists within the company or unit studied. Here Data are generated iterated from the activities within a firm. For example, the record of sales, budget, advertising expenses, previous market research studies etc.

(b) External Source of Data

It refers to information which is collected by a source external in unit. It may consist of both private and public documents. These documents may be both published and unpublished in nature. Such external secondary sources comprise government publications, business reference sources, and commercial agencies. The private documents may consist of life history, diaries, letter, and memories etc. Public documents may consists of the documents published by the journals, magazines newspaper etc.

The difference between primary and secondary data is a matter of relativity. Data which are primary in the hands of one become secondary in the hands of other.

Choice between primary data and secondary data Sources of data

The researcher should decide what data he will use for his study. That is primary data or secondary data. The selection of the data source depends upon the following:

- Nature and scope of enquiry or study.
- Accessibility of financial resources.
- Availability of time.
- Degree of accuracy necessary for the study.
- The status of the investigator or researcher
- The availability of trained investigators.

Generally primary data is used where the secondary data is not providing sufficient basis of analysis. In certain cases both primary and secondary data is used for study. Secondary data provides readily available (published) data to the researcher.

The following points are also considered while comparing the selection of primary source or secondary source:

- The primary source gives a detailed data compared with secondary source.
- In the secondary source there is a possibility of mistakes due to errors while transcripting figures, which were copied from primary sources.
- The primary source includes the definitions of terms and units used for study.

Sources of Data

The sources of information to be tapped depend upon the type of study. In general sources of data can be classified into two. They are: (a) Primary Source and (b) Secondary Sources.

Primary Source

These are original sources from which the researcher directly collects data that have not been previously collected.

e.g., data is collected to know the brand awareness of the customers.

Secondary Sources

These sources contain data, which has already published or compiled for another purpose of study. It includes not only published record and reports, but also unpublished records.

According to Pauline V. Young, the sources on information can be classified into two namely documentary source and field source. But we can classify sources of data into three types. They are:

(i) Documentary sources (both official and non-official nature)
(ii) Personal source
(iii) Library source

A document is everything is writing which contains materials of sociological importance. Paper or documentary source provides a vast wisdom of usable information. Historical records, books, journals and periodicals, thesis, statistical records, reports, manuscripts, letters, published and unpublished forms etc are the documentary sources or secondary sources.

Classification of documentary source

We can classify the documentary sources into two.

1. Individual documents and
2. Public documents

1. Individual documents

These are the documents which are recorded by individuals. A person records his thoughts and views about various problems either in diary or in note books. Later it becomes documents for subject of study. It may be an indispensable document to the researcher.

Kinds of Individual documents

These documents can be classified as; (i) Life history (ii) Diary (iii) letter and (iv) memory.

(a) Life history: It contains all kinds of biographical information. It is an autobiography. In that sense it consists of report and views about social and personal events.

(b) Diary: A number of people keep diaries to record certain events, day to day affairs, their feelings, reactions etc. some of the diaries may be published later. The diary provides the life of the person. It is the most revealing source first-hand information. So it can be taken as an evidence for our study.

(c) Letters: It provides intimation about the stands taken by the concerned individual relate to the problems. So it gives an idea about the attitude of that individual and trends of his mind. It can be taken as prima facie evidence of the attitude of the writer. The letter is a powerful and useful material related to social problems. But utmost care must be taken to select appropriate letters for the study.

(d) Memories: Certain people will write their memories concerned with certain events, travel, and other significant phenomena. These memories provide material for study of the social phenomena.

2. Public documents

(a) Published Records

It consists of newspapers, journals and magazines, public records and statistics, historical documents, survey reports are case histories.

(b) Newspapers

Information published in newspapers such as editorial discussion or news on contemporary issues, various reports essays, letters to reader etc. are valuable source of information. All these are usable for various types of social research.

(c) Journals and magazines

These are one of the important sources of information, includes wide variety of information which can be utilised social research. The researcher should select usable information from the information supplied by these journals.

(d) Public records and statistics

These are the most reliable sources of data. It includes census reports, annual statistical reports published by various authorities, business and legal papers provides useful data for study. The reports published by government are considered as the most reliable research data. While collecting such data the researcher should assure that the definition of categories used in the available statistics are coincided with the definition used for the study.

(e) Historical Documents

These documents provide data or events of the past; Manuscripts, palm leaves, copper plate, stone inscriptions etc. are coming under this category.

(f) Other sources

Apart from the above documents film, television, radio and public speeches are also contributing as the source of information. It supply information related to contemporary flumes.

3. Unpublished Records

Those records deals the matters related with public interest. These records are not available for public in published form e.g. proceeding of the meeting, noting of files etc.

Merits of Secondary Data

The secondary data has the following merits:

- The secondary data provides an insight to the totals situation studied. While exploring the available secondary sources, the researcher may come across many unexpected information. It will contribute significant information for the study.
- The secondary information derived from various sources may be helpful to the researcher to formulate the hypotheses which is necessary for study.
- It is also useful to test the formulated hypothesis.
- The secondary sources also provide complementary information to the researcher which is needed for study.

Limitations

The secondary data has the following limitations:

- The secondary data is the already collected information for some other study. So it may not be suited for the study proposed by the researcher.
- These are the data collected in past. They may not be the current information and there are not uptodate information which are necessary for the purpose of study.

- The available data may not be as accurate as desired.
- The secondary data are not uptodate.
- Information about the whereabouts of sources may not be available to all social scientists.

Precautions to be taken by the researcher while using secondary data

Researcher must be very careful while using secondary data sometimes the secondary data may be unsuitable or inadequate in the context of the problem which the researcher wants to study. So he must make minute scrutiny of the available data. According to Dr A .L. Bowley, it is never safe to take published statistics at their face value without knowing their meaning and limitations and it is always necessary to criticise arguments that can be based on them. Before using the secondary data the researcher must ensure that the following features are possessed by the data which is collected from the secondary sources.

1. Reliability

He wants to verify whether this data is reliable or dependable for his study. He should find the person or firm or organisation or agencies collected data. He should also verify from where data is collected, on what methods, at what time, whether there is any bias in compilation, the level oil accuracy desired etc.

2. Suitability

The data which are suitable for one enquiry may be suitable for other enquiry. So the researcher should see whether the collected data are suitable for his study. If is unsuitable for study it should not be used by the researcher for his study. He should carefully scrutinise the definitions of various terms and units for collection used at the time of collecting of data. Similarly, he should study the object, scope, and nature on original enquiry. If the researcher finds any difference in these, it is unsuitable for the present study and he should not use it.

3. Adequacy

If the level of accuracy achieved in data is inadequate, then it should not used for the study. So the researcher should use if it suitable, adequate and reliable for his study.

Sources or Methods of Collecting Primary Data

The different methods of data collection vary in terms of their cost, the quality and depth of information they supply, and the level of response they are likely to secure. For example, face to face surveys should result in a higher response rate than a general postal questionnaire, but they are time consuming to administer and need a team of trained administrators (and are therefore relatively expensive). They may also allow respondents to give better-considered answers, and they are more accessible to the non-literate. Overall, they may therefore be more cost effective for some purposes. The first consideration when selecting methods is the kind of information needed by the researcher. There are two basic approaches namely, quantitative and qualitative.

Quantitative Methods

These methods are centred on the quantity of certain responses. They are most appropriate when the potential range of answers the researcher can expect to each question is shown in advance, and typical questions involve ticking boxes of filling in numbers. Quantitative data is also particularly useful for measuring change, because it is relatively easily to ask the same questions again at a later date and to compare the Bulls. For quantitative information to be reliable (and especially when measuring change), it needs to be based on relatively large numbers of responses.

Qualitative Methods

These methods are less focused on numbers and offer the opportunity to explore issues and gain more in-depth information about them particularly where the range possible answers is not known beforehand.

Being less dependent on numbers, qualitative approaches not require such large numbers of responses for their results to be useful, provided the researcher be sure that the respondents are sufficiently typical or insightful. On the other hand, they are more demanding in terms of the analysis required the extract the required information. It is possible to combine both approaches in a single data collection exercise.

Methods of collecting the data collection

In general, there are several methods of collecting primary data especially in surveys and descriptive research. The following are the important primary sources of collecting data.

A. Observation
B. Experimentation
C. Simulation
D. Interview
E. Use of telephone
F. Panel method
G. Mail survey
H. Projective techniques
I. Sociometry
J. Focus group discussion
K. Content analysis.

Choice of the Methods of Data Collection

One of the questions faced by a researcher while collecting primary data is which of the above methods are to be selected. Out of the above methods one or more methods have to be chosen. The selection of method depends upon the following factors:

1. The nature of the subjection matter under study: If the study is related with opinion or preference of individuals, it is better to choose interview or mailing. It also depends upon the educational level of dependents. If an experimentation, then it is better to choose impact study. The study is related with behavioural pattern, and then chooses observation.

2. The unit of enquiry: If the unit of enquiry is an individual, or a household, then choose interview. Data from institutions may be collected by mail survey. Studies concerned with communities require observation.

3. The size of the sample: If the sample is small, and the area covered is solid, interviewing is preferable. In the large samples, which is scattered over a wife area, mailing is preferable.

4. Scale of survey: A large scale survey requires mailing or interviewing through trained investigators.

5. Respondent's educational level: In the case of simple data among educated respondents, a mail survey is suitable.

In the case of illiterate persons, interviewing is the only suitable method.

6. The type and intensity of the information to be collected: For collecting factual and non-emotional data, interviewing or mailing is suitable. For an in-depth survey, in-depth interview is essential. To collect data related with life style, culture, custom etc. observation method may be adopted.

7. Availability of skilled personnel: The skilled manpower is essential in order to get correct response.

8. Required accuracy: Depending upon the desired accuracy, the mode of collecting data is also to be determined. For example, For collecting accurate data personal interview is the most suitable among all methods with least biasness.

A. Observation

Observation is one of the important methods of acquiring knowledge in social and physical sciences. It is one of the important sources of information to any scientific investigation or research. These are methods for gathering data that involve watching test subjects without interacting with them; there is no verbal communication with the respondents. Observation refers to the recording of data as they come to the notice of the investigator or researcher. In other words it is the careful and systematic watching of facts as they occur in the course of nature. The Concise Oxford Dictionary defines observation as, "accurate watching and noting of phenomena as they occur in nature with regard to cause and effect or mutual relations."

Observation may be defined as, "a systematic viewing of a specific phenomenon in its proper setting for the specific purpose of gathering data for a particular study." The scope of direct observation is limited. Observation can provide accurate data, free of biases introduced by interviewers. This method is particularly useful in continuously collecting data about routine consumer behaviour.

Features of observation

- Observation is a physical and mental activity.
- It is selective. A researcher selects the range of things to be observed. It is done on the basis of nature, scope and objectives of the study.

- It is purposive and not informal.
- It grasps the significant events and occurrences that effect social relation of the participants.
- It should be exact. It should be based on standardised tools of research such as observation schedule, socio-metric scale etc.

Types of observation

There are different types of observations such as simple and systematic observation, subjective and objective observation, intra subjective and inter subjective observation, casual and scientific observation, factual and inferential observation, direct and indirect observation, behavioural and non-behavioural observation.

1. Simple and systematic observation

Observation is done to collect data at exploratory stages of research is termed as simple observation. In systematic observation standard procedures, training to observers, schedules for recording and other devices to control observers are employed.

2. Subjective and objective observation

If one observes one's own immediate experience it is termed as subjective observation. It is also known as self-observation. When a person observes things in investigations which are not related with him is called objective observation.

3. Casual and scientific observation

In casual observation there is no previous preparation; investigator observes things as a matter of chance. That he observes the right thing at right time. If observations carried on the basis of certain measurement tools it is called scientific observation.

4. Intra-subjective and inter-subjective observation

If repeated observation of a constant phenomenon is done by the same investigator which yields constant results it is known as intra-subjective observation. If repeated observations constant phenomenon by different observers yield constant data, such observation is known as inter-subjective observation.

5. Factual and inferential observation

If factual information is collected through observation: it is known as factual observation e.g. Identification of period. Inferential observation is the observation which done to draw inferences.

6. Direct and indirect observation

In direct observation, the observer is physically present, observe the particular situation. He personally monitors situation. Researchers actually watch a behaviour as it occurs and reports what they see. May be obtrusive or undisguised (respondents are aware they are being observed) or unobtrusive or disguised (respondents are unaware they are being observed). When observation is done by using mechanical devices such as eye cameras, close circuit TV etc, it is termed as indirect observation. Here the researchers observe the results of behaviour rather than the actual behaviour.

7. Participant and non-participant observation

When the observer participates with the activities of the group under study, it is known as participant observation. The observer penetrates into the thought, emotions and actions of the observed group. When the observer does not actually participate in the activities of the group to be studied, but simply present in the group, it is known as non-participant observation. Here he keeps himself as a disconnected ambassador and observes things. In this case the observation does not make any effort to create relationship with the group.

8. Structured and unstructured observation

In structured observation, there is a careful definition of the units to be observed, information to be recorded, the selection of the relevant data for observation and standardisation of conditions of observation. Observers record only certain well-defined behaviour, typically on a checklist or standardised form; that behaviour not listed on the form would not be recorded. It is mostly used in studies designed to provide systematic observation or to test casual hypothesis. In unstructured observation the conditions are not standardised. It is mostly used as an exploratory technique. It is most Flexible.

9. Controlled observation and non-controlled observation

In controlled observation, the observation is done as per pre-Wronged plan. In this case the mechanical aids for obtaining data are used. The conditions of observations are standardised. In uncontrolled observation there is no prearranged plan. No formal mechanical tools are used for observation. The data are collected without standardising procedure. It is also known as simple or natural observation. The observer visits the places of occurrence of phenomenal in order to observe things.

Components or process of observation

Observation involves three components namely: (i) Sensation (ii) attention and (iii) perception.

Sensation: It is the first step in observation. It is gained through sense organs. It depends upon the physical attentiveness and keenness of the observer. The personality of the observer is more responsible for accurate observations.

Attention: It depends upon the ability of the observer to concentrate or concerned studies. The concentration is largely a matter of will power which depends upon adequate training, experience etc.

Perception: It comprises the interpretation of sensory reports. Perception helps the mind to recognise the facts by grouping and identifying sensation.

Objectives of Observation

The observation is most useful for collecting facts. The process of observations helps the study in the following ways:

- It studies collective behaviour and complex social.
- Following up of individual units composing the situations.
- Understanding the whole and parts in their interrelation.
- Getting the out of the way details of the situations.

Success of observation

A reliable and successful observation is only possible if the following conditions are satisfied:

- The observed problem should be clearly and precisely formulated.
- The observer must develop a free mind. It will help to observe and formulate a clear and correct opinion.
- The facts observed are always interrelated. So the observed should consider only vital facts.

Advantages

The advantages of observation method are as follows:

- The researcher is collecting observed information rather than relating to intentions or preferences.
- The actual actions or habits of person are observed.
- There is a reduction or elimination of recall error.
- It can obtain information from those who are unable to effectively communicate in written or oral form.
- There may be no better way to gather information than through observation.
- The method is applicable when it is undesirable for people to know an experiment is taking place since their actions would change and the experiment would be spoiled.
- Observation provides one of the most reliable methods of data collections especially under the circumstances where other methods may not be feasible.

Disadvantages

Following are the disadvantages of observation method:

- Result of observation depends on the skill of the observer.
- Opinions and attitudes cannot be obtained by observation.
- Forms of behaviour such as the frequency of a person's purchase, church going, smoking and crossing roads cannot obtained by 'one-time' observation, but by a continuous lengthy period of observation.
- It would be expensive to tie up personnel in such tasks.
- The researcher's findings are limited to those observed.
- These techniques do not usually examine motives for feelings toward particular behaviour.
- The data is usually accepted as accurate and objective although sample sizes may be small, so statistical representation of those observed is suspect.
- Time and energy to implement the research can lead fatigue and jeopardise accuracy.

B. Experimentation Method

It is the least-used method for collecting primary data. This method is commonly used by marketers is *test-marketing*. Suppose that a company intends to introduce a firefighting equipment using a new technique, they are unable to speak to anyone who has used it in the past. It may be that the only way they can gather data will be to carry out some experiments using the new firefighting equipment. A set of experiments could be designed and carried out with the results being carefully logged.

All experiments involve three types of variables. First there is liable whose effect upon some other variable experiment is designed to measure. It is often referred as independent variable. The second type of variable: an experiment is the effect of interest. It is the outcome or variable. The last category of variable consists of those other than the manipulated independent variable that could influence the observed effects. These are known as extraneous variables, and unless controlled adequately they are the source of error in an experiment.

Planning to conduct experimentation

1. First of all the researcher wants to determine the hypotheses to be tested. Thereafter to determine the dependent and independent variables involved in it.
2. Operationalise the variables.
3. Select the type of experimentation plan.
4. Choose the setting. The setting may be a laboratory or field.
5. Make the experimental conditions as nearly as the expected real life conditions.
6. Introduce suitable method for controlling extraneous variables, which are not manipulated in experiment.

Advantages

Following are the advantages of experimental method:

- The power to determine causal relationship between variables is more compared with other methods.
- The human errors can be reduced to the minimum.
- It helps to produce exact measurements.

Limitations

Following are the limitations of experimental method:

- It is difficult to establish comparable control and experimental group.
- The scope for experimentation with human beings is limited. It lacks realism.
- It cannot be used for studies related to future.
- It cannot be used to determine the opinions, motives and intension of individuals.

Types of Experiment

1. Laboratory Experiment

A laboratory experiment is an investigation conducted in situation created specifically for that purpose. This experiment is mainly conducted to found out casual relations under clean conditions, to test the predictions derived from theory and other researches. This method is used in physical as well as social science research. It helps to yield specific results and it is replicable.

2. Field Experiment

This is an experiment conducted in real life situation in which the experiments manipulate an independent variable in order to test a hypothesis. It is suitable for testing theory and finding solutions for practical social problems. This method is particularly suitable for studying methods of social influence, social process and social changes in real life situation.

C. Simulation

Simulation is a realistic enactment of roles in an imagined situation. There are three uses of simulation.

- Assessment of a situation,
- Understanding a situation,
- Decision-making in a situation.

Enacting a simulation increases member's awareness and understanding of their interpersonal skills; facilitates in providing feedback to the member regarding his/ her behaviours/ actions; and, provides an opportunity to practice improved responses in a sheltered academic environment.

In a structured simulation, members are called upon to enact prescribed roles in a predetermined vignette. At the same time the actual actions of and decisions made by the members are spontaneous.

In other words, Simulation involves the construction of model representing the situation and in effect, experimenting with it rather than the actual situation. This approach is borrowed from physical sciences.

Simulation can be defined as a set of techniques of manipulating a model of some real world process for purpose of finding numerical solutions that are useful in a real process that is being modelled.

Steps of Simulation

1. Identify the process or system to be stimulated.
2. Decide the purpose of simulation.
3. Develop a mathematical model on the basis of available information on the process or system.
4. Collect several sets of input data for use. Inputs may be samples of actual data or synthetic data based on the general features of the real input data.
5. Determine the type of simulation required.
6. Operate the simulation with the various sets of input data.

Types of simulation

There are three types of stimulation.

(1) Computer stimulation
(2) Man stimulation and
(3) Man computer stimulation

A simulation may be a computer model that mimics the operation of a real or proposed system, such as the day-to-day operation of a bank, or the running of an assembly line in a factory, or the staff assignment of a hospital or call centre. It provides information from an imitation of a particular situation.

Man stimulation model is a game played in a laboratory setting to stimulate people in real world. For example, a number of persons are divided into certain groups. Each group is asked to imagine that they are representing each country. Simulated international situations involving treaties, wars etc are then played by the groups.

If both are used to imitate a situation, it is called man computer simulation.

With simulation we can quickly try out our ideas at a fraction of the cost of trying them in the real organisation and, because we can try ideas quickly, we can have many more ideas, and gain many insights, into how to run the organisation more effectively.

Simulations may be used for research, instruction, decision-making, or some combination of these applications. The analyst view a simulation model as an imitation of the process or system under study and attempts to run the system on paper or by means of a computer to see what would happen if a particular policy was put into effect.

A simulation may be a computer model that mimics the operation of a real or proposed system, such as the day-to-day operation of a bank, or the running of an assembly line in factory, or the staff assignment of a hospital or call centre. It provides information from an imitation of a particular situation.

With simulation we can quickly try out our ideas at a fraction of the cost of trying them in the real organisation, because we can try ideas quickly, we can have many more ideas, and gain many insights, into how to run the organisation more effectively.

Simulations may be used for research, instruction, decision-making, or some combination of these applications. The analyst view a simulation model as an imitation of the process or system under study and attempts to run the system on paper or by means of a computer to see 'what would happen if' a particular policy was put into effect.

D. Interview

The interview is one of the important and power tools of collection of primary data. This method is best suited to the problems of developing countries like India. The interview technique is a verbal method of securing data specifically in the field research connected the social problems; it is an important tool for data collection in social research. It is a direct method of enquiry. In interview, there is face-to-face communication.

The person who is interviewing is called interviewer and the prison who is giving interview is called interviewee or respondent or informant. The respondent is asked to provide ml urination in the form of facts, attitudes, opinions and intensions. Interview is an interactional process. The researcher is able to gather different types of data intensively and extensively.

Process of Interview

Interview process consists of the following steps.

(i) Preparation
(ii) Introduction
(iii) Developing relationship
(iv) Carrying the interview
(v) Recording the interview
(vi) Closing the interview.

(i) Preparation

Some preplanning and preparation is required to carry on an interview. The interviewer should keep a copy of interview schedule for ready use. He should also keep a list of the names and address of the respondents. He should regroup the list of names of the respondents according to the place. It will save time and the cost of travelling. He should mentally prepare for the interview. He also should determine the way of approach, the way of introduction, what situations are to be faced etc. He is bound to face situations like suspicion, avoidance, reluctance, indifference, inadequate response, distortion etc. If he is not suitable prepared such situation, he is not able to get necessary information from the respondents.

(ii) Introduction

As the respondents are concerned interviewer is a stranger. So he will be properly introduced to the respondents. There is no universal mode for introduction. It depends upon the situation and the group of persons who are going to be interviewed. If the study is related with an organisation, it is better to approach the head of the organisation and get the cooperation to meet the sample employees. If the study is related with a community, then it is better to approach the community leaders first.

After introducing himself to the respondents in a suitable manner, the interviewer should follow the following steps for motivating the respondents.

- Greet the respondents with a smile.
- Identify the respondents by name.
- Explain the method of selection of respondent as sample.
- If it is for organisation, tell the respondents the name of the organisation.
- Explain the confidential nature of the interview.
- Describe the use of
- Give stress on the value of the cooperation of the respondents for gathering information.

(iii) Developing rapport

Before stating the interview, a good relationship must be developed with the respondents. Then start the conversation with general topic of interest. It is helpful to create a friendly atmosphere.

(iv) Carrying the interview

After establishing a friendly relationship, questions are asked from the interview schedule. Care, self-restraint, alertness, ability to listen with understands is required to ask questions. Questions are to be explained if it is not understand by respondent. If the conversation is going out of the track, then the interviewer should try to get it on track.

(v) Recording the interview

All the required responses are to be noted as they take place. Noting of information should be done in the schedule under respective question. Any modern recording device like smart phone, camcorder can be used to note the responses.

(vi) Closing of the interview

After the interview, close the interview by saying thanks with a smile to respondent. If the respondent wants to know the result of the whole responses, then note his address for sending the result after the study.

Types of interview

The interview methods can be classified as follows:

1. On the basis of their function, interview can be classified as diagnostic interview, research interview and sample interview.
2. On the basis of number of person participating interview be classified as group or individual interview.
3. On the basis of length of interview, the interview can be classified as short interview or long interview.
4. On the basis of nature of approach, the interview can be classified into structured or directive interview and unstructured interview.

Personal interview

The personal interview may be defined as an effective informal verbal and non-verbal conversation initiated for specific purpose and focused on certain planned content areas. In this case a single person is interviewed to establish close personal contact. Knowledge about the confidential personal aspects of an individual is collected through this way. It may be a structured or unstructured one. Generally personal interview is conducted in a structured way.

Benefits of personal interview

The following are the main benefits of personal interview:

- More information can be collected.
- In-depth information can be collected.
- The information secured through personal interview are more reliable than the information collected through other methods.
- It can be made to yield an almost perfect sample of general population.
- There is greater flexibility. The interviewer can modify the questions according to his needs.
- Personal information can be gathered without any difficulty.
- The interviewer can secure the spontaneous reaction of the respondent.
- The interviewer can collect the supplementary information from the respondent.

Limitations

Even though there are number of advantages for this method it has certain weakness. They are given below.

- It is an expensive method.
- There is the possibility of bias of interviewer as well as that of the respondent.
- Certain higher groups like officials and high income group personal are not easily accessible.
- It is time consuming process.
- Sometimes the respondent gives imaginary pictures just make the interview interesting.
- A number of specialised trained staff is required to conduct interview.
- There is a possibility of occurring systematic errors.

Group interview

This interview is conducted for gathering routine or customary information by interviewing two or more persons simultaneously.

Formal interview

In this case the interview is conducted for collecting information by presenting a set of well-defined questions.

Informal interview

It is a flexible form of interview. The interviewer has full freedom to make adequate alterations in the questions to sun the specific needs of the interviewer.

Focused interview

It is meant to focus attention on the given experience of respondent and its effects. Here also the interviewer freedom to decide the manner and sequence in which questions may be asked and has also the freedom to exploit is reasons and motives. In other words it focuses on the background of emotional and intellectual atmosphere of the problem, usually with unstructured questions.

Non-directive or unstructured interview

It is a type of interview in which the interviewer exercises no control, provides no direction, and has no predetermined questions. He simply acts as a catalyst by encouraging the respondent to tell about his/her experiences and feeling, does not follow any standardised technique of recording information. The interviewer asks questions only if there is a need to do so.

Diagnostic interview

This type of interview is carried out among patients. In this case the interviewer tries to understand the causes of problem.

Treatment interview

This type of interview is carried out to make the patients are of the causes of their deceases and advices them to change the mode of life.

Research interview

These types of interviews are conducted to gather information Tinted to a specified problem. The questions are asked on a predetermined basis.

Mixed interview

This type of interview is applied when customary and specified type of data is required.

Telephone Interview

Telephone is used for conducting personal interviews. It is one of the least cost methods for obtaining primary information.

This method is widely adopted by the houses, advertising firms etc. the respondent is contacted through telephone to gather information.

Merits

The important merits of telephone interview are as follows:

- It is more flexible compared with questionnaire methods.
- It is faster.
- It is cheaper.
- Call backs be simple and economical.
- There is highest rate of response, because the respondent is contacted through telephones.
- The researcher can record the replies without causing humiliation to respondents.
- The study can be covered in a wider geographical area.
- The interview bias is less because there is no face to face to contact.

Limitation

However there are certain limitations in the telephone Interview.

- This method has limited use as it is possible to conduct study among telephone holders.
- Relatively small amount of information can only be gathered.
- It is also not possible to use visual aids while conducting interview.
- Limited time is given to respondents to answer the questions.
- It is not suitable for comprehensive surveys, in which detailed information is required.
- Questions asked through telephones may be short and it will create problems while answering.

In-depth Interviews

These are typically unstructured, one-to-one conversations between a skilled interviewer and a member of a target population. This type of interview is designed to discover underlying motives and desires and is often used in motivational research. Such types of interviews are held to explore needs, desires and feelings of respondents. In other words, they aim to elicit unconscious as also other types of material relating especially to personality dynamics and motivations. To effectively operate an in-depth interview, the following guidelines should be followed:

1. Allow between a half hour and two hours for each session.
2. Each respondent should be screened carefully.
3. It is to make sure that the interviewer is capable of conducting an in-depth interview.
4. A tape or video recorder is to be used to record the interview.
5. It is the duty of the interviewer to make the interview setting comfortable.
6. Proper rewards are given to participants of interview.

Advantages of in-depth interviews

- The respondents feel more comfortable with discussing sensitive topics in in-depth-interview.
- It can be more detailed one and it will reveal more information than in group discussions.
- It is easier to schedule.
- It can handle more complex topics than other techniques.

Disadvantages of in-depth interviews

- The participants are unable to interact with others.
- Cost of implementation is high.
- The success of the in-depth interview depends upon the reliability of interviewers.
- It will deplete the energy of the interviewer.
- It lacks consistency.
- It lacks statistical validity.

Delphi Techniques

There are sometimes occasions when expert answers are needed for questions which are ill-defined and / or for which little data has been gathered and analysed. Executives often want "the answer" before the research is done. Delphi techniques can be used to remedy this problem.

Identification of the panel of experts

The Delphi technique is a group process involving a panel of experts. A facilitator chooses a set of experts. Once the experts are chosen, the facilitator then organises a series of exchanges among the experts on a topic of interest. Typically the initial sets of exchanges are usually in response to a formal set of questions. Subsequent exchanges are based on experts reach "consensus" on the issues. Sometimes it is difficult to identify experts to participate in a Delphi process. One approach is to start with one or two experts and use a reputational technique to identify other experts. This should be done with care. Problems often cross-disciplines boundaries and people with expertise from different disciplines may not be known to each other. If a problem is ill-defined, there may be several competing explanatory paradigms. Experts may dismiss opposing or distinctive views out of hand and may not identify those who hold such views as being potential experts.

A reasonable alternative is to look for discussions of an issue in the broadest possible forums and to use those places as a starting point for identify expertise. It is also appropriate to approach those with dissenting views or those who have been critically reviewed for their nomination. Often there will be interest groups that form around an issue and it may be useful to solicit name from those groups. A search of the internet may turn of people with different approaches to a problem. The selection of the nominees can be tricky one and it will depend upon goal of the panel. Depending on how well define the problem is, one may one to choose a panel that is more or less heterogeneous. Even the most diverse panel can and do reach consensus position.

Response of the experts

Once a panel of experts is identified they are typically asked to respond to a questionnaire or protocol. Their view are collected and distributed to all other experts on the panel. The experts then react to each other's ideas. The purpose is to exchange view until some consensus about an issue is reached.

Develop an adequate protocol

One of the keys to using the Delphi technique is developing an adequate protocol. It is important to identify the issues and to frame them in a way that elicits credible responses. With ill-defined problems there is often controversy about what constitutes the important issues. The protocol may be a subject of debate among the experts.

A Delphi process may go through several stages and require several weeks or months. Often the initial stages involve one- on-one contact between the expert and the organiser of the Delphi process. Typically, this includes sending an Interrogatory or protocol and requesting a response. This may be done by mail or by using electronic mail. Traditionally, Delphi processes have involved bringing experts together in *one* place after an initial round of communications. The initial rounds of exchanges are used to identify where there is agreement and disagreement and to facilitate the preparation of a protocol for a face-to-face meeting where the less tractable issues can be resolved. As intractable issues are identified, the experts are asked to identify alternatives. The introduction of the alternatives often leads to the identification of potential resolutions.

When experts meet, they usually start by following a prepared agenda. Discussions may be interspersed with some type of voting or rating procedure which may be used to narrow in choices and force some level of consensus.

A report or a paper is usually produced representing the consensus. This may then be the subject of further discussion.

There are numerous variations on these processes. In some instances the views may exchanged but the experts may not physically meet. With the advent of the internet, it may impossible to "meet" electronically.

E. Panel Method

In this method, data is collected from the same sample respondents at intervals either by mail or by personal interview. This is used for longitudinal studies on economic situations, consumer behaviour, advertisement effectiveness, etc. the panel members are contacted for information for several months or years. The nature of contact depends upon the nature of the study.

The main feature of the panel method is successive collection of data on the same items from the same persons over a period of time. In the same way this method requires carefully selected and well-trained field workers and effective supervision over their work.

Merits

- This method helps to collect more accurate data for longitudinal studies.
- This method is suitable for studying trends in events, behaviour or attitudes.

- It provides evidence on the casual relationship between variables.
- It provides depth interviews.

Demerits

- This method is very expensive.
- It is very difficult to keep a representative panel and to keep it as representative.
- There is a possibility of declining the quality of reporting.

F. Mail Surveys

Mail survey is the other method of collecting primary data. The survey is a non-experimental, descriptive research method. Surveys can be useful when a researcher wants to collect data on phenomena that cannot be directly served (such as opinions on library services). Surveys are used extensively in library and information science to assess attitudes and characteristics of a wide range of subjects, from the quality of user-system interfaces to library user reading habits. In a survey, researchers *sample* a *population.* Since populations can be quite large, researchers directly question only a *sample* (i.e. a small proportion) of the population.

In this method of data collection there is no field worker and no personal interface for communication. Here there is an impersonal contact. That means the questionnaire is sent through post to the respondent. Questionnaire-based surveys are one of the most common tools used by market researcher to establish consumer preferences. Bad questionnaires are misleading and likely to yield meaningless data, therefore an awareness of the techniques of questionnaire design is essential to any student or researcher wanting to establish opinions on their subject specialism. In addition, you will find that a sound awareness of the principles of questionnaire design will allow you to look more critically at other people's research and to begin to question the methods and tools of analysis that they use.

A questionnaire is prepared and it is mailed to respondents. The respondents are expected to read and understand the questions and write down the reply in the space meant for the purpose in the questionnaire itself. This method of collecting data by mailing the questionnaires are widely employed in various and economic business surveys. Response rates are typically much lower than for personal interviews. It usually takes a long time to conduct. Questionnaire cannot answer unanticipated questions that occur. In this case the archers must worry about bias. It is a cost-effective alternative. The lack of personal communication between those conducting the study and the respondents is the main constraint of this method. Another problem is related to its impendence on the person's own willingness to fill out the form and return it. The return envelope should be pre-addressed with adequate postage stamp.

Types of mail survey

The following are the important mail surveys conducted in industrial and business field.

1. **Industrial and consumer survey:** Industries surveys are the studies conducted among manufacturers, wholesalers or liens or suppliers of products which are used for industrial use.
2. **Media studies:** Advertisers, their agents and media itself want to know the effectives of their advertisement. So they conduct a mail survey among the readers to know the effectiveness.
3. **Multiple surveys:** In this case survey is conducted among several groups of people.

Advantages of Mail Survey

The following are the important advantages of a mail survey:

1. Wider area coverage: In personal interview surveys a limited number of rural areas are selected and interviewers are sent to collect data. It is a costly affair. But the mail order covers a wider area, because the cost of income in mail survey is very much less their personal interview.

2. Less bias: The interviewer is not able to reach all person's house to conduct interview. So there is chance of bias. In the case of mail survey the questionnaire is sent by post to the concerned parties. The parties can take timer to answer the questions. So there is less chance bias.

3. Thoughtful reply: In the case of personal interview, the respondent is required to answer the questions immediate.

But in the case of survey the respondent has sufficient time to think answering questions.

4. Centralised control: Mail survey is done through an office. So every phase of survey is under strict supervision.

5. Saving in cost: The cost of the services for mail is less than the cost incurred for an interviewer to conduct interviews. The investigator is required to pay remuneration. In this case there is no problem of remuneration.

Demerits

It consists of the following limitations:

- A readymade mailing list is not available for conducting mail survey. The available list may also incomplete. It will make problems.
- It is difficult to conduct a mail survey if the questionnaires are too long.
- It is seen that a number of respondents are not responding in time, not giving wrong answers or not sending reply.
- The respondents may not cooperate if the questionnaires are too long.
- Several questionnaires contain unanswered questions and incomplete responses.

G. Projective Techniques

These techniques provide verbal or visual stimuli which, through their indirection and concealed intent, encourage respondents to reveal their unconscious feelings and attitudes without being aware that they are doing so. Marketers use these techniques to tap the subconscious minds of consumers.

The projective tests are defined and relatively unstructured standard situation in which a candidate is asked to respond. It is also called indirect intervening techniques. These tests are generally used to project the personality traits of subjects. Here the candidates are asked to project his/her own interpretations in certain standard situations. The way in which the subject responds to these stimuli depends upon his own values, motives and personality. Projective techniques are used by psychologists. They develop these techniques to project the respondents underlying motives, urges or intensions which are not revealed by the respondents. Sometimes they are reluctant to reveal them. In projective techniques the respondent in supplying information tends unconsciously to project his own attitudes or feelings on the subject under study. These techniques play an important role in motivational researches or in attitude surveys.

Intensive specialised training is required to use these techniques. The following are the important projective techniques.

(i) Word Association Test

It is a projective technique in which the researcher says a word and the participant is to respond with the first word that comes to mind. These tests are used to extract information regarding such words which have maximum association. Here the respondent is required to express the first word which is coming out of his mind. The general technique is to use a list of as many as 50 to 100 words. The matching words expressed by the respondent are analysed. It will indicate whether the given word should be used for the study purposes. For example, this technique is used in market research to find out the quality that is mostly associated with a brand of the product. Firstly, a number of qualities of product are listed. Then the informants are asked to write the brand names possessing one or more of these qualities.

(ii) Sentence Completion Test

It is extension of the word associated test. Researchers present a series of incomplete sentences and ask respondents to complete them. The way they complete the sentence reveals their feelings. Several sentences of this type of the same subject may be put on informants and they are asked to complete it. The replies given by the informant is analysed. It reveals the attitude of the informant towards the same subject. All the sample informant views are taken and analysed. The result represents the views of the population. This technique is easy to use.

(iii) Story Completion Test

In this method the researcher plot stories instead of sentences. Then the informants are asked to complete the story.

(iv) Verbal Projection Test

Under this method the respondents are asked to comment on or to explain what other people do. The answer given by the respondents will reveal his motivations.

(v) Cartoon

Researchers show characters in a particular situation and ask respondents to describe what the characters are doing and explain the situation depicted. Often "bubbles" appear above the cartoon characters but without their speech filled in. Respondents fill in what the characters would say.

(vi) Pictorial Techniques

There are number of pictorial techniques. Some of the techniques are given below:

(a) Thematic Appreciation Test (TAT): This test is administered to reveal some of the dominant drives, emotions, sentiments, complexes and conflicts of personality. This "thematic appreciation test" uses pictures to depict an ambiguous situation, and respondents are asked to describe what is going on in the pictures and what will happen, is a result of the situation. For example, the informant is asked to write a story on the basis of picture shown to him. This will lead to the interpretation of what the characters are feeling and thinking. On the basis of reply the investigator can draw inferences about the personality structure, attitudes etc of the respondents.

(b) Rorschach Ink Blot Test: The test was developed by the Swiss scientist Herman Rorschach. He used 10 original ink blot cards which are still in use today. There is no picture made in these blots. Five of these are black, two black and red, and the other three multicoloured. To investigate personality traits, these cards are exhibited before the informants one after another. Then the informants are asked to describe everything he seen in the blot. The blots are shown in a fixed interval of time. Further the blots are shown again and the informant is asked to point out the location, of whatever he has seen on the blot. The reaction of the candidate after seeing blots is analysed by a psychologist. He analyses the location and determining the factors and the object. Analysis of the determining factor indicates whether the reaction of the subject is related with the shape of the blot or colour or motion in the blot. Analysis of the object shows whether the subject has seen a figure of man, or an animal or anything else in the blot. This test is frequently used.

(c) Holtzman Inkblot Test (HIT): It is a modification of Rorschach test. This test consists of 45 inkblots instead of 10.

It is based on colour, movement, shading and other factors involved in inkblot perception. Only one response per card is obtained from the subject or respondent. The responses are interpreted by the researcher in three levels of form appropriateness. Form responses are interpreted for knowing the accuracy or inaccuracy of respondent's percepts, shading and colour to ascertain his effectional and emotional needs and the movement responses to assess the dynamic aspects of his life. This test facilitates studying the responses of a respondent to different cards in the light of norms of each card instead of group them together.

(d) Rosenzweig Test: This test uses cartoon format. We have a series of cartoons with words inserted in "balloons" above. The respondent is asked to write his own words in an empty balloon space provided for the purpose in the picture. From this the respondents' attitude may be studied.

Disadvantages of Projective Techniques

- This tests have low reliability.
- It has low validity.
- It lacks substantiating evidence.
- Considerable training is needed to administer, score and interpret the tests.

H. Sociometry

The word Sociometry comes from the Latin "socius", meaning social and the Latin "metrurn", meaning measure. As these roots imply, Sociometry is a way of measuring the degree of relatedness among people. Measurement of relatedness can be useful not only in the assessment of behaviour within groups, but also for interventions to bring without positive change and for determining the extent of change. For a work group, Sociometry can be a powerful tool for reducing conflict and improving communication because it allows the group to see itself objectively and to analyse its own dynamics. It is also a powerful tool for assessing dynamics and development in groups devoted to therapy or naming.

Sociometry is one of the methods of socio-psychology developed by the psychiatrist Jacob Levi Moreno (1934). He developed methods to analyse interpersonal (motive relationships within a group. Moreno used sociometric techniques to assign residents to various residential cottages. He found that assignments on the basis of sociometry substantially reduced the number of runaways from the facility. Many more sociometric studies have been conducted since, by Moreno and others, in settings including other schools, the military, therapy groups, and business corporations.

Sociometry is a method for the study and observation of the interpersonal relations in small groups of people. Basically consists in graphically representing the relations using a set of points (individuals) connected by one or more lines (interpersonal relations). His methods can be used to identify informal leaders, social rankings and isolated individuals.

Sociometry can be defined as a methodology for tracking the energy vectors of interpersonal relationships in a group. It shows the patterns of how individuals associate with each other when acting as a group toward a specified end or goal. Moreno himself defined sociometry as "the mathematical study of psychological properties of populations, the experimental technique of and the results obtained by application of quantitative methods".

Sociometry is based on the fact that people make choices in, interpersonal relationships. Whenever people gather, they make choices-where to sit or stand; choices about who is perceived as friendly and who not, who is central to the group, who is rejected, who is isolated. As Moreno says, "Choices are fundamental facts in all ongoing human relations, choices of people and choices of things. It is immaterial whether the motivations are known to the chooser or not; it is immaterial whether the choices are inarticulate or highly expressive, whether rational or irrational. They do not require any special justification as long as they are spontaneous and true to the self of the chooser. They are facts of the first existential order.

J. L. Moreno investigated the structure of groups and society and developed Sociometry—the scientific measurement of social relationships in groups. As in systems models, the individual is viewed in relationship to others. Sociometry in us most basic sense can be best characterised as a collection of methods to investigate and evaluate networks of existing and preferred relationships. Specifically, sociometry is the study of interpersonal choices regarding criteria of interest to the investigator. Sociometry is not a study of formal group structure (e.g., official hierarchies), rather it is a phenomenological study of people's interpersonal choices. Sociometric explorations measure, observe, and intervene in the natural attraction/rejection processes within a given group, e.g., family, social, work, community. These explorations may be didactic or action oriented and includes social atoms, role diagrams, interpersonal relations, Sociograms, and social networks.

Objectives of sociometry

The goals of Sociometry include:

1. To facilitate constructive change in individuals and groups.
2. To increase awareness, empathy, reciprocity and social interactions.
3. To explore social choice patterns and reduce conflicts.
4. To clarify roles, interpersonal relations, and values.
5. To reveal overt and covert group dynamics.
6. To increase group cohesion and productivity.

I. Focus Groups

It is a qualitative research technique in which a skilled facilitator or moderator leads a small group of participants in an unstructured discussion about a particular topic. The Moderator or facilitator is the leader of the focus group sessions. The focus groups are used for the following:

- To generate information for questionnaires
- To assess needs
- To test new programmes
- To find what customers consider when making decisions
- To recruit new members for the organisation
- To test existing programmes
- To follow-ups to mail surveys
- To understand an organisation's image
- To assess products
- To learn about market segments about which little is known.

Participants in a focus group may be asked to discuss their needs, talk about what they may want in a product category, tell how they use a certain product, visualise scenarios, react to descriptions of products, react to physical objects, etc.

Purpose

One of the purposes of a focus group is to get at the range of responses. A second is to get people in an environment where they will stimulate each other's things. A third purpose is to get at the associations, depth of feelings, beliefs and attitudes, and emotion that may be tied to an issue.

Focus groups usually involve from 7-15 people who have been invited to participate in a session lasting from 1 - 3 hours. The session is run by a facilitator who follows a script called a focus group guide. The script is usually defined Wound a well-defined set of issues.

Selection ofparticipants

To get good focus group results participants are recruited. The potential participants are chosen on the basis of the goals of in focus group. Generally, focus group recruitment is oriented to selecting people so that the full range of issues are covered and is less concerned about proportionally representing certain segments of a population. Focus group participants' selection may be manipulated to make a group more or less heterogeneous with respect to some issue.

In some cases participants may be drawn at random from a population. In other cases, it may be important to recruit participants with particular experiences. It is important to define exactly what target group the focus group is supposed to represent. Is it all consumers or all distributors? Is it some sub-group within a population such as people who are comfortable with technology or large distributors who sell only motors? Further, it is important to get participants who represent a cross-section of the segment of interest. There is sometimes a tendency to invite people to focus groups who are familiar or who are known. This can lead to biased results and limit the information that is gathered.

There are a variety of ways to recruit participants to focus groups. One method is to draw samples from a specific target population. This may be difficult if there are no readily available lists of that target population and the population of interest is one about which little is known.

Intimation to participants

It is usually helpful to send a letter to potential participant explaining the purpose of the focus group and indicating that someone will be contacting them by telephone about participating. The purpose of the letter is to legitimise the telephone call. The telephone call to a potential participant should provide an explanation of the goal of the focus group and a description of what will be required of the respondent along with a request to participate. If there is a need to select people representing special qualifications, the telephone-recruitment call may include a set of screening question before inviting participation. In some instances it may be necessary to conduct a screening survey to develop a list of candidates.

Information about the purpose, time and location should be provided during the call. The person chosen to do the calling should be skilled at telephone recruiting. Once a potential participant agrees to participate, there should be a follow-up letter confirming the details and providing a map (if appropriate) to the location where the focus group will be held.

Fee and refreshments

The focus group participants are given a fee for participating in discussions. The amount of the fee will depend upon the population, the difficulty of recruiting people, and the amount of effort required on the part of the participants. Refreshment are provided at the beginning of sessions to help break the ice and / or midway if the session is to be a lengthy one.

Location

The details of the setting for the focus group are extra important. The goal of a focus group is to obtain information usually that requires a setting where people can comfortable. The location of the focus group should be accessible both from a physical and a safety standpoint. The setting should be one that is attractive but not overwhelming. The layout of the room will depend on the purpose of the Session.

Facilitator

Focus groups have one and sometimes more facilitators. The role of the facilitator(s) is to direct the discussion, moderate the meeting, and to encourage all parties to participate. The facilitator should be viewed as a neutral party. It should be made clear to participants that the role of the moderator is to encourage people to contribute. A good moderator will be able to read body language and direct a question at an opportune moment. A good facilitator will also know how to limit rambling and repetitive comments without offending participants. The moderator should be prepared to deal with conflict and with disruptive behaviours. Sometimes these behaviours can be productive but they can also cause other participants to hold back.

Protocol

It is essential to have a protocol for the session and for the moderator to be intimately familiar with the protocol. The protocol is a list of the important topics to be addressed. Such a protocol may take the form of a list of key questions. For each key question there may be an extensive subset of questions or topics. The protocol may be based on prior knowledge or may be generated as a result of interviews with knowledgeable persons.

The protocol should provide the structure for a session. The session may not follow the same order as the protocol. The facilitator will have to decide whether to follow the flow and cover topics later or to limit discussion on certain points and return to them later. Most importantly, the facilitator needs to understand the import of new ideas and elicit additional information so that the ideas do not get lost.

Recorder

Persons staffing a focus group session should be identified to the participants. There may be a "recorder" present. Focus groups may be audio or video taped. It is unobtrusive all possible while taping a session because the audio and video taping process can be distracting and inhibit focus group participation. There are specially equipped rooms available in most localities which have microphones and one-way mirror that will permit video recording. Usually these can be rental for a nominal fee. As an ethical matter, participants in focus groups should be informed about how the contents of session are to be recorded and used and whether or not the session is being taped. Many people will assume it is and the failure in say one way or the other may make people feel that they are being deceived.

Follow up

Finally, it is important to follow-up with participants after a focus group session. A letter is nearly always appropriate.

Focus Group Sessions via the Internet

Online focus groups or "chat sessions" have proven effective in getting elusive groups to participate in discussions. Online focus groups lose the advantages of group dynamics. Security is a problem with online focus groups since no one knows for sure who is participating in online chat sessions.

Advantages of Focus Group Research

- Focus groups can observe respondents.
- It is a flexible method.
- They are controllable.
- Group interaction among participants is possible.
- The openness motivates participants to be honest and direct.
- There is an opportunity for quick execution.

Disadvantages of Focus Group Research

- It lacks scientific validity.
- It is prone to bias.
- A False sense of security is created.
- There is difficulty in measuring the results.

J. Content Analysis

Under content analysis the contents of documentary material which as books, magazines, newspapers and the content of all other material which can either be spoken or printed are analysed. Prior to 1940's content analysis was quantitative in nature. But since 1950's it is mostly qualitative analysis in nature. A review of research in area involves content analysis of the articles published in journal, magazines etc. According to Pauline V. Young, "content analysis is a research technique for systematic, objective, quantitative description of content of research procured through interviews, questionnaires, schedules, and other linguistic expressions, written or oral. It means categorisation or classification of data into different categories or groups.

It is usually applicable to sociological analysis; it requires the researcher to use his judgment in making decisions about the data. The objective of content analysis is to convert that recorded raw phenomena into data which can be treated essentially in a scientific manner so that body of knowledge may be build up. A comparative study of various communication levels is possible through content analysis.

Tools for Data Collection

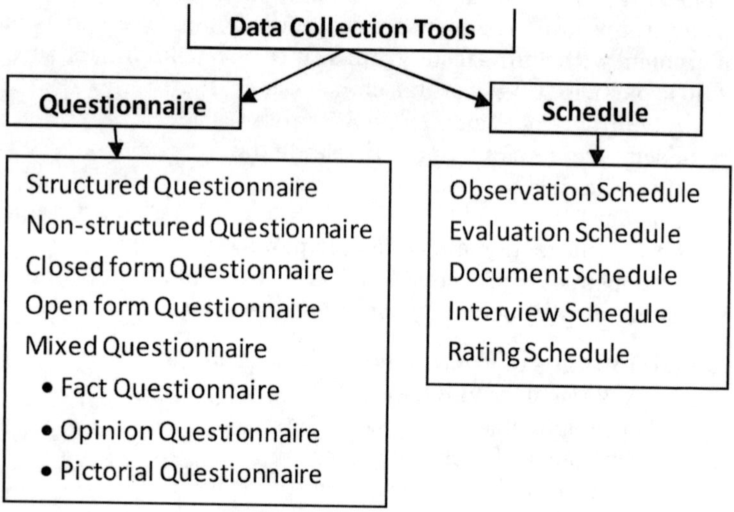

The tools of the data collection help to translate the research objectives into specific questions or items. Information collected through these tools provides explanations of characteristics of persons, organisations, or the phenomena under study. The characteristics help to explain the differences in behavioural pattern and performance of objects under the study.

Questionnaire and Schedule

A schedule or a questionnaire is a devise that is most frequently used in collecting primary data or information by using survey technique. It is used particularly in case of big enquiries. It is being adopted by private individuals, research workers, private and public organisations and even the government. In this method a questionnaire is sent (usually by post) to the persons concerned with a request to answer the question and return the questionnaire. It is an important instrument in normative survey research. It is used to gather information from widely scattered sources.

Comparison between Questionnaire & Schedule

1. The questionnaire can be sent via mail but the schedule is done only Personally
2. The questionnaire is a cheaper method than schedule (for schedule you have to move everywhere
3. The questionnaire can be returned without answering all the questions but, in schedule, enumerator ensures the filling all the questions.
4. The questionnaire can be filled in by anyone but the schedule is always filled by enumerator.
5. Respondent should be literate & co-operative in Questionnaire but schedule can be administered even to illiterates as it is filled in by the enumerator by asking responses.
6. Risk of incomplete & wrong information is more in Questionnaire as compared to schedule.
7. Physical appearance of Questionnaire has to be attractive but it is not necessary with schedule because the person is physically available in front of the respondents.
8. Success of Questionnaire depends on its design but in case of Schedule it depends on honesty & competency of Enumerator.

Questionnaire

A questionnaire is a device for securing answers to question by using a form which the respondent fills himself. It consists of a number of questions printed or typed in definite order on a form or set of forms. The main purpose of a questionnaire is to collect information from people who are widely distributed and to achieve success in collecting reliable and dependable data.

Forms of questionnaires

It consists of the following forms:

1. Structured questionnaires

It contains definite, concrete and direct questions. The questions are presented with exactly the same wording and in the same order to all respondents. A sort of standardisation is adopted to ensure that the all respondents reply to the same set of questions. It is simple to administer. It is relatively in expensive to analyse.

2. Non-structured questionnaires

It may consist of partially completed questions or statements. It is often used as an interview guide. The following are the non-structured questionnaires:

3. Closed form questionnaire

The questions that call for a short check responses are known as close form. It provide for marking 'yes' or 'no' answers or short response to check an item out of a given list of responses. In other words, the respondent is asked to make choices among a set of alternatives given by the researcher. The respondent may simply select the answer which is supplied to him. In this type of questionnaire less time is required to fill it. It is relatively more objective. It is very convenient to the respondent. He is not bothered to give lengthy answers. It is fairly easy to tabulate and analyse.

4. Open form questionnaire

It is open end or unrestricted type questionnaire. It calls for free response of the respondent. That means the respondent can answer the questions in any way they choose. No clues are provided to answer. It probably provides a greater depth of response. It is difficult to interpret, tabulate and summarise. When a respondent is allowed to express his response, it may take it in a unique direction and it may not be find any uniformity with other responses.

5. The mixed questionnaire

It contains both close and open type questionnaires. This method is useful in social research.

Fact questionnaire

Questionnaire of fact requires certain information of facts from the respondent without any reference to his opinion or attitude about them.

Opinion questionnaire

Through this type of questionnaires, informant's opinion, attitude or preference regarding some phenomena is sought.

Pictorial questionnaire

In this case pictures are used to get answers. It will inspire the respondent to answer the questions. It is used widely in studies where the respondents are children or illiterate persons.

Pointers for Developing Questionnaires

The following points are kept in mind while developing questionnaires:

I. Structure

The structure of the questionnaire should be attractive. Adequate importance should be given to the physical form of questionnaire.

(i) ***Size:*** The size of the questionnaire depends upon the scope of the survey and the number of items to be included.

(ii) ***Length:*** Generally the respondents do not like to take too much time to fill a questionnaire. So the length of the questionnaire should be quite reasonable so that it can be completed in less than half an hour.

(iii) ***Use one side of the paper:*** It is better to use only one side of the paper, the reverse may be put as blank for special marks.

(iv) ***Margin and spacing:*** There should be proper margin and spacing among various questions. Title, sub-titles and column for noting may be included.

2. Brevity

The questionnaire should be as brief as possible. Nobody likes to face with a ten-page questionnaire. The respond rate is low enough without giving a further disincentive.

3. Simplicity

A complicated form may well conceal the real point of the questionnaires. There is a mistaken idea that, in the design of questionnaires, one has to use extremely complicated language. It is not necessary to use four or five words when would suffice.

4. Ambiguity

The respondent must be in no doubt as to what a question means. A question such as "Have you ever been involved in an accident in the past?" is open to a number of different interpretations. The definition of accident is not given and so to how far back the respondent will be unsure as to whether it is intended to embrace thefts, fires, accidents, or windscreen breakage.

5. Leading Questions

It is unwise to lead the respondent to provide a certain response to a question you have posed. This would occur where you frame a question such as, "Responsible jewellers always use the machine guards, do you use guards?" This would therefore reflect the respondent's perception of what you think is right, rather than what he really does.

6. Sequence

While preparing questionnaires importance should be given for sequence of questions. A proper sequence of questions reduces considerably the chances of individual questions being misunderstood.

7. Personal Questions

It is always wise to avoid the use of personal questions unless they are absolutely necessary. Most people need very little excuse for not completing a questionnaire and if you were to ask a question that they considered too personal, this might be enough for them to reject the entire form.

8. Double barrelled questions

A question that lends itself to different possible responses its subparts is called a double barrelled question. Such questions should be avoided. Instead of that two or more separate questions are asked.

9. Loaded questions

Another type of bias in question occurs when they are phrased in an emotionally charged manner. Such type of questions should also be avoided.

10. Arrangement of questions

The questions of the same category should be arranged together.

11. Nature of the response

The questions should always be designed with the eventual analysis in mind. Most questionnaires will be analysed by computer and the questions will have to reflect this. Computers operate best in term of numbers. The respondents would be presented with a number of options, leaving him to select the bone that matches his circumstance. The final analysis would be carried out by the computer. Not only is the analysis of the responses to this particular question made simple, it is also possible to carry out other forms of analysis. For example, we could ask the computer to select the people who are living in Odisha and then the computer provides other information of these people.

Guidelines for the Preparation of the Questionnaire

Delbert C Miller has given certain guidelines for preparing a questionnaire. The sixteen commandments which are to be observed while formulating the questions are given below:

(i) Keep the language pitched to the level of the respondent.
(ii) Try to pick words that have same meaning for everyone.
(iii) Avoid long questions.
(iv) Do not prior assume that your respondent possesses factual information, on first hand opinions.
(v) Establish the frame of reference you have in mind.
(vi) Informing a question, either suggest all possible alternatives to the respondent or do not suggest any.
(vii) Protect your respondent's ego.
(viii) If you are after unpleasant orientations, give your respondent a chance to express his positive feeling first so that he is put in an unfavourable light.
(ix) Decide whether you need a direct question, an indirect question or an indirect followed by a direct question.
(x) Decide whether the question should be open or closed.
(xi) Decide whether general or specific questions are needed.
(xii) Avoid ambiguous wording.
(xiii) Avoid biased or leading questions.
(xiv) Phrase questions so that they are not unnecessarily objectionable.
(xv) Decide whether a personal or impersonal question will obtain the better response.
(xvi) Questions should be limited to a single idea or single reference.

Contents of Questionnaire

The questionnaire should contain the following information.

1. Introductory part

The details regarding the name of the survey, the address of the surveyor, serial number of the case, place, address etc. are given in detail in the introductory part of the questionnaire.

2. Social background and factual information

The details regarding age, marital status, education, religion, political preference, size of the family, composition of the family and occupation, employment details, family income, economic status etc. are to be collected are given in this section.

3. Main part of the questionnaire

The information to be collected is given in this part. It is asked through questions.

Merits of Questionnaire

The following are the merits of questionnaire :

1. **Economical:** The mailed questionnaire is popularly used when the respondents are located in faraway places. So it is more economical in terms of money and time and energy.
2. **Uniformity:** The questionnaire is an impersonal technique, the uniformity can be provided by standardised wording of the questions. This method place less pressure on the subject of immediate response and provided more time to the respondent to answer.
3. **Free from bias:** It is free from bias of the interview because the answers are given by the respondent in his own words.
4. **Enough time:** The respondent gets enough time to answer the questions.
5. **Convenient access:** The respondents, who are not easily accessible, can be conveniently reached.
6. **Reliable results:** Large number of samples can be made use of and thus the results can be made dependable and reliable.

Limitations

The following are the limitations of questionnaire :

1. **Limited in use:** It is possible only among respondents who are well educated and ready to cooperate with the investigator or the researcher.

2. **Lower percentage of returns:** In the case of mailed questionnaire the proportion of return questionnaire with reply is too low.

3. **Misinterpretation:** There is a chance of misinterpretation of questions. So replies may be suitable for the study.

Schedule

A schedule is a set of questions which are asked and filled in by the interviewer in a face-to-face situation with another person. Enumerators go to respondents along with as schedule. He put the questions on them from the Proforma in the order of the questions listed and record the replies in the space meant for the same in the Proforma. In certain situations the schedule is handed over to the respondents and enumerator may help them in recording these answers to the various questions mentioned in the schedule. Enumerator explains the objects and aims of such investigation to the respondents. He also tries to remove the difficulties faced by the respondent while answering the questions. The investigator interprets the questions wherever necessary.

The schedule may contain two types of questions such as direct questions and form of a table. For data collection by using schedules enumerators are to be appointed. They are to be carefully selected. They should be given proper training to perform their job well. The nature and scope of data collection should be clearly spelled out to them. Then only they will be well understood about the implications of the different questions put in the schedule. The enumerators are to be intelligent. They must possess the capacity of cross-examination in order to find out the truth. Above all they should be honest, sincere, hardworking and trustful. They should have patience and perseverance.

Purpose of a schedule

A schedule is prepared to fulfill the following objectives :

1. To offer a consistent instrument for observation or interview in order to achieve objectivity.

2. To act as a memory reminder.
3. To assist the work of tabulation and analysis.

Schedule Preparation Process

The following steps are considered while framing a schedule:

1. The problem is to be studies should be split into different portions. A clear understanding of the problem is necessary for the sub-division of the problem into different aspects.
2. These portions or aspects are further sub-divided into number of sub-parts. The sub-parts should be able to provide clear picture of the different aspects of the study.
3. The next step is the preparation of proper questions related with the study. Proper care should be taken to see that the questions framed convey its exact meaning to the responders.
4. All the questions are well ordered. The validity of the schedule can only be assessed at the time of operation.

Types of schedules

1. Observation schedule

It is used for recording observations. It is mainly used to verify information. They offer an opportunity for uniform classification in recording the activities and social situation of groups or persons.

2. Evaluation schedule

It is used to gather information about specialised institutions or agencies. It is used in sociological or psychological research. The form and size of this schedule is determined on the basis of nature and complexity of the problem faced by the institution. If it is more complex, the size of the schedule may be bigger.

3. Document schedule

It is used to record data obtained from documents.

4. Interview schedule

This type of schedule is used by the interviewer to gather information from informants. It includes standard questions which are asked by the interviewer while interviewing the respondents. He enters the answers in the blank spaces provided for answers in schedule.

5. Rating schedule

The rating schedule is used to assess the attitudes, opinions, preferences, inhibitions, and other like elements in the field of business guidance, psychological research and social research.

Merits of schedules

- It can be adopted in those cases where informants are illiterate.
- When there is very little non-response, the enumerators go personally to obtain the information.
- The information received through schedules is more reliable and dependable.

Demerits of schedules

- This method is quiet costly. Enumerators are to be appointed to collect data.
- The success of the data collection depends upon the efficiency of the enumerators. They will be given training to collect data.

Comparison between Questionnaire and Schedule:

Though the questionnaire and schedule are designed on similar grounds, yet in practice they differ significantly. Some of the important points of comparisons are:

1. The questionnaire can be sent via mail but the schedule is done only personally
2. The questionnaire is a cheaper method than schedule (for schedule you have to move everywhere
3. The questionnaire can be returned without answering all the questions but, in schedule, enumerator ensures the filling all the questions.
4. The questionnaire can be filled by anyone but the schedule is always filled by enumerator.
5. Respondent should be literate & co-operative in Questionnaire but schedule can be administered even to illiterates as it is filled in by the enumerator by asking responses.
6. Risk of incomplete & wrong information is more in Questionnaire as compared to schedule.
7. Physical appearance of Questionnaire has to be attractive but it is not necessary with schedule because the person is physically available in front of the respondents.
8. Success of Questionnaire depends on its design but in case of Schedule it depends on honesty & competency of Enumerator.

Pre-Testing of the Questionnaire and Schedule

After preparing the questionnaire or schedule it is to be pre-tested before sending it to respondents. Pre-testing is a process of an advance testing of the study design after the preparation of the schedule or questionnaire. It is very much useful and necessary. It provides a test for the clarity of the questions and correctness of the interpretations put upon them by the respondents, it helps to find out the new aspects of that problem to be studied which are not anticipated at the time of planning stage of the study. So it is a trial and error procedure where in successful trials are repeated and the errors are avoided.

The following are the important symptoms that may be noticed while pre-testing the questionnaire or schedule.

- Absence of the proper order of the response.
- No response for certain questions.
- Large number of 'do not know' or 'do not understand answers' can be seen.
- Irrelevant answers may also be seen.
- Refusal of answering questions.
- Higher degree of variance in answers.
- Similar type of people gives different responses to the same question.

The work of the pre-testing must be done with due care and caution, otherwise unnecessary and unwanted changes may be introduced. Proper testing, revising and pre-testing questionnaire would yield high dividends.

Merits of Pre-test

There are many merits for the pretest:

- The investigator or researcher can find out what are the strengths and weaknesses of the questionnaire. That means which question are ought to be deleted and which one ought to be added.
- An idea can be formed about the extent of the response likely to take place.
- It helps to improve the design and effectiveness of the questionnaire in terms of format, quality etc.
- Pre-testing helps to resolve many problems of the measurement. It will show how to develop proper lines of inquiry in a logical manner.
- It provides right estimate of the resources needed to

complete the survey in terms of time, money, personnel, and equipments.

Review Questions

1. What is meant by primary data and secondary data?
2. What are the factors which are to be taken into consideration while selecting data source?
3. What are the important sources of data?
4. Explain the different documentary source.
5. What are the merits and demerits of Secondary Data?
6. What are the precautions to be taken by the researcher while using secondary data?
7. What are the sources or methods of collecting primary data?
8. Define interview. What are the types of interview used for data collection?
9. What is observation? Explain the process of observation.
10. What are the merits and demerits of observation?
11. Define experimental method.
12. What is Simulation?

5

Measurement Scales

Introduction

Measurement is a systematic way of assigning numbers or names to objects and their attributes. It is easy to assign numbers in respect of properties of some objects. But it is relatively difficult in respect of others. Properties like weight, height etc. can be measured directly with some standard unit of measurement. But it is not easy to measure qualitative aspects like motivation. In social phenomena there are two types of variables. One is related with variables which can be converted into quantitative variables and it can be measured with standard units or scales. Another type is related with items which cannot be converted into quantitative data. For example, we can't measure the social status, standard of living etc.

Technically speaking, measurement is a process of mapping aspects of a domain on to other aspects of a range according to some rule of correspondence. For measuring we use certain scales in the range and then transform or map tin-properties of the object from the domain on to this scale.

Scaling

The term scaling is used to indicate measuring of something. It is a device used for measuring various things. Scaling is the procedure for determining the quantitative measure of abstract concepts like leadership style, brand image of the product etc. It explains the procedure of assigning numbers to various degrees of opinion, attitude and other concepts. This can be done in two ways:

(i) To make the judgment about some characteristic of individual and then place him directly on a scale that has defined in terms that characteristic.

(ii) Construct questionnaires in such a way that the scores individual responses allocate him in a place on a scale.

A scale consists of a set of statement logically related referring to the same attitude that is being studied and is used to study simultaneously a number of observations which are dependent. Individually these observations are not useful.

A scale may be used to measure the characteristic of a respondent or to evaluate object presented to him.

Types of Measurement Scales

There are different types of scales which can be applied to measure different variables. A scale is a tool or mechanism by which individuals are distinguished as to how they differ from one another on the variables of interest to our study. Variables differ in "how well" they can be measured, i.e., in how much measurable information their measurement scale can provide. There is obviously some measurement error involved in every measurement, which determines the "amount of information" that we can obtain. Another factor that determines the amount of information that can be provided by a variable is its "type of measurement scale." Specifically variables are classified as (a) nominal, (b) ordinal, (c) interval or (d) ratio.

Nominal scales

It is simply a system of assigning number symbols to events in order to label them. For example, numbers are assigned to volleyball players in order to identify them or to distinguish one player the other. The numbers provided to them are just lenient labels. So it has no quantitative value. Nominal levels of measurement are used to distinguish between features only on the basis of qualitative information.

Nominal data does not imply quantitative differences. We can only say that A is different to B. It is meaningless to add, subtract, multiply or divide nominal data. If points on a map were coded to represent towns, buildings, population clusters or mountains they would represent nominal data. In other words nominal scales are used to measure the property of difference.

It is a scale of measurement with two more categories that have no numerical (less than, greater than) properties. Objects are measured by determining the category to which they belong. The only operation that can be performed on a nominal scale is that of counting. There are no numeric properties to nominal scales. The information obtained from a nominal scale is qualitative, meaning object are classified by name only.

This scale classifies individuals, companies, products, brands or other entities into categories where no order is implied. It is often referred to as a categorical scale. It is a system of, classification and does not place the entity along a continuum. It involves a simply count of the frequency of the cases assigned to the various categories, and if desired numbers can be nominally assigned to label each category as in the example below:

An example of a nominal scale

Which of the following food items do you tend to buy at least once per month? (Please tick)		
Meat	Coconut Oil	Raw Rice
Chilly	Prawns	Pasteurized Milk

Nominal scale is the least powerful measurement. The numbers have no arithmetic properties and act only as labels. The only measure of average which can be used is the mode because this is simply a set of frequency counts. Hypothesis tests can be carried out on data collected in the nominal form. The most likely would be the Chi-square test. However, it should be noted that the Chi-square is a test to determine whether two or more variables are associated and the strength of that relationship. It can tell nothing about the form of that relationship, where it exists, i.e. it is not capable of establishing cause and effect relationship.

Ordinal Scales

The ordinal scale places events in order. Ordinal scales involve differentiation by class, but they also differentiate within a class of features on the basis of rank according to some qualitative measure. Only rank is involved in ordinal scales. We are able to say that object 'A' has a higher rank than object 'B', but we cannot say by how much. Examples might be differentiating between major roads and minor roads or small, medium and large cities. This scale measures differences in magnitude (i.e., rank order). It's a scale of measurement in which the measurement categories form a rank order along a continuum. If P < Q and Q < R, then P < R. There are only crude numeric properties to ordinal scales, numbers assigned *cannot* be meaningfully added or subtracted. However, the extent to which P is less than Q may not *be* the same as the nil-lit to which Q is less than R. We can rank-order the objects according to whether they possess more, less of the same amount of the variable being measured. Thus, we can determine whether P > Q, P = Q, or P < Q. The information obtained from an ordinal scale is rank order. Thus, the use of an ordinal scale implies a statement of "greater than or less than" but it does not mention how much greater or less. The differences among objects are valid only relative to the other objects measured.

Ordinal scales involve the ranking of individuals, attitudes or items along the continuum of the characteristic being scaled. For example, if a researcher asked women to rank five brands of detergents in order of preference he/she might obtain responses like those in table given below.

An ordinal scale is used to determine women preferences among five brands of detergents in the following table:

Table-1

Order of preference	*Brand*
1	Henko
2	Surf
3	Tide
4	Areal
5	Nirma

From the Table 1 the researcher is able to know the order of preference but nothing about how much more one brand is preferred to another. That is there is no information about the interval between any two brands. All of the information nominal scale would have given is available from an ordinal scale.

In addition, positional statistics such as the median, quartile and percentile can be determined.

It is possible to test for order correlation with ranked data. The two main methods are Spearman's Ranked Correlation Coefficient and Kendall's Coefficient of Concordance. Using either procedure one can, for example, ascertain the degree in which two or more survey respondents agree in their ranking of a set of items. Consider again the ranking of detergents given in the Table 1. The researcher might wish to measure similarities and differences in the rankings of detergent brands according to the income pattern of respondents. The resultant coefficient takes a value income range 0 to 1. A zero would mean that there was no agreement between the two groups, and 1 would indicate total agreement. It is more likely that an answer somewhere between these two extremes would be found.

The only other permissible hypothesis testing procedures are the runs test and sign test. The runs test (also known as the Wald-Wolfowitz. Test is used to determine whether a sequence of binomial data - meaning it can take only one or two possible values e.g. Indian /non-Indian, yes/ no, male/ female - is random or contains systematic 'runs' of one or other value. Sign tests are employed when the objective is to determine whether there is a significant difference between matched pairs of data. The sign test tells the analyst if the number of positive differences in ranking is approximately equal to the number of negative rankings, in which case the distribution of rankings is random, i.e. apparent differences are not significant. The test takes into account only the direction of differences and ignores their magnitude and hence it is compatible with ordinal data.

Interval Scales

Interval scales is also known as the cardinal level of measurement, interval scales add information about the distance between ranks. To employ an interval scale we must use some kind of standard unit. For example, we differentiate between temperatures by using the standard unit of degrees Celsius. We cannot multiply or divide interval scale data. For example, it would be incorrect to say 40 °C = 2 * 20°C. Interval scales have no true or absolute zero. A temperature of 0°C does not imply an absence of heat; it is just the point at which water freezes.

It measures differences in magnitude, but also possesses the property of equal intervals. It's a scale of measurement in which the intervals between numbers on the scale are all "equal" in size. There are numeric properties to interval scales, and the numbers assigned can be meaningfully added or subjected, but not multiplied or divided. We can determine if A - B = B - C. The information obtained from an interval scale is the exact amount of the underlying construct that one object differs from another.

It is only with an interval scaled data that researchers can justify the use of the arithmetic mean as the measure of average. The interval or cardinal scale has equal units of measurement, thus making it possible to interpret not only the order of scale scores but also the distance between them. However, it must be recognised that the zero point on an interval scale is arbitrary and is not a true zero. This, of course, has implications for the type of data manipulation and analysis we can carry out on data collected in this form. It is possible to add or subtract a constant to all of the scale values without affecting the form of the scale but one cannot multiply or divide the values. It can be said that two respondents with scale positions 1 and 2 are as far apart as two respondents with scale positions 4 and 5, but not that a person with score 10 feels twice as strongly as one with score 5. Temperature in interval scaled, being measured either in Centigrade or Fahrenheit. We cannot speak of 50°F being twice as hot as 25°F since the corresponding temperatures on the centigrade scale, 10°C and -3.9°C, are not in the ratio 2:1.

Interval scales may be either numeric or semantic. Most of the common statistical methods of analysis require only interval scales in order that they might be used. These are not recounted here because they are so common and can be found in virtually all basic texts on statistics.

Ratio Scales

Ratio data is the highest measurement scale. All forms of arithmetic operations can be meaningfully applied to ratio scale data. Distance, tonnes of wheat, number of people is examples of ratio scale measurements. Zero has real meaning in ratio level measures. It is not possible to have less than zero people or to travel less than 0 km. Ratio scale represents the actual amount of variables. This has the properties of an interval scale together with a fixed origin or zero point. It's a scale of measurement in which there is an absolute zero point, indicating an absence of the variable being measured.

Examples of variables which are ratio scaled include weights, lengths and times. Ratio scales permit the researcher to compare both differences in scores and the relative magnitude of scores. For instance, the difference between 5 and 10 minutes are the same as that between 10 and 15 minutes, and 10 minutes is twice as long as 5 minutes.

There are numeric properties to interval scales, and the numbers assigned can not only be meaningfully added or subjected, but also multiplied and divided. The information obtained from a ratio scale is an absolute indication of how much of the underlying construct being measured an object has.

Differences between different scales

Nominal variables allow for only qualitative classification. That is, they can be measured only in terms of whether the individual items belong to some distinctively different categories, but we cannot quantify or even rank order those categories. For example, all we can say is that two individuals are different in terms of variable A (e.g., they are of different race), but we cannot say which one "has more" of the quality it-presented by the variable. Typical examples of nominal variables are gender, race, colour, city, etc.

Ordinal variables allow us to rank order the items we measure. In terms of which has less and which has more of the quality represented by the variable, but still they do not allow us to say "how much more." A typical example of an ordinal variable is the socioeconomic status of families. For example, we know that upper-middle is higher than middle but we cannot say that it is, for example, 18 per cent higher. Also this very distinction between nominal, ordinal, and interval scales itself represents a good example of an ordinal variable. For simple, we can say that nominal measurement provides less information than ordinal measurement, but we cannot say "low much less" or how this difference compares to the difference between ordinal and interval scales.

Interval variables allow us not only to rank order the items that are measured, but also to quantify and compare the sizes differences between them. For example, temperature, as measured in degrees Fahrenheit or Celsius, constitutes an interval scale. We can say that a temperature of 40 degrees is higher than a temperature of 30 degrees, and that an increase from 20 to 40 degrees is twice as much as an increase from 30 to 40 degrees.

Ratio variables are very similar to interval variables; in addition to all the properties of interval variables, they feature an identifiable absolute zero point, thus they allow for statements such as x is two times more than y. Typical examples of ratio scales are measures of time or space. For example, as the Kelvin temperature scale is a ratio scale not only can we say that a temperature of 200 degrees is higher than one of 100 degrees; we can correctly state that it is twice as high. Interval scales do not have the ratio property. Most statistical data analysis procedures do not distinguish between the interval and ratio properties of the measurement scales.

Given that sociological and management research seldom aspires beyond the interval level of measurement, it is not proposed that particular attention be given to this level of analysis. Suffice it to say that virtually all statistical operations can be performed on ratio scales.

Essentials of the Measurement Scale

A sound measurement scale must meet the requirements like test of validity, reliability and practicability. These are the important three major considerations the researcher must use in evaluating a measurement tool.

1. Test of validity

It is the most important critical criterion. It indicates the degree to which an instrument measures. There are two types of validity in this connection.

(a) Content validity: It is the extent to which a measuring instrument provides adequate coverage of the topics under study. If the instrument contains a representative of the filiations, the content validity is good. The content validity can also be judged by a panel of persons. This panel judges how well the measuring instrument meets the standards.

(b) Criterion related validity: It relates to the ability of researcher to predict some outcome or estimate the existence of the current situation. The concerned criteria should process the following qualities like relevance, free from bias reliability and availability.

2. Test of reliability

It is the other important criteria for sound measurement. If the measuring instrument gives consistent results we can say that it is reliable. It may be noted that the reliable instrument need not be a valid instrument. But a valid instrument may be reliable. Reliability of measurement depends upon two aspects namely, stability and equivalence. The stability aspect concerned with securing consistent results with repeated measurements of the same person and with the same instrument. The equivalent aspect considers how much error may get introduced by different investigators or different samples of items being studied. Reliability can be achieved in two ways.

I. Standardise the conditions under which the measurer takes place.
II. Design carefully the directions for measurement. Trained and motivated persons are employed to conduct the research. Likewise the sample size may be enlarged.

3. Test of practicability

The practicability of measuring instrument depends upon its convenience, economy, and interpretability features. The measuring instrument should be easy to administer. For till purpose the researcher or investigator should give proper attention to the layout of the measuring instrument. It indicates that the measuring instrument is a convenient one. The measuring instrument must be interpretable. In order to posses such feature, it must be supplemented by (i) detailed inn-lions to administer the test (ii) scoring keys (iii) evidence about the reliability and (iv) guides for using the test and interpretation of the results. If it is affordable within the limits of budget, then it has economy.

4. Appropriateness of scales

To become scaling suitable or appropriate the researcher should have full knowledge of the universe from where sample is taken for study. If various factor are logically related and in the form of continued measurement we can say that it is measurable or scalable.

5. Continuum

It means judging the scalability of the phenomenon under study. A scale in continuum if the scale consists of highest point (in terms some features like preference, favourableness etc.) and the lowest point with intermediate points.

Approaches Related with Construction of Scale

Generally there are five major approaches related to construction of scales.

1. Arbitrary approach

In this case the researcher develops a scale on ad-hoc basis. He collects a number of statements which he believes that they are unmistakable and suitable to a given topic. He chooses some of them and forms a scale. This approach can be adopted to develop any type of scale. The main advantage of methods is that they can be developed easily and it is less expensive. At the same time it has certain limitations.

1. The reliability depends upon the respondent's subjective logic.
2. The scale is constructed on the basis of an assumption that the statements selected are representing the entire universe. It may not be correct in all cases.

2. Consensus approach

Under this method the statement are selected by a panel of judges by considering the following facts.

1. Whether they come under the topic of study.
2. Whether they are meaningful and clear.
3. The level of the attitude that the scale represents.

After developing the scales, the respondents are asked to check the statements with which they agree.

Differential scales developed by *L.L. Thurstone* are coming under this category. This method is widely used for developing differential scales which are utilised in measuring attitude towards varied issues like war, religion etc.

3. Item analysis approach

As per this approach the actual responses are analysed on the basis of statements for determining their accessibility. A particular item is evaluated on the basis of how well they discriminate between those persons whose total scores are high and those whose scores are low. Those items or statements which meet best to this sort of discrimination tent are included in the final statement. Summated scales or Likert scales are developed by utilising this approach.

4. Cumulative scale approach

This scale contains a series of statements to which the respondent expresses his agreement or disagreement. The special feature of this type of scale is that they are cumulative in nature. The statements are related with one another. respondent replies favourably to item No. 3 also replies durably to item No. 2 and 1 the other person replies favourable to item No. 4 may also replies favourable to item numbers 3, 2, and 1 so on. It is being so, an individual whose attitude is at a certain point in a cumulative scale will answer favourable all the items of the one side of this point and answer unfavourably on all items of other side. The score of the individual is worked out by counting the number of point concerning the number of statements he answers favourably. If the investigator knows this total score, he can estimate as to how a respondent has answered individual statements constituting cumulative scales. Louis Guttmann's scalogram analysis is coming under this category. This approach is a complex one. So it is not widely used for study.

5. Factor analysis approach

As per this approach, factor scales are designed to inter-correlate items to determine their degree of independence between items. An important scale based on factor analysis is semantic differential scale and the other one is dimensional scaling. These tools are not widely used in the business research problems.

Sources of Error in Measurement

The researcher should always be aware of the sources of error in measurement. In an ideal research study the measurement should be precise and unambiguous. The following are the possible types or errors which are occurring while measurement.

1. Respondents reluctance

In certain times the respondent may be reluctant to express their strong negative feelings. Likewise in certain cases it has no little knowledge about a particular topic and he does not admit it. It will lead to make guesses at the time of interview. Apart from this, fatigue, anxiety etc will limit the ability of the respondent to express the ideas and feeling correctly. All this will lead wrong measurements.

2. Situational factors

It is another hindrance which will make constraint in measurement. The condition which places strain on interview will make serious effects on the interviewer-respondent rapport. If someone else is present at the time of interview, the respondent is reluctant to express his feeling and ideas fully.

3. Fault with interviewer

The interviewer can twist replies by rewording or reordering questions. His behaviour, style, and looks will encourage or discourage certain replies from respondents. In certain times careless mechanical processing may distort the findings. Errors may also occur if incorrect coding and faulty initiations are adopted.

4. Defective measurements

If defective measurements are adopted, it will make error. The use of the complex words, poor printing, inadequate space for replies etc may cause creating errors. Likewise if poor sampling is done it will also create mistakes.

RATING SCALES

Rating means measuring an attribute by judgment in continuum e.g. rating students by their teachers. While making rating the judges should be impartial. Rating scales are used for measuring the attitudes and the intensity of the attitudes. For example, a consumer is asked to rate a model of TV set as to its performance. The following types of rating scales are used in organisational research.

1. Dichotomous scale

Dichotomous scale is used to draw one out of set of two conjugate binary responses. i.e. Yes or No, Agree or Disagree,

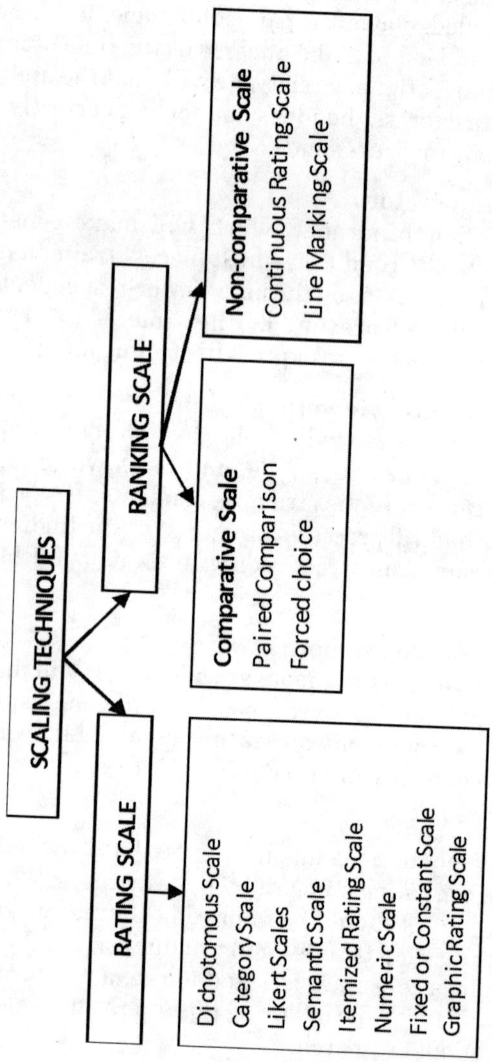
SCALING TECHNIQUES
RANKING SCALE
RATING SCALE
Comparative Scale
Paired Comparison
Forced choice
Non-comparative Scale
Continuous Rating Scale
Line Marking Scale
Dichotomous Scale
Category Scale
Likert Scales
Semantic Scale
Itemized Rating Scale
Numeric Scale
Fixed or Constant Scale
Graphic Rating Scale

Accept or Reject etc. The Kuder-Richardson Co-efficient of Reliability K-R 20 is used to test the consistency and reliability of such measure using nominal scale to elicit the response.

For example

Do you have a bike? Yes/ No.

2. Category Scale

This scale uses multiple items to draw out a single response. In this case also a nominal scale is used to elicit the response.

Where do you reside?

- Bhubaneswar
- Cuttack
- Balasore
- Berhampur
- Others

3. Likert scales

Rensis Lickert developed summated rating scale based on item analysis. A Likert scale is what is termed a summated instrument scale. This means that the items making up a Likert scale summed to produce a total score. In fact, a Likert scale is a composite of itemised scales. It consists of number statements which expresses either a positive or negative attitude towards the object of interest. The respondent is asked to agree or disagree with each statement. Each response is a numerical score to reflect its degree of attitude favourableness. Typically, each scale item will have 5 categories, with scale values ranging from -2 to +2 with 0 as neutral responses.

In Likert scale, the respondent is asked to respond to each of statements in terms of several degrees, usually five degrees of agreement or disagreement.

Steps in construction of a Likert scale

It consists of five steps.

A. Collection of statements

The researcher should collect a large number of statements which are relevant to the attitude being studied. Each of the statement expresses definite favourable or unfavourable to a particular point of view or the attitude that the number of favourable and unfavourable statements is approximately equal.

B. Wording

Greater care should be taken while forming sentences in the Complex sentences, ambiguous words, and sentences to be avoided. It is better to use phrases relating to emotions, feelings, fears, hopes and wishes.

C. Pilot study

After the collection of the statements the next step is to administer a trial test. Items to be included in the final scale should de done on the basis of a pilot study.

D. Scrutiny and editing

The pilot studies conducted for this purpose are to be scrutinised and edited to check the suitability of appropriateness of the statements. The statement which give Responses like do not now, uncertain etc are to be corrected or changed. The statements which are ambiguous or faulty must be discarded.

E. Final selection

At the time of final selection of the statement, it must be ensured that the statement represents the whole universe.

Merits of Likerts' scale

Following are the merits of using Likert's scale:

- It is relatively easy to construct.
- It is considered more reliable.
- This scale permits the use of statements that is noticeably related to the attitude being studied.
- It can easily be used in respondent centred and stimulus centred studies.
- Less time is required to construct this scale. It is widely used by research students.

Limitations

Following are the limitations of using Likert's scale:

- With the help of the scale a researcher is able to examine whether the respondents are more or less favourable to a topic but it is not able to tell how much more or less they are.
- There is no basis to believe that the five position indicated on the scale are equally spaced.
- The total score of an individual respondent has little clear meaning since a given total score can be secured by a variety of answer patterns.

Example of Likert scale

	Strongly Agree	*Agree*	*Neither Agree*	*Disagree*	*Strongly Disagree*
If the price of raw materials fell firms would reduce the price of their food products.	1	2	3	4	5
Without government regulation the firms would exploit the consumer.	1	2	3	4	5
Most food companies are so concerned about making profits they do not care about quality.	1	2	3	4	5
The food industry spends a great deal of money making sure that its manufacturing is hygienic.	1	2	3	4	5
Food companies should charge the same price for their products throughout the country	1	2	3	4	5

4. Semantic scales

This type of scale makes extensive use of words rather than numbers. Respondents describe their feelings about the products or brands on scales with semantic labels. When bipolar adjectives are used at the end points of the scales, these are termed semantic differential scales. The semantic scale and the semantic differential scale are illustrated below:

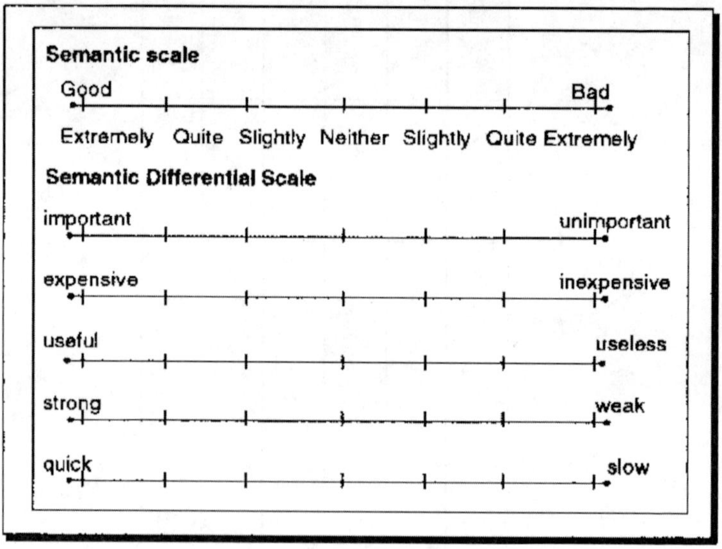

Semantic and Semantic Differential Scales

Several bipolar attributes are identified at the extreme of the scale, and respondents are asked to indicate their attributes on semantic space, toward a particular object, individual or event on each of the attributes. The bipolar adjectives like Good-Bad, strong-weak etc are employed. Semantic differential scale was developed by Osgood and his associates. It attempts to measure the psychological meanings of the concept to individuals. It consists of a set of bipolar rating scales usually seven points, by which groups of subjects are asked to rate one or more concepts relevant to the selected research problem.

Steps

The steps of the semantic differential scale are represented with reference to an organisation are:

(a) Identify the attributes on which the organisations are to be judged by respondents.
(b) Decide on the number of descriptive phrases and define them.
(c) Design a questionnaire containing semantic differential scale.
(d) Give the questionnaire to the respondents and seek their judgements.
(e) Sum of the judgement scores of each attribute across respondents and find average.
(f) Plot the average score of each attribute on schematic differential scale.

5. Itemised rating scales

The respondents are provided with a scale having numbers and/ or brief descriptions associated with each category. Then the respondents are asked to select one of the limited numbers of categories, ordered in terms of scale position, which best describes the product, brand, company or product being studied. This uses interval scale. The itemised scale provides the flexibility to use as many points in the scale as considered necessary. Research indicates that a five point scale is frequently used in business research. The increase in number of points does not improve the reliability of the ratings. An example of the itemised rating scale is given below:

6. Numerical scale

It is similar to semantic differential scale. The difference is that numbers on a five points or seven points scales are provided with bipolar adjectives on both ends. This is also an interval scale.

7. Fixed or constant scale

Here the respondents are asked to distribute a given number of points across various items. For example: The respondents

Colour	-------------------
Smell	-------------------
Size	-------------------
Shape	-------------------
Quality of foam	-------------------
Total Points	---------------------

are asked to indicate importance to the five aspects by allotting points for selecting toilet soap.

8. Graphic rating scale

This is a common and simple form to use. A graphical scale helps the respondent to mark on their scale their answers to a particular question by placing a mark on the appropriate point on the line.

RANKING SCALES

These scales are used to tap preferences between two among more objects or items. Such ranking may not give ultimate clues to some of the answers required by the researcher. There are generally three approaches of making scales.

Comparative scale

- Paired comparison
- Forced choice.

Comparative scale

It provides a benchmark or a point of reference to assess towards the current object, event or situation under study.

Paired comparison

Under this method the respondent can express his attitude by making a choice between two objects e.g. choice between new flavour of a soft drink or established brand of a product. As the number of the objects compared increases, the following formula is used.

The paired choice of 'n' objects will be [(n) (n-1)/2].

The greater the number of objects the greater the number paired comparisons presented to the respondents. It will enhance the fatigue of the respondent. So paired comparison is good when the number of stimuli or objects are small.

The paired comparison scale gives ordinal data. It may be converted into the interval scale by the method of the 'law of comparative judgment' developed by L.L. Thurstone.

Forced choice

It enables the respondents to rank the objects relative to one another among the alternatives provided. This is easier and faster as the respondents are concerned. For example, under paired comparison method, with 10 items, 45 paired comparisons are required to complete the task. In the method of ranking, 10 items are to be ranked. In certain cases complete ranking of items is not needed when the respondent is asked to rank only their first, second and third choice. The main limitation of the method is that, sometime respondent give ranks carelessly.

Non-comparative scales

Non-comparative scales include continuous rating itemised rating scales, semantic differential scales and Likert scales.

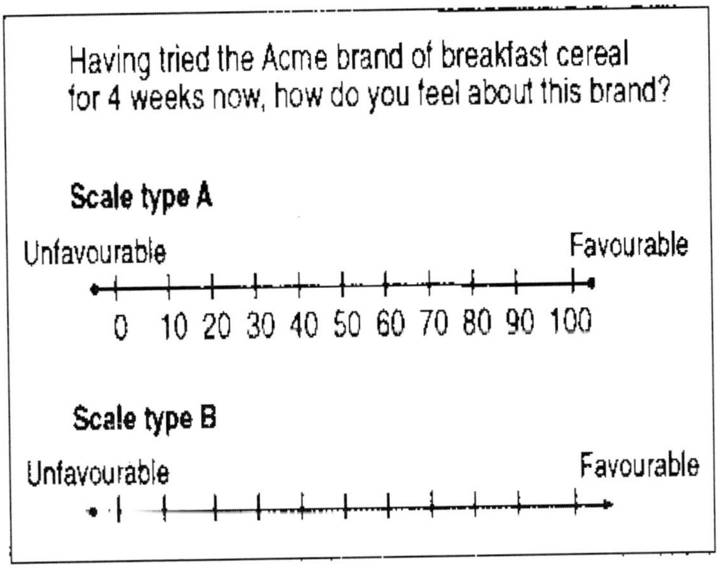

Continuous rating scales

The respondents are asked to give a rating by placing a mark at the appropriate position on a continuous line. The scale can be written on card and shown to the respondent during the interview. Two versions of a continuous rating scale are depicted in the following chart:

When version B is used, the respondent's score is determined either by dividing the line into as many categories as desired and assigning the respondent a score based on the category into which his/her mark falls, or by measuring the distance, in millimeters or inches, from either end of the scale.

Whichever of these forms of the continuous scale is used, the hills are normally analysed as interval scaled.

Line marking scale

The line marked scale is typically used to measure perceived similarly differences between products, brands or other objects. Technically, such a scale is a form of what is termed a semantic differential scale since each end of the scale is labelled with a word/phrase (or semantic) that is opposite in meaning to the other. For example, consider the products below which can be used when frying food. In the case of each pair, indicate how similar or different they are in the flavour which they impart to the food. The following chart depicts this scale.

For some types of respondent, the line scale is an easier format because they do not find discrete numbers (e.g. 5, 4, 3, 2, and 1) best reflect their attitudes/ feelings. The line marking scale is a continuous scale.

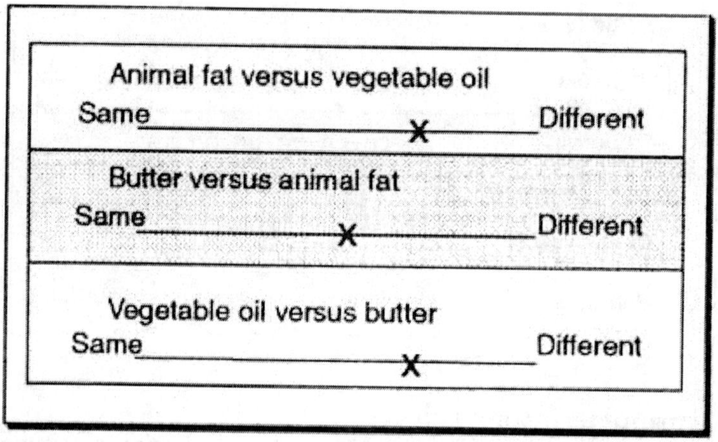

PILOT STUDY

It is a mini study before the main study to eliminate all the bugs. It is the preliminary study conducted on a limited scale before the original studies are carried out in order to gain some primary information, on the basis of which the main project would be planned and formulated. The preliminary study of the population under the study will give knowledge about the problem to researcher. It eventually helps to know the nature and different aspects of the problems.

The pilot study is undertaken on a smaller sample size without formulating a hypothesis. The sample for the study should be selected from the population. Sometimes different population may be used in order to preserve the sample size.

The study enables the researcher to gain some systematic knowledge of the universe and its population under study. The researcher is able to frame schedule or questionnaire on the basis of information gathered through pilot study. Pilot study can be used to find out the best method of data collection (especially in ethnographic research). Pilot study gives a novice opportunity for research skill development. However, the size and design of the pilot study depends upon the convenience, time and money. The researcher studies the field in a very non-directive fashion.

Pilot study can be used to get the answers of the following questions:

1. Has the problem adequately defined? (Scientific logic can be tested)
2. Are the variables clear?
3. Will the result address the purpose adequately?
4. Methodological issues will be tested through pilot study (questions clear?)
5. Are the research methods adequate?
6. Are the Subjects selections adequate?
7. Is the Variables adequately measured?
8. Are the Instruments accurate?
9. How long it takes to complete the survey?

Case study research can be conducted as pilot study for the purpose of generating hypotheses to be tested later through experimental methods. In historical research pilot study may not be appropriate because we may use all the available data because we may not have too much, data for piloting (1 event or 1 chain of events) and do not want to eliminate the data used in pilot study.

Advantages of the pilot study

Following are the advantages of pilot study:

- Helps in selection of the respondents.
- It helps to expose the inadequacies of the questionnaire.
- It helps to know the non-response rate, reasons for desirable time for interviewing etc.

- The pilot study provides necessary training and motivation for the investigators to carry out the planned job.
- The pilot study provides an opportunity the researcher to learn about the local culture and build self-confidence.
- It helps the interviewer to learn a variety of tactics and code of conduct which they would follow to get the rapport of respondents.
- It provides a trial rehearsal to test the work of interviews.
- It helps to identify the tools and equipment's needed for the survey. The climate of the region decides the need of the different equipment which may range from a rain coat to lanterns.
- It helps to estimate the time and cost for completing the work successfully.
- It helps to decide the superior to interviewer ratio.

FIELD WORK

Management of the field work aims to maximise the flow of pertinent, accurate data. It also aims to minimise the errors committed by the interviewers. So the twin objectives of the field work are:

o Maximising the low of accurate data.
o Minimise the errors committed by the interviewers.

There are six phases in the field work. They are

1. Pre-testing
2. Simplifying procedures
3. Interviewer recruitment and selection
4. Instructing field workers
5. Supervision and
6. Control

1. Pre-testing

Every important project should be pre-tested on the basis of a Standard procedure. There are possibilities of errors in survey. It may come in the form of wrong order of questions, awkward terminology, leading questions, and weak stimulation of response. In some cases the sampling plan is in appropriate. The instructions for the field work may be in vogue. Pre-testing of questionnaire and schedules will help to identity all this defects. So pre-testing is a very important aspect as the project is concerned.

2. Simplify procedure

A number of simplifying procedure is available to simplify the field work.

(a) The interviewer may be equipped with sufficient aids to demonstrate the desired responses and to establish relationship.

(b) Self-administered interview method is to be adopted to simplify the field work. The interviewee himself writes the answers in the questionnaire. The interviewer has to wait till the interviewer complete the answers.

(c) Tape records are to be used to record the answers of the questionnaires. It enhances the fidelity of the recorded responses. It eases the interviewer role also.

(d) Previous appointment should be fixed with interviews through telephone. It will help to complete the interviews as per time schedule.

(e) The design and legibility of the questionnaire must be enhanced to ease the work and to achieve the accuracy.

3. Recruitment and selection of the interviewer

In every research work including project work, data collection is entrusted with an interviewer. The interviewer recruitment is an important step required for data collection. The quality of the collected data depends upon the efficiency of the interviewer for receding responses and appropriate probing. Tho following factors are kept in mind while selecting an interviewer.

(a) Education: The interviewer should possess good academic qualifications. Good reading and writing skills are required for an interviewer.

(b) Gender: Field survey is a part time or intermittent work. So majority of the survey organisation prefers women for field work.

(c) Age: The age of the interviewer is important. Generally persons within the age group 25-45 are preferable.

(d) Quality of the voice: The voice of the interviewer should be such that which could be listened comfortably by the respondent over a long time. It is free from harshness or features that could irritate others.

(e) Experience: An experienced interviewer can perform better in the field work. They are capable to follow instruction in a better way. They can record the responses accurately, and conduct interview smoothly.

(f) Personal Qualities: The following qualities are considered while selecting interviewers:

(i) **Honesty:** An interviewer must be honest and sincere.

(ii) **Interest:** Interest in the work is highly desirable.

(iii) **Accuracy:** An interviewer should be accurate to follow the instructions. He/she should understand the objectives accurately.

(iv) **Temperament:** Pleasantness is always a necessity.

(v) **Intelligence:** An interviewer should have sufficient intelligence to follow instruction whether it is complicated or not.

(vi) **Communication skill:** The interviewer must possess communication skill. That means he/she should have interviewing ability.

Selection Procedure:

The selection procedure of an interviewer includes:

(I) Selection test

(II) Trial Interview

(III) Personal Interview

Selection test is intended to measure reading ability, arithmetic ability, and ability to follow instructions, accuracy in recording, summarising, checking and classifying data.

If a candidate passes selection test, he/she is asked to interview certain strange persons with an interview schedule. It is observed to assess his/her ability. It is known as trial interview.

When the candidate complete trial interviews successfully, he/she is called for a personal interview. Personal interview is conducted to study their personality, manners and temperament.

4. Instruct field workers

Proper instruction should be served to field workers to conduct the work properly. Sufficient instructional material should be provided to field workers to conduct field surveys. Training should be imparted to interviewers for the purpose of proper conduct of the field work. There are mainly four basic methods for teaching interviewers. They are as follows:

(a) **Provision of written materials:** It can be used in two ways: (i) Provision of a complete written description of interviewer procedures, (ii) Provision of written description for each particular research project.

(b) **Lectures and demonstrations:** It offers the trainees an opportunity to ask questions on procedures that are not clear. Demonstration of an interview helps the trainees to understand the various aspects of the interview and the purpose of the survey.

(c) **Role playing:** It gives an opportunity to the trainee to handle different interview situations set by the trainer.

(d) **Field practice:** It helps the interviewer to understand the actual procedure for conducting a survey. The supervisor accompanies trainees an as observer. He gives proper evaluation of the way of interview conducted by the interviewer.

5. Supervision

The supervisor has to perform various duties such as briefing the field staff, directing the sample selection, scheduling the field work, allotting to work to field staff, attending to their quarries and difficulties, and receive the complete schedules in time. It is the duty of the supervisor to maintain regular contact with the interviewer working in miserable locations.

6. Control

A good control will lead to the survey a grand success. To achieve control the programme should be scheduled and validated. Validation refers to the verifying that the interviewers are submitting authentic interview of acceptable quality. When there is no field supervision, the head office has primary responsibility to check the field work. The head office should see: (i) whether the interviewer has studied and understood the instructions property, (ii) whether the reported interviews are genuine. It should also appraise the quality of the interviewing and reporting.

Review Questions

1. Explain the types of Measurement scales?
2. What are the possible types of errors which are occurring while measurement?

3. What are the essentials of a sound measurement Scale?
4. What are the approaches related with Construction of scale?
5. What are the frequently used scaling techniques?
6. What are the steps involved in construction of a Likert's scale?
7. What is pilot study? Explain advantages and limitations of the pilot study.
8. What is meant by field work? What are the objectives of the field work?

6

Data Processing

(Editing, Classification and Coding of Data)

After collecting data, it has to be processed. Processing is essential for scientific study and for ensuring that all the data are gathered for making comparisons and analysis. Processing operations involves the following steps.

(i) Editing
(ii) Coding
(iii) Classification
(iv) Tabulation

(i) Editing

It is the first step in data processing. It is the process of examining the data collected in questionnaires or schedules to detect the errors and omissions and to correct these as far as possible. It involves a careful scrutiny of the completed questionnaires and schedules. It is done to ensure that the data is accurate, consistent with the other facts gathered, uniformly entered, as complete as possible, acceptable for tabulation and arranged for facilitating for tabulation and coding.

Editing is also undertaken to determine whether or not a specific interview is acceptable in the light of the objectives of the project.

There are two stages in editing

1. Field editing,
2. Central editing.

Field editing

In field editing the investigator makes appraisal of the reporting forms for completing what the latter has written in abbreviated and /or in illegible form at the time of recording the respondent's responses. This type of editing is necessary because an individual writing style may be difficult for others to interpret. This type of sorting should be done after the interview preferably on the same day or on the next day. The investigator should not indulge to correct errors of omission by mere guessing what the respondent would have said.

Central editing

Central editing is done after getting all completed forms or schedules in office. This type of editing is done by one editor if the study is a small one. If the study is large, then the editing is done by the team of editors. Editors may correct the obvious errors such as an entry in wrong place; entry recorded in months when it should have been recorded in weeks and the like. If there is missing replies the auditor can determine, the proper answer by reviewing the other information in the schedule. In certain times the editor is required to contact the respondents for getting clarification with certain matters which are written in schedule or questionnaire. The editor can strike out answers which are inappropriate and has no basis for determining the correct answer. The clear wrong replies must be dropped from the final results. In the doubtful cases also the incorrect reply should be discarded.

Every study contains numerical answers. The entire respondents are not thinking the answers in terms of the same base, it is necessary to convert the numerical answers into a common base.

The following points are kept in mind by the editor while performing the editing work.

1. The editors should be familiar with the instructions are given to interviewers and coders. They are also familiar with the instructions given to them with regard to editing.
2. When they wipe out the original entry for one reason or other, they should draw a single line on it to become it legible.
3. When they are making entries in the form, it should be with a distinctive colour and in a standard form.

4. They should initial all changes which have done by then in the firm. They should also put the date of editing on each completed form of schedule.

(ii) CODING

The next step is to code the responses. Coding is the process of assigning figures or other symbols to answers so that responses can be put into a limited number of categories or classes. In other words, coding involves two main operations (i) decide the category to be used and (ii) to allocate individual answers to them. Such classes should be appropriate to the research problem under study. They must also possess the features of exhaustiveness, mutual exclusivity and undimensionality. Exhaustiveness indicates that there must be a class for every data item. Mutual exclusivity means that a specific answer can be placed in only one cell in a given category set. Undimensionality means every category is defined in terms of only one concept. Coding can be recorded on the questionnaire/ schedule themselves. In such cases, the code numbers are receded in the margin if the questionnaire with a colour pencil.

Coding is necessary for efficient analysis. The coding eliminates much of information in raw data. That means several replies are reduced to a small number of classes which contains critical information required for analysis.

Coding decision is usually taken at the designing stage of the questionnaire. This makes it possible to pre-code the questionnaire choices and which in turn is helpful for computer tabulation.

Steps in coding

1. The first step in coding is to study the answers. In the case of pre-coded questions coding begins at the time of the preparation of the questionnaire.
2. Develop a coding frame. It is the outline of what is coded and how it is to be coded. It is asset of explicit rules and conventions that are used to base classifications of observed variables into values which are transformed into numbers. Coding frame is framed by listing the possible answers to each question and assigning code numbers of symbols to each of them which are the indicators used for coding.

3. After the preparation of the sample frames the next step is gradual fitting of the answers to the questions.
4. The next step to transfer the information from the schedule to a separate sheet named transcription sheet. This sheet is a large summary sheet which contains the answers /codes of all the respondents. If simple tables are used, no transcription is required.

Coding rules

The following are the coding rules in data collection process:

- Code numbers are to be provided to each respondent for the purpose of identification. Generally digits are used to identify the area, the institution department etc.
- Provide code number for each question.
- Confer code numbers off each response. Qualitative responses are also given code numbers.
- Researcher himself does the work of assigning code. It should not be delegated to others.
- Arrange a coding frame.
- Prepare instructions for coders.
- Get readies the supply coder's instruction manual.
- Arrange the services of the trained coders under close supervision.
- Vigilantly inspect every coded item in the early stages of coding.
- Random checking should be done to see that the coding process is going on smoothly.
- The researcher should take decision when any change is needed at the process of coding.

(iii) CLASSIFICATION

After coding the data the next step is classification of responses. In most research studies there is large volume of data. All these data are classified into homogenous groups to get meaningful relationships. Classification of data is the process of grouping of related facts into classes on the basis of certain common characteristics. Data having common characteristics are placed in one class. In this way the entire data is divided into a number of groups or classes. A good classification should have the qualities of clarity, homogeneity, equality of scales, purposefulness and accuracy.

Objectives of classification

The following are the important objectives:

- To condense the mass of data in such a manner that similarities and dissimilarities can be readily apprehended.
- To organise complex, scattered and haphazard data into concise, logical and intelligible form.
- To facilitate comparison.
- To identify the most significant features of the data glance.
- To give prominence to the important information by dropping the unnecessary elements in the data.

Types of classification

The data can be classified on the following basis:

1. Qualitative classification (on the basis some attributes).
2. Geographical classification (on the basis of area).
3. Chronological classification (on the basis of time).
4. Quantitative classification (on the basis of quantity).

In geographical classification data are classified on the basis of geographical or locational; difference between the various items. If the data are observed over a period of time it is better to classify data on the basis chronology. Such a classification is known as chronological classification. In qualitative classification data are classified on the basis of some attribute or quality such as sex, literacy, religion etc quantitative classification refers to the classification of data according to some characteristic that can be measured such as height, weight etc.

The other types of classification is multiple and dichotomous classification. The type of classification where only two classes are formed is called dichotomous classification. If instead of forming two classes we further subdivide the data on the basis of some attribute or attributes so as to form several classes it is known as multiple classifications. Grouping the workers of a factory under the various income groups is the example of multiple classifications.

Classification according to attributes

Data can be classified on the descriptive nature of data. Descriptive characteristics refer to qualitative aspects which cannot be measured quantitatively. Only the presence or absence of it in an individual item is to be noticed. Literary, sex, honesty, etc are coming under the descriptive nature. Such classification may be simple or manifold classification. In simple classification we divide the universe into two classes. One class includes only items which possess one quality and the other class includes items which do not possess that quality. In manifold classification two or more attribute are considered simultaneously and the data is divided into number of classes.

Classification according to class interval

This type of classification is most popular in practice. Data relating to income, production, age, height, weight etc are classified on the basis of class intervals. Such data are known as statistics of variables. For example, data relating to income in between 101 to 200 can be one class and 201 to 300 may be in another class. In this way the entire data is classified into different classes which are usually called *class intervals.*

Each class interval has upper limit and lower limit. So the difference between upper class limit and lower class limit is termed as *class magnitude.*

Class limit may be generally stated in the following ways.

1. *Exclusive type class intervals*

In exclusive type class interval, the items whose values are equal to the upper limit of a class are grouped in the next higher class. For example:

100-200
200-300
300-400
400-500
500-600
600-700

The above interval can be read as 100 and under 200 and so on. In this case the item whose value is exactly 200 is included in 200-300 classes and not in 100-200.

2. Inclusive type class intervals

In this case the upper limit of the class interval is included in the same class interval. For example:

101-200
201-300
301-400
401-500

501-600
601-700

An item whose value is 200, then it is included in the group of 100-200.

Inclusive type of classification is included if the data under consideration is discrete one. But the phenomena are a continuous one, and then exclusive types of class interval are to be adopted.

Size of the class interval

The size of the class interval is determined by the number of classes and the total range in the data. Several systems have been devised to determine the width of the class interval. One method suggested by H.A Sturges is given below:

$$C = \frac{Highest \quad Value - Lowest \quad Value}{1 + 3.222 \quad Log \quad N}$$

Where N = number of items grouped.

We may have classes with equal magnitudes or unequal. There is no specific answer with regard to the number of classes. It depends upon the skill and experience of the researcher. However, the objective should be to display data in much a way as to make a meaningful analysis.

Frequency Determination

The number of observations corresponding to particular class is termed as its frequency. If the lowest limit 100 and highest limit is 150, it means the frequency in between these two is 50. Frequency of each class can be determined by using tally sheets.

Class	*Tally Sheet (Tallies)*	*Frequency (f)*
20-25	*I*	1
25-30	*III*	3
30-35	*~~IIII~~*	5
35-40	*~~IIII~~ II*	7
40-45	*~~IIII~~ ~~IIII~~*	10
45-50	*~~IIII~~ III*	8
50-55	*IIII*	4
55-60	*II*	2
		$\Sigma f = 40$

The class groups are written in a sheet of paper and for much item a stroke (vertical line) is marked against the class group in which the item falls. The general practice is that upto lour items strokes are marked and for fifth item which falls in the same group is marked by drawing a cross line on four strokes.

Example of a tally sheet

Yellow	////	4
Red	~~////~~	5
Blue	~~////~~ /	6
Green	/	1
Pink	////	4

In the case of large scale surveys the sorting is done by machines.

Principle of classification

It is difficult to lay down hard and fast rules for classifying data. In general the type of classification of data depends upon the nature of the given data and the object of classification.

The following general considerations may be kept in mind to classify data into a meaningful one:

1. The number of classes should be preferably in between 5 and 15.
2. Preferably one should have classifications either five or its multiples.
3. The starting point may either be zero or five or multiples of five.
4. It is better to adopt exclusive method of calculation if we want ensure continuity and to get correct class interval.
5. The interval should be equal for all classes.
6. If possible open end class such as below 100, 100-200, 200-500, above 500 should be avoided.

Review Questions

1. What is editing? What are its stages?
2. What is coding? What are the steps involved in coding?
3. What are the rules that are followed in coding?

4. What is classification of responses? What are its objectives and types?
5. What are the principles of classification?
6. Write a short note on:
   a. Size of the class interval
   b. Frequency determination
   c. Quantitative classification.

7

Tabulation

Introduction

A table is a systematic arrangement of data into vertical column and horizontal rows. So the process of arranging data into rows and column is called tabulation. Tabulation is the process of summarising raw data and displaying it in a compact form for further analysis. In other words it is the arrangement of data in some kind of concise and logical order. Broadly speaking, tabulation is an orderly arrangement of raw data in columns and rows. Tabulation can be done by hand, or by mechanical devices or through computer. It is essential due to the following reasons:

1. It helps to simplify complex data.
2. It preserves space and reduces explanatory and descriptive statement at minimum.
3. It facilitates the processes of comparison.
4. It gives an identity to data. When the data is arranged and giving a title to it, it can be identified distinctively.
5. It helps to detect errors and omissions.

Meaning and Definitions

Tabulations are defined as the information arranged in a tabular manner. It is also defined as the process of arranging data, facts, statistics, etc in an orderly form of rows and columns. Tabulations can be defined as the cutting or forming with a plane surface or a flat surface.

Tabulation refers to the systematic arrangement of the information in rows and columns. Rows are the horizontal arrangement. In simple words, tabulation is a layout of figures in rectangular form with appropriate headings to explain different rows and columns. The main purpose of the table is to simplify the presentation and to facilitate comparisons.

According to Neiswanger, "A statistical table is a systematic organisation of data in columns and rows."

According to Connor, "Tabulation involves the orderly and systematic presentation of numerical data in a form designed to elucidate the problem under consideration."

From the above cited definitions, it is clear that tabulation refers to the systematic arrangement of data in rows and columns. The arrangement of data obtained after this process is called a table.

Objects and Importance of Tabulation

Tabulation is a technique to present and interpret the complex information in a simple and systematic form. The main objectives of the process of tabulation are as follows:

- The main purpose of the tabulation is to simplify the complex information so that it can be easily understood.
- Under tabulation, data is divided into various parts and for each part there are totals and sub-totals. Therefore, relationship between different parts can be easily known.
- Since data are arranged in a table with a title and a number so these can be easily identified and used for the required purpose.
- Tabulation makes the data brief. Therefore, it can be easily presented in the form of graphs.
- Tabulation presents the numerical figures in an attractive form.
- Tabulation makes complex data simple and as a result of this, it becomes easy to understand the data.
- This form of the presentation of data is helpful in finding mistakes.
- Tabulation is useful in condensing the collected data.
- Tabulation makes it easy to analyse the data from tables.
- Tabulation is a very cheap mode to present the data. It saves time as well as space.

- Tabulation is a device to summaries the large scattered data. So, the maximum information may be collected from these tables.

Parts of a Table or Preparation of a Table

Preparation of a table is an art which needs an expert handling of data. Following general principles may be followed for the purpose of preparing a perfect table:

Table Number: When a table or a book contains more than one table, each table must have a number. The tables are numbered in a sequence so that they may be easily referred to. The number of the table should be placed at the middle on the top of the table.

Title: Every table must have a suitable heading. The heading should be short, clear and convey the purpose of the table. It should contain four types of information:

- The subject matter
- Time
- Basis of classification
- Sources.

Besides, the main heading, there may be some sub-heading also.

The title should be so worded that it permits one and only one interpretation. Its letters should be the most prominent of any lettering on the table.

Long titles cannot be read as promptly as short titles, but they may have to be used for the sake of clarity when necessary. In such a situation a "catch title" may be given above the main title.

Captions and stubs: Captions refer to the vertical column's headings, whereas stubs refer to the horizontal row's headings. Captions generally give the basis of classification e.g. sex, occupation, meters, kms, etc. It may consist of one or more column headings. Under a column heading, there may be sub-heads. The captions should be clearly defined and placed at the middle of the column. It is desirable to number each column and row for reference and to facilitate comparisons.

Head notes: Head Note is a statement given below the title which clarifies the contents of the table. It gives an explanation concerning the entire table or main parts of it, e.g., the units of measurement are usually expressed in a head note such as 'in hectares', 'in millions', 'in quintals' etc.

Body: The body of the table contains the figures that are to be presented to the readers. The table must contain sub-totals of each separate class of data and grand total for the combined classes.

Source: The source is given in case of secondary data. It gives the sources from which the data were obtained. The source should give the name of the book, page number, table number etc. from which the data have been collected.

Limitations of Tabulation

Tabulation suffers from the following limitations:

- Tables contain only numerical data. They do not contain details.
- Qualitative expression is not possible through tables.
- Tables can be used by experts only to draw conclusions. Common men do not understand them properly.

Types of tabulations

Tabulation may be classifies as simple and complex tabulation. In simple table only one characteristic is shown. Hence this type of table is known as one way table. In a complex table two or more characteristics are shown. When two or more characteristics are shown it is called two way table. When three characteristics are shown in a table it is known as treble tabulation. The following example indicates the simple table.

Age in years	*No. of employees*
Below 25	-----
25—35	-----
35—45	-----
45—55	-----
Above 55	-----
Total	**XXXXXX**

Example of Two way table

Mark	*Number of Students*		
	Male	*Female*	*Total*
I.	**II.**	**III.**	**IV.**
Below 25			

Mark	Number of Students		
	Male	Female	Total
V.	VI.	VII.	VIII.
25-- 35			
35--45			
45--55			
55—65			
Above 65			
Total			

Principles of Tabulation

It is difficult to lay down hard and fast rules for tabulating data because much depends upon the given data and requirements of the survey. General consideration which can be followed in tabulation is given below:

1. The table should suit the size of the paper usually with more rows than columns.
2. The table should have a clear, concise and adequate title. It should always place just above the body of the table.
3. Every table should have a distinct number for easy reference.
4. The captions and stubs should be arranged in a systematic manner in all types of tables. It would make the table easier to read and allow more important items to be emphasised.
5. The unit of measurement should be clearly defined and is given in the table such as income in rupees.
6. Figures should be rounded to avoid unnecessary details in the table and footnote should be given in this effect.
7. Explanatory footnotes if any should be given as footnote along with reference symbols used in the table.
8. Sources from which data in the table is obtained are to be indicated just below the table.
9. The columns drawn are to be separated by lines which make the table more attractive and legible.
10. The data under one class is separated from the data another class by drawing thick lines. The lines used to separate subdivision of data may be thin.
11. The columns may be numbered for reference.

12. The data which are to be compared is to be kept side by side in columns. Similarly, percentages, or averages are kept close to the data.
13. The items related to each other should be placed new about and if possible in the same group.
14. To give emphasis of certain data, different kinds of type, spacing and indentations are to be used.
15. All items in the table should be logically arranged.
16. All the column figures are to be properly aligned.
17. Abbreviations should be avoided especially in the title and headings. For example 'yr' should not be used for 'year'.
18. A column named miscellaneous column should be added for data which do not fit in the classification model.
19. Table should be clear, accurate and simple. It should not be overloaded with details.
20. Total of the rows should be placed extreme right column.
21. Do not use ditto marks. If figures are to be repeated it should be shown in each time.
22. The data in a table may be arranged in chronological, geographical, alphabetical or according to the magnitude to facilitate comparison.

Graphical Representation of Data

Suitable forms of graphic presentation are desirable to present data of frequency distributions and statistical computations. It is done along with tabular presentation of data. Graphic presentation involves use of graphics, charts and other pictorial devices. These forms are very helpful to condense large quantity of statistical data to a form that can be quickly understood at a glance. Properly drawn charts and graphs helps to understand the data easily by general public. Graphic presentation should be drawn with care and diligence. The forms used should be simple, clear, accurate and also suitable for data.

Rules for Graphical Representation

The following rules are to be followed in graphic representation:

1. The chart must have a title. The title of the chart should be placed above the chart.
2. The title should be clear, brief, and simple and should portray the nature of the data presented.

3. Numerical data on which graphic is done must be supplemented as a table.
4. The scale intervals should be equal.
5. Each curve or bar on the chart should be labeled.
6. If there are more than one curves or bar, they should be differentiated with colours or pattern.

Type of Graphs

The following graphs are commonly used to represent data:

1. Charts or Line Graphs
2. Histograms
3. Bar Charts
4. Circle charts or Pie Charts
5. Frequency Polygon
6. Lorenz Curve
7. Pictograms
8. Ogive Curve

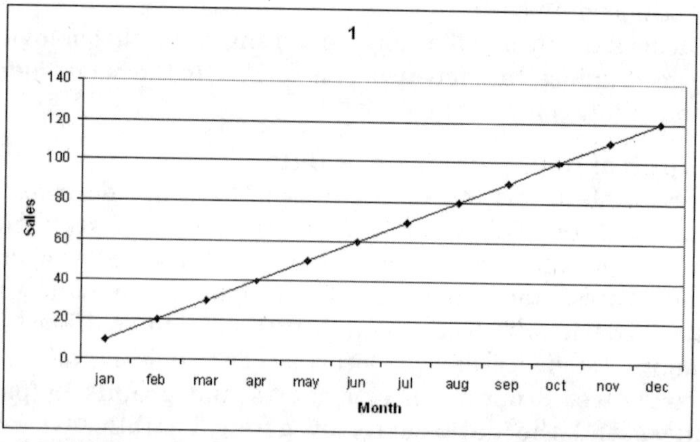

Charts or line graphs

Tables, charts and graphs are convenient ways to clearly show the data. A line graph is used to show continuing data; how one thing is affected by another. It's clear to see how things are going by the rises and falls a line graph shows. This kind of graph is needed to show the effect of an independent variable on a dependent variable.

A line graph of the per cent change in the CPI over time. Each line represents per cent increase for the three months ending at the date indicated.

Histogram

In statistics, a histogram is a graphical display of tabulated frequencies. A histogram is the graphical version of a table that shows what proportion of cases fall into each of several or many specified categories. It is a graphical representation of a frequency distribution. The range of the variable is divided into class intervals for which the frequency of occurrence is represented by a rectangular column. The height of the column is proportional to the frequency of observations within the interval. The histogram differs from bar charts in that it is the area of the bar that denotes the value, not the height, a crucial distinction when the categories are not of uniform width (Lancaster, 1974). The categories are usually specified as non-overlapping intervals of some variable. The categories (bars) must be adjacent.

The word histogram comes from the Greek *histos*, meaning pole or mast, and *gram*, which means a chart or graph. Hence, the direct definition of Histogram is Pole Chart. A histogram is used to display the distribution of data values along the real number line. It is a traditional way of displaying the shape of

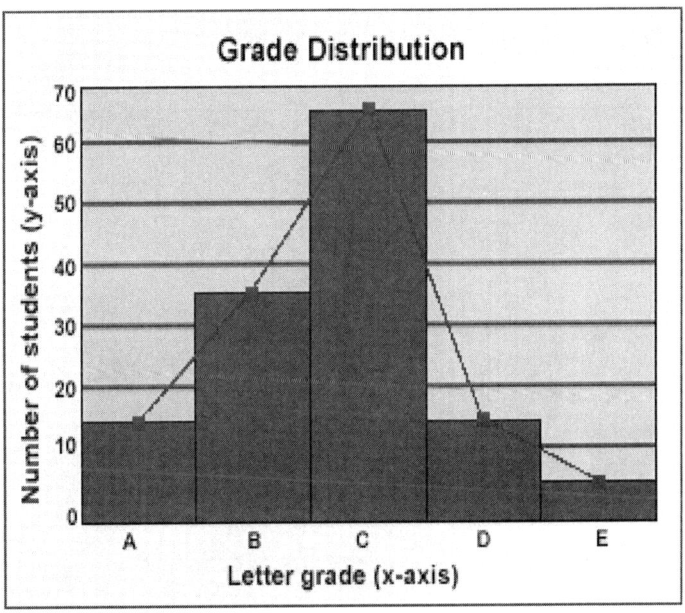

data and competes with the probability plot as a method of assessing normality.

Histogram is a graph of the frequency distribution in which the vertical axis represents the count (frequency) and the horizontal axis represents the possible range of the data values. It is constructed from a frequency distribution, where choices on the number of classes and class width have been made. These choices can drastically affect the shape of the histogram. The histogram is one of the seven basic tools of quality control, which also include the Pareto Chart, Check Sheet, Control Chart, Cause-and-effect diagram, Flow Chart and Scatter diagram. A generalisation of the histogram is kernel smoothing techniques. This will construct a very smooth probability density function from the supply data.

Bar Chart

A bar chart, also known as a bar graph, is a chart with rectangular bars of lengths usually proportional to the magnitudes or frequencies of what they represent. Bar charts are used for comparing two or more values. The bars can be horizontally or vertically oriented. Sometimes a stretched graphic is used instead of a solid bar. The following bar chart indicates the per cent change in the Consumer Price Index (CPI) over time.

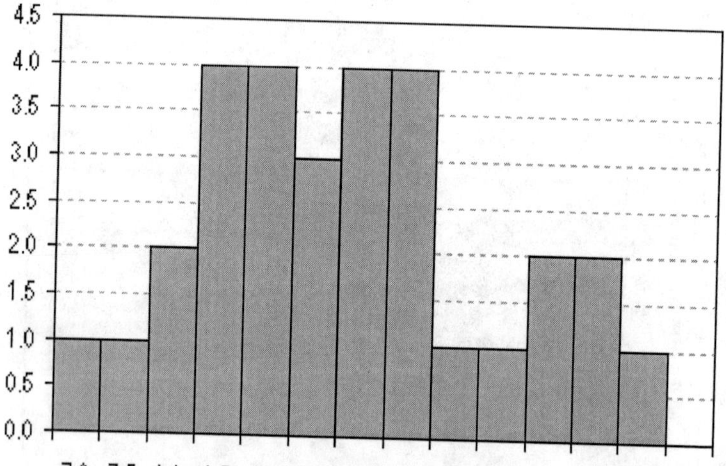

Bar Graph

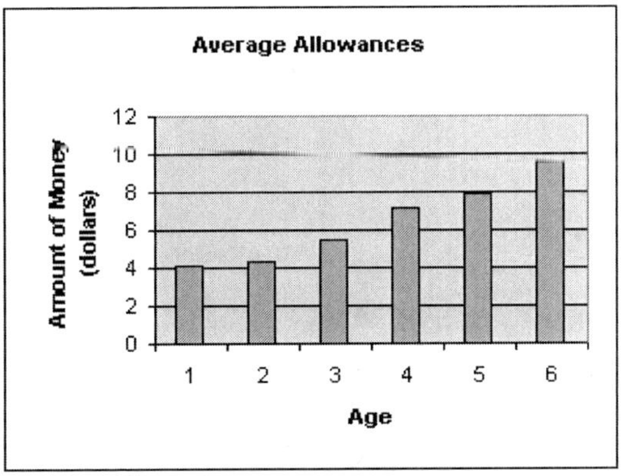

Line Graph

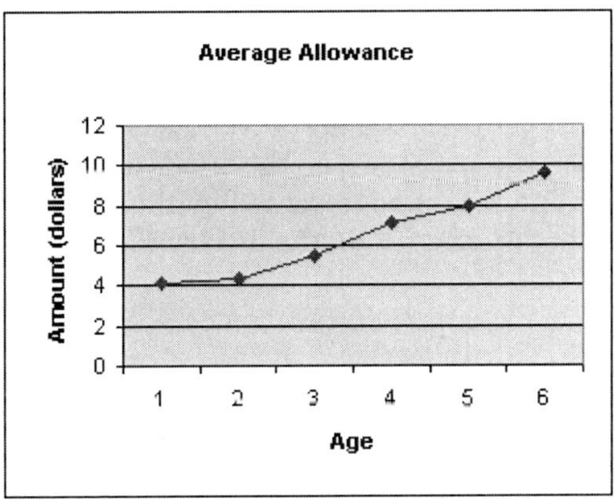

Pie Chart

A Pie Chart is a circular chart divided into sectors, illustrating relative magnitudes or frequencies. In a Pie Chart, the arc length of each sector (and consequently its central angle and area), is proportional to the quantity it represents. Together, the sectors create a full disk. It is named for its resemblance to a pie which has been sliced. While the pie chart is perhaps the most omnipresent statistical chart in the business world and the mass media, it is rarely used in scientific or technical publications. It is commonly used for presenting the sectorial distribution of national income.

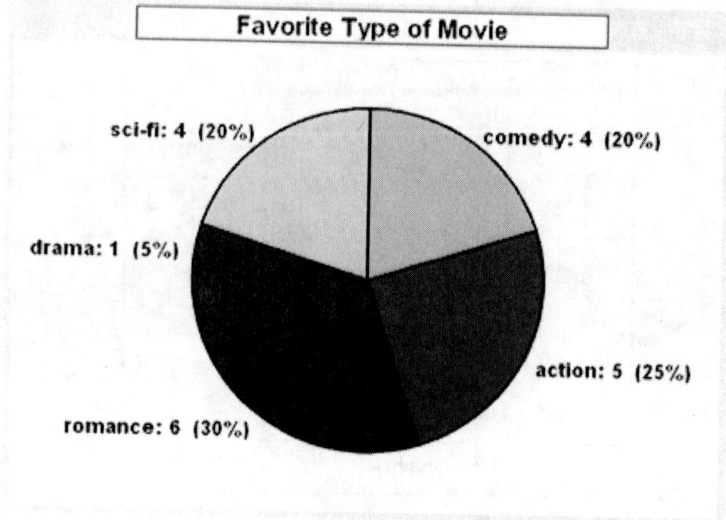

Frequency Polygon

A frequency polygon is a graphical display of a frequency table. The intervals are shown on the x-axis and the number of scores in each interval is represented by the height of a point located above the middle of the interval. The points are

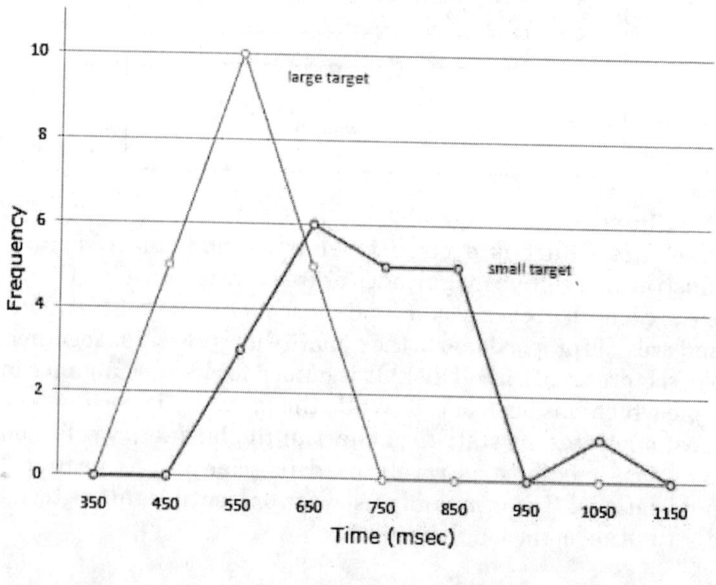

connected so that together with the x-axis they form a polygon. If two or more series are shown on the same graph, the curves can be made with different kind of ruling. The frequency polygon is suitable for portraying continuous series.

The Lorenz Curve

The Lorenz curve is a line chart. It is a graphical representation of the proportionality of a distribution (the cumulative percentage of the values). In other words the Lorenz curve is a graphical representation of the cumulative distribution function of a probability distribution. To build the Lorenz curve, all the elements of a distribution must be ordered from the most important to the least important. Then, each element is plotted according to their cumulative percentage of x and y, x being the cumulative percentage of elements. The Lorenz curve is compared with the perfect equality line, which is a linear relationships that plots a distribution where each element has an equal value in its shares of x and y.

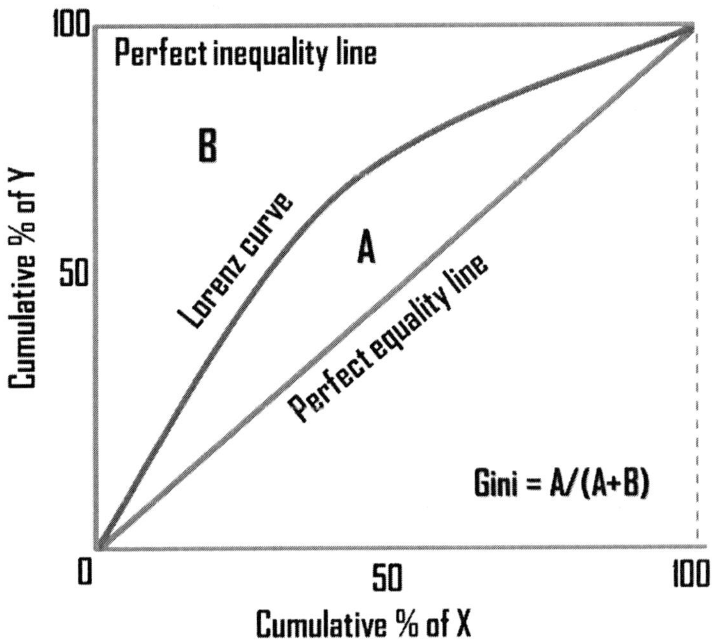

Pictograms

Pictograms are a variation of the bar chart. The values presented in chart are represented by identical pictures or symbols. Each picture represents a fixed size of variable. The symbols or picture used must be suitable to the type of data. The following rules are to be observed while drawing a Pictogram:

- The picture or symbols used should be self-explanatory.
- Each symbol stands for a suitable sum of units.
- The chart should be clear and simple.

Ogive Curve

Ogive curve is a cumulative frequency curve. It is a line chart plotted on arithmetic graph paper. There are two ways of constructing an Ogive or cumulative frequency curve. (Ogive is pronounced as O-jive). The curve is usually of "S" shape.

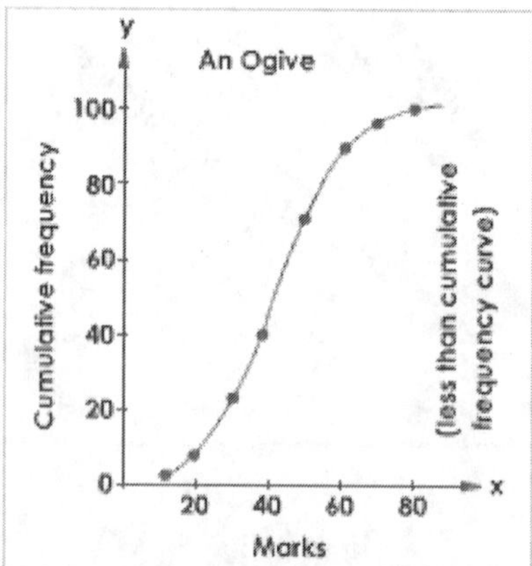

It is useful in representing population, per capita income etc. We can compare two or more distributions by converting data of the distributions to percentages to the total, then cumulating the percentages and plotting the Ogive on the same grid. The difference in steepness and the shape of the Ogives help to compare observations.

The details of Tabulation is explained in the following Chapter.

Review Questions

1. What is tabulation? What principles do we follow for tabulation of data?
2. What are the common methods for tabulation?
3. What are various diagrams and charts used for depicting research results?
4. What is graphical representation of data and what rules those are to be followed for it?
5. Write a short notes on:
   (a) Histogram
   (b) Bar chart
   (c) Pie Chart
   (d) Frequency Polygon
6. Define Lorenz Curve and Ogive Curve. What are the similarities and differences in these two curves?

8

Hypothesis

Introduction

A Hypothesis is an assumption about relations between variables. It is a tentative explanation of the research problem or a guess about the research outcome. Before starting the research, the researcher has a rather general, diffused, even confused notion of the problem. It may take long time for the researcher to say what questions he had been seeking answers to. Therefore, an adequate statement about the research problem is very important. What is a good problem statement? It is an interrogative statement that asks: what relationship exists between two or more variables? It then further asks questions like: is A related to B or not? How are A and B related to C? Is A related to B under conditions X and Y? Proposing a statement pertaining to relationship between A and B are called hypothesis.

Meaning and Examples of Hypothesis

Hypothesis is usually considered as the principal instrument in research. Its main function is to suggest new experiment and observation. Before we explain how hypothesis are tested through different tests meant for the purpose. It will appropriate to explain clearly the meaning of the hypothesis and the related concept for better understanding of the hypothesis testing techniques.

What is a Hypothesis?

The word hypothesis consist of two words

HYPO+ THESIS

'HYPO' means tentative and 'THESIS' means statement about solution of problem.

According to G.A. Lundberg, "a hypothesis is a tentative generalisation, the validity of which remains to be tested. In its most elementary stage, the hypothesis may be any hunch, guess, imaginative idea, which becomes the basis for action or investigation". Formulation of hypothesis gives a definite point to the inquiry, and it helps in establishing direction in which to proceed. Hypothesis provides the basis for investigation, and ensures proper direction in which the stuffy should proceed. K facilitates the collection of data, and helps one to arrive at suitable conclusions, suggestions and observations.

It helps to delimit the field of enquiry by singling out the relevant facts on which to concentrate. So the formulation of hypothesis is very crucial and the success of the failures of a research study depends upon how best it has been formulated by the researcher.

Importance of Hypotheses

The following are the importance of hypothesis in research:

1. It gives direction to research. It helps to define what is relevant and what is irrelevant. It prevents wastage in the collection of data.
2. A hypothesis gives a definite point to the investigation, and it guides the direction on the study.
3. It focuses research.
4. It determines the data needs.
5. A hypothesis specifies the source of data which shall be studied, and in what context they shall be studied.
6. A hypothesis suggests which type of research is likely to be most appropriate.
7. It prevents blind research. It helps to prevent collection of data indiscriminately.
8. It places specific goals and clear foal before us. It acts as a basis for selection of samples and research procedures to meet the goals.
9. It enables the investigator to understand the problem under study with great clarity.
10. It serves as a frame work for drawing conclusions.
11. It gives a definite point to the investigation.
12. It specifies the source of data.
13. It determines the suitable technique of analysis for study.
14. It contributes to the development of the theory.

Criteria for Selection of a Good Hypothesis

A hypothesis, which fulfills the following conditions, can be selected as good hypothesis.

1. **Conceptual clearness:** A hypothesis should contain clearly defined and understandable concepts.
2. **Simplicity:** It should be simple.
3. **Testability:** A hypothesis should be testable. It should be possible to collect empirical facts to test the hypothesis.
4. **Available techniques:** A hypothesis should be connected to available techniques. Otherwise they will not be researchable.
5. **Theoretical relevance:** A hypothesis should be related to a body of theory. Research based on a body on existing theory is able to contribute genuine knowledge.
6. **Reliability:** hypotheses should be logically reliable.
7. **Impartiality:** A hypothesis should be free from value judgment.
8. **Exact:** A hypothesis should be specific. It should explain the expected relation between variables and the conditions under which these relations will hold well.
9. **No conflict:** A hypothesis should not make conflict with the law of nature. It should describe one issue only.

Nature of Hypothesis

A scientifically justified hypothesis must meet the following criteria:

- It must accurately reflect the relevant sociological fact.
- It must not be in contradiction with approved relevant statements of other scientific disciplines.
- It must consider the experience of other researchers.

Types of Hypothesis

There are many kinds of hypothesis the researcher has to be working with. One type of hypothesis asserts that something is the case in a given instance; that a particular object, person or situation has particular characteristics. Another type of hypothesis deals with the frequency of occurrence or of association among variables; this type of hypothesis may state that X is associated with Y. A certain Y proportion of items e.g. urbanism tends to be accompanied by mental disease or than something are greater or lesser than some other thing in specific settings. Yet another type of hypothesis asserts that a particular characteristics, i.e. X is the producer of Y. Hypothesis of this type are called casual hypothesis.

Null Hypothesis and Alternative Hypothesis

In the context of statistical analysis, we often talk null and alternative hypothesis. If we are to compare method A with method B about its superiority and if we proceed on the assumptions that both methods are equally good, then the assumption is termed as null hypothesis. As against this we may think that the method A is superior, it is alternative hypothesis symbolically presented as:

Null hypothesis = $\mathbf{H_0}$ and alternative hypothesis = $\mathbf{H_a}$

Suppose we want to test the hypothesis that the population mean is equal to the hypothesis mean ($\mu\ H_0$) =100. Then we would say that the null hypothesis is that the population mean is equal to the hypothesised mean 100 and symbolical we can express as $\mathbf{H_0{:}\mu = \mu\ H_0 = 100}$

Alternative Hypothesis	To be read as follows
$H_a : \mu?\ \mu\ H_0$	(The alternative Hypothesis is that the population mean is not equal to 100 i.e. it may be more or less 100)
$H_a : \mu > \mu\ H_0$	(The alternative hypothesis is that the population mean is greater than 100)
$H_a : \mu < \mu\ H_0$	(The alternative hypothesis is that the population mean is less than 100)

If our sample results do not support these null hypotheses, we should conclude that something else is true. What we conclude rejecting the null hypothesis is known as alternative hypothesis. If we accept $\mathbf{H_0}$, then we are rejecting $\mathbf{H_a}$ and we reject $\mathbf{H_0}$, then we are accepting $\mathbf{H_a}$. For H_0: $\mu = \mu\ H_0 = 100$, we may consider three possible alternative hypotheses as follows:

The null hypothesis and the alternative hypothesis are chosen before the sample is drawn (the researcher must avoid the error of deriving hypothesis from the data he collects and testing the hypothesis from the same data). In the choice of null hypothesis, the following considerations are usually kept in view:

- Alternative hypothesis is usually the one which wishes to prove and the null hypothesis are ones that wish to disprove. Thus, a null hypothesis represents the hypothesis we are trying to reject, the alternative hypothesis represents all other possibilities.
- If the rejection of a certain hypothesis when it is actually true involves great risk, it is taken as null hypothesis because then the probability of rejecting it when it is true is a (the level of significance) which is chosen very small.
- Null hypothesis should always be specific hypothesis i.e., It should not state about or approximately a certain value.
- Generally, in hypothesis testing we proceed on the basis of null hypothesis, keeping the alternative hypothesis in view. Why so? The answer is that on assumption that null hypothesis is true, one can assign the probabilities to different possible sample results, but this cannot be done if we proceed with alternative hypothesis. Hence the use of null hypothesis (at times also known as statistical hypothesis) is quite frequent.

Hypothesis can also be classified in the following manners according to the nature, function, level of abstraction, analysis etc.:

Descriptive Hypothesis

These are propositions, which describe the characteristics of a variable. (Size or form) the variables may be an individual, organisation, event or objects. For example, the rates of unemployment among graduates are higher than postgraduates.

Relational Hypothesis

These are propositions, which describe the relationship between two variables. For example, labour productivity decreases as working duration increases.

Causal Hypothesis

It indicates the existence of or a change in, one variable causes or leads to an effect on another variable. The first variable is called independent variable and the other variable is known as dependent variable.

Working hypothesis

At the initial stage of research, the researcher fixes a hypothesis, which may not be very specific. These hypotheses are known as working hypothesis. These hypotheses are subject to modification when the research is in progress.

Statistical hypotheses

These are statements about a statistical population. It is quantitative in nature. So they are quantitatively measurable. It may be a hypothesis of difference or hypothesis of association. The association can be measured by the co-efficient of correlation.

Common sense hypothesis

This type of hypothesis states the existence of empirical uniformities perceived through day-to-day observations.

Complex hypothesis

This type of hypothesis tests the existence of logically derived relationships between empirical uniformities.

Analytical hypothesis

These are related with the relationship of analytic variables.

RULES FOR CONSTRUCTING HYPOTHESIS

Smith, H.J. gives certain rules for constructing good hypothesis in his book strategies of social research. They are given below.

1. Search for variable measurement with the quantitative characteristics available.
2. Make the variable scale properties explicit by stating all of the variables, which are mutually exclusive and totally inclusive categories by degree. E.g., income of an individual may be stated as up to Rs 2000, 2001 to 4,000, 4001 to 8000.
3. Describe the means used to sort observation into variable categories in sufficient detail.
4. Always consider alternative operations, which might be more appropriate for a given variable.
5. Analyse variables through their relationships.
6. Link two or more formal propositions through a shared independent or dependent variable where possible.

Concepts of Hypothesis Testing

Basic concepts in the context of testing of hypothesis need to be explained.

The Level of significance

This is a very important concept in the context of hypothesis testing. It is always some percentage (usually 5 per cent) which should be chosen with great care, thought and reason. In case we take the significance level at 5 per cent, then this implies that H_0 will be rejected when the sampling result (i.e. observed evidence) has less than 0.05 probability of occurring if $\mathbf{H_0}$ is true. In other words, the 5 per cent level of significance means that researcher is willing to take as much as 5 per cent risk rejecting the null hypothesis when it ($\mathbf{H_0}$) happens to be true. Thus, the significance level is the maximum value of the probability of rejecting $\mathbf{H_0}$ when it is true and is usually determined in advance before testing the hypothesis.

Decision Rule of Test of Hypothesis

Given a hypothesis $\mathbf{H_0}$ and an alternative hypothesis $\mathbf{H_0}$ we make rule which is known as decision rule according to which we accept $\mathbf{H_0}$ (i.e., reject $\mathbf{H_a}$) or reject $\mathbf{H_0}$ (i.e. accept a). For instance, If($\mathbf{H_0}$ is that a certain lot is good (there are very few detective items in it) against $\mathbf{H_a}$ that the lot is not good(there are many detective items in it), that we must decide the number of items to be tested and the criterion for accepting or rejecting the hypothesis. We might test 10 items in the lot and plan our decision saying that if there are none or only 1 defective item among the 10, we will accept $\mathbf{H_0}$ otherwise we will reject $\mathbf{H_0}$ (or accept $\mathbf{H_a}$). This sort of basis is known as decision rule.

Type I and Type II Errors

In the context of testing of hypothesis there are basically two types of errors that researchers make. We may reject $\mathbf{H_0}$ is true and we may accept $\mathbf{H_0}$ when it is not true. The former is known as Type I and the later is known as Type II. In other words, Type I error mean rejection of hypothesis which should have been accepted. Type I error is donated by α (alpha). Also called as level of significance of test; and Type II error is donated by β (Beta).

	Decision	
	Accept **H_0**	Reject **H_0**
H_0 (true)	Correct decision	Type I error (α error)
H_0 (false)	Type II error (β error)	Correct decision

The probability of Type I error is usually determined in advance and is understood as the level of significance of testing the hypothesis. If type I error is fixed at 5 per cent, it means there are about chances in 100 that we will reject **H_0** when **H_0** is true. We can control type I error just by fixing it at a lower level. For instance, if we fix it at 1 per cent, we will say that the maximum probability of committing type I error would only be 0.01.

But with a fixed sample size, n when we try to reduce type I error, the probability of committing type II error increases. Both types of errors cannot be reduced simultaneously. There is a trade-off in business situations, decision-makers decide the appropriate level of type I error by examining the costs of reworking a batch of chemicals that should have been accepted, where as type II error means taking a chance that an entire group of users of this chemicals compound will be poisoned, then in such a situation one should prefer a type II error. As a result, one must set very high level for type I error in one's testing techniques of a given hypothesis. Hence, in testing of hypothesis, one must make all possible effort to strike an adequate balance between Type I and Type II error.

Two Tailed Test and one Tailed Test

In the context of hypothesis testing these two terms are quite important and must be clearly understood. A two-tailed test rejects the null hypothesis if, say, the sample mean is significantly higher or lower than the hypnotised value of the mean of the population. Such a test inappropriate when we have **H_0**: $\mu = \mu$ **H_0** and **H_a**: $\mu \neq \mu$ **H_0** which may $\mu > \mu$ **H_0** or $\mu < \mu$ **H_0**. If significance level is % and the two-tailed test to be applied, the probability of the rejection area will be 0.05 (equally split on both tails of curve as 0.025) and that of the acceptance region will be 0.95. If we take μ=100 and if our sample mean deviates significantly from μ, in that case we shall accept the null hypothesis. But there are situations when only one-tailed test is considered appropriate. A one-tailed test would be used when we are to test say, whether the population mean in either lower than or higher than some hypothesised value.

Procedure for Testing Hypothesis

To test a hypothesis means to tell (on the basis of the data researcher has collected) whether or not the hypothesis seems to be valid. In hypothesis testing the main question is: whether the null hypothesis or not to accept the null hypothesis? Procedure for hypothesis testing refers to all those steps that we undertake for making a choice between the two actions i.e., rejection and acceptance of a null hypothesis. The various steps involved in hypothesis testing are stated below:

Making a Formal Statement

The step consists in making a formal statement of the null hypothesis ($\mathbf{H}_0$) and also of the alternative hypothesis ($\mathbf{H}_0$). This means that means that hypothesis should clearly state, considering the nature of the researcher problem. For instance, Mr Ravi of the Civil Engineering Department wants to test the load bearing capacity of an old bridge which must be more than 10 tons, in that case he can state his hypothesis as under:

Null hypothesis $\mathbf{H}_0$: μ=10 tons

Alternative hypothesis $\mathbf{H}_a$: μ>10 tons

Take another example: The average score in an aptitude test administered at the national level is 80. To evaluate a states' education system, the average score of 100 of the state's students selected on the random basis was 75. The state wants to know if there is a significance difference between the local scores and the national scores. In such a situation the hypothesis may be state as under :

Null hypothesis $\mathbf{H}_0$: μ=80

Alternative hypothesis $\mathbf{H}_a$: $\mu \neq 80$

The formulation of hypothesis is an important step which must be accomplished with due care in accordance with the object and nature of the problem under consideration.

It also indicates whether we should use a tailed test or a two tailed test. If $\mathbf{H}_a$ is of the type greater than, we use alone tailed test, but when $\mathbf{H}_a$ is of the type "whether greater or smaller" then we use a two-tailed test.

Selecting a Significant Level

The hypothesis is tested on a pre-determined level of significance and such the same should have specified. Generally, in practice, either five per cent level or one per cent level is adopted for the purpose. The factors that affect the level of significance are:

- The magnitude of the difference between sample ;
- The size of the sample;
- The variability of measurements is directional or non-directional (A directional hypothesis is one which predicts the direction of the difference between, say, means). In brief, the level of significance must be adequate in the context of the purpose and nature of enquiry.

Deciding the Distribution to use

After deciding the level of significance, the next step in hypothesis testing is to determine the appropriate sampling distribution. The choice generally remains between distribution and the **t** distribution. The rules for selecting the correct distribution are similar to those which we have stated earlier in the context of estimation.

Selecting A Random Sample and Computing An Appropriate Value :

Another step is to select a random sample(s) and compute an appropriate value from the sample data concerning the test statistic utilising the relevant distribution. In other words, draw a sample to furnish empirical data.

Calculation of the probability

One has then to calculate the probability that the sample result would diverge as widely as it has from expectations, if the null hypothesis were in fact true.

Comparing the probability

Yet another step consists in comparing the probability thus calculated with the specified value for α, the significance level. If the calculated probability is equal to smaller than α value in case of one tailed test (and α/2 in case of Two-tailed test), then reject the null hypothesis (i.e. accept the alternative hypothesis), but if the probability is greater than accept the null hypothesis. In case we reject $\mathbf{H_0}$ we run a risk of (at most level of significance) committing an error of type I, but if we run some risk of committing error type II.

FLOW DIAGRAM FOR HYPOTHESIS TESTING

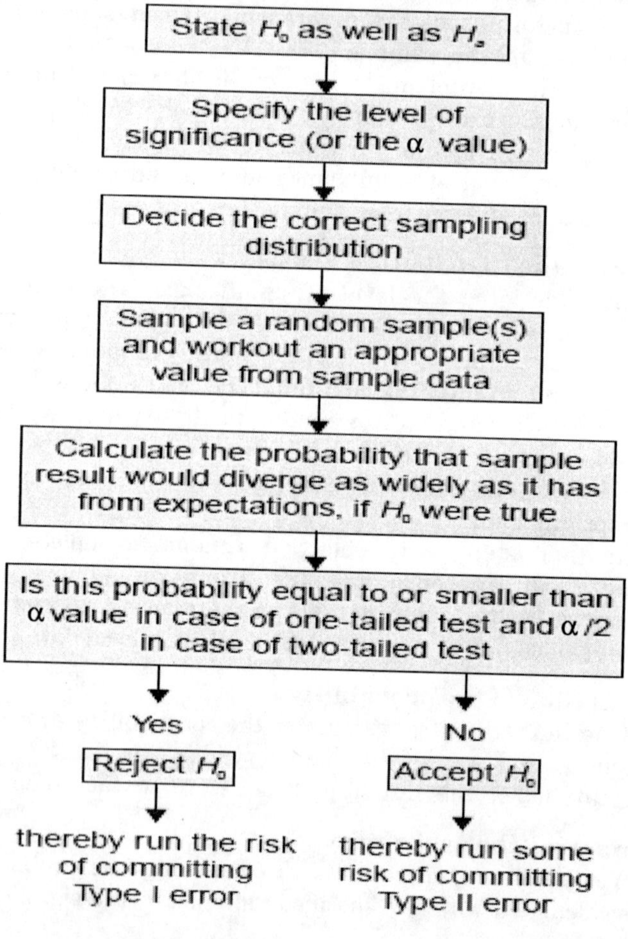

TESTING OF HYPOTHESIS

The worth of the hypotheses lays in its ability to meet the test of validity. The process of testing hypothesis embodies the major part of the research process. Only after testing, the hypothesis may be accepted or rejected, it fails to meet the test of validity, and it must be modified or rejected. The process of testing hypothesis involves operationalisation of concepts, construction of data gathering tools, collection of data, statistical analysis of data, and drawing inferences from the results. If observed facts are consistent with the hypothesis, it should be accepted.

Defining Concepts

Specific definition of concepts is vital for planning the subsequent steps in the research process. Concepts are included in the title of the research problem, the objectives of the study, the investigation questions, and hypothesis. All these concepts should be well defined. Defining concepts precisely is an important step in the formulation of research problem. The definitions of concepts decide the information needs of the study.

Features of concepts

- Concepts are symbols, which represent an object or a certain phenomenon.
- Different individual have different concepts in relation with an object.
- It represents various degree of abstraction. Abstract concepts refer to properties or features of objects such as weight, height, altitude etc.

Steps in operationalisation of concepts

It is the way to quantify, the operational definitions of concepts. It is a difficult task. Wide knowledge and meditative thinking is necessary for this purpose. A series of steps are there to operationalise the concepts. First of all the researcher should select the major concepts from the title of the problem, the objectives of the study, the investigative questions and the hypotheses. He should try to operationally define each concept in the following process.

- Examine the definition of concepts in the published literature such as research reports, books etc.

- Find out the various usages of the concept. Then analyse the obvious meaning elements of the concept.
- Identify the measurement criteria relating to the meaning element and specify the quantitative measurement for those criteria.

MEASUREMENT OF VARIABLES

Measurement of variables is one of the important stages of the research process. Measurement of social and psychological variables is a complex task. Measurement is the assignment of numbers to objects. According to Torgerson, W.S. measurement is the assignment of numbers to objects represents amounts or degrees of property possessed by all objects.

The assignment of numbers to objects is done according to rules. In research process the properties of objects are measured. For example, measurement of psychological properties like intelligence, attitude etc or physical properties like height, weight etc.

Measurable devices help to quantify variables. The psychological and social variables are measured for verifying hypothesis statistically.

The following are the objectives of measurement:

- To facilitate empirical explanation of social and psychological phenomena. Measuring devices helps the researcher to classify variables, which he observes.
- It renders data amenable to statistical manipulation and treatment. The application of statistical techniques for comparing and studying the relationship between variables is possible only if the data collected can be manipulated and amenable for quantification.
- It facilitates testing of theories and hypotheses. Theories are formulated to predict and explain a social or psychological phenomenon. For example, to explain and predict about communal harmony, job satisfaction etc. Hypotheses are derived from these theories. Then it is to be tested by using statistical techniques. It is possible only when the hypotheses are quantified through measuring devices.
- It enables the researcher to differentiate between objects or people in terms their specific properties. That means the measurement performs a classificatory function.

For example we can compare to see whether girls perform well in examination compared with boys in an educational institution.

Levels of Measurement

Stanley Smith Stevens proposed the levels of measurement in his 1946 article on the theory of scales of measurement. According to him, there are four levels of measurement.

1. Nominal measurement
2. Ordinal measurement
3. Interval measurement
4. Ratio measurement

1. Nominal Measurement

In this type of measurement, names are assigned to objects as labels. It is often referred to as a categorical scale. This level involves the categorisation of a variable into several nominal sub-classes by assigning numerals such as 1.2.3... or any other symbols to mutually exclusive sub classes. It involves a simply count of the frequency of the cases assigned to the various categories, and if desired numbers can be nominally assigned to label each category.

Nominal data commonly identifies groups of two members, e.g., male or female, left or right, yes or no, young or old, normal or abnormal, etc. There is no rank or order, no better or worse, and no mathematical operations that can be applied to numbers used in grouping in this manner.

The only comparisons that can be made between variable values are equality and inequality. There are no "less than" or "greater than" relations among the classifying names, nor operations such as addition or subtraction. "Nominal measurement" was first identified by psychologist Stanley Smith Stevens in the context of a child learning to categorise colours (red, blue and so on) by comparing the similarity of a perceived colour to each of a set of named colours previously learned by ostensive definition. Other examples include: geographical location in a country represented by that country's international telephone access code, the marital status of a person. Variables that are measured only nominally are also called categorical variables. In social research, variables measured at a nominal level include gender, race, religious affiliation, political party affiliation, and birthplace.

Hypothesis tests can be carried out on data collected in the nominal form. The most likely would be the Chi-square test. However, it should be noted that the Chi-square is a test to determine whether two or more variables are associated and the strength of that relationship. It can tell nothing about the form of that relationship, where it exists, i.e. it is not capable of establishing cause and effect.

2. Ordinal Measurement

Ordinal scales involve the ranking of individuals, attitudes or items along the continuum of the characteristic being scaled. In this classification, the numbers assigned to objects represent the rank order (1st, 2nd, 3rd etc.) of the entities measured. The numbers are called ordinals. The variables are called ordinal variables or rank variables. Ranks are assigned in ascending or descending orders: The highest category '1' and the next lowest category '2' etc. Comparisons of greater and less can be made, in addition to equality and inequality.

All of the information a nominal scale would have given is available from an ordinal scale. In addition, positional statistics such as the median, quartile and percentile can be determined. It is possible to test for order correlation with ranked data. The two main methods are Spearman's Ranked Correlation Coefficient and Kendall's Coefficient of Concordance. Using either procedure one can, for example, ascertain the degree to which two or more survey respondents agree in their ranking of a set of items.

3. Interval Measurement

The numbers assigned to objects have all the features of ordinal measurements, and in addition equal differences between measurements represent equivalent intervals. It is only with an interval scaled data that researchers can justify the use of the arithmetic mean as the measure of average.

The interval or cardinal scale has equal units of measurement, thus making it possible to interpret not only the order of scale scores but also the distance between them. However, it must be recognised that the zero point on an interval scale is arbitrary and is not a true zero. This of course has implications for the type of data manipulation and analysis we can carry out on data collected in this form.

It is possible to add or subtract a constant to all of the scale values without affecting the form of the scale but one cannot multiply or divide the values. Variables measured at the interval level are called interval variables.

More powerful statistical techniques such as arithmetic mean, standard deviation, and test of significance test like "t" test and "F" test can be used with interval scales.

4. Ratio Measurement

The numbers assigned to objects have all the features of interval measurement and also have meaningful ratios between arbitrary pairs of numbers. Operations such as multiplication and division are therefore meaningful. The zero value on a ratio scale is non-arbitrary. Variables measured at the ratio level are called ratio variables. Most physical quantities, such as mass, length or energy are measured on ratio scales. The central tendency of a variable measured at the ratio level can be represented by its mode, its median, its arithmetic mean, or its geometric mean; as with an interval scale, however, the arithmetic mean gives the most useful information. Social variables of ratio measure include age, length of residence in a given place, number of organisations belonged to or number of church attendances in a particular time.

The interval and ratio measurement levels are sometimes collectively called "true measurement", although it has been argued that this usage reflects a lack of understanding of the uses of ordinal measurement. Only ratio or interval scales can correctly be said to have units of measurement.

Criteria for determining good measurement

A measurement should satisfy certain criteria. They are given below.

1. **One-dimensional:** The scale should measure one characteristic at a time.
2. **Linear:** A scale should follow the straight liner model.
3. **Validity:** A scale is able to measure what it is supposed to measure.
4. **Reliability:** A scale should give consistent results.
5. **Accuracy:** The measurement should be precise and accurate.
6. **Simple:** A scale should be simple.
7. **Administrable:** It should be easily administrable.

TESTS OF HYPOTHESES

As has been stated above that hypothesis testing determines the validity of the assumption (technically described as null hypothesis) with a view to choose between two conflicting hypotheses about the value of a population parameter. Hypothesis testing helps to decide on the basis of a sample data, whether a hypothesis about the population is likely to be true or false. Statisticians have developed several tests of hypotheses (also known as the tests of significance) for the purpose of testing of hypotheses which can be classified as:

(a) Parametric tests or standard tests of hypotheses; and
(b) Non-parametric tests or distribution-free test of hypothesis.

Parametric tests usually assume certain properties of the parent population from which we draw samples. Assumptions like observations come from a normal population, sample size is large, assumptions about the population parameters like mean, variance, etc., must hold good before parametric tests can be used. But there are situations when the researcher cannot or does not want to make such assumptions. In such situations we use statistical methods for testing hypotheses which are called non-parametric tests because such tests do not depend on any assumption about the parameters of the parent population. Besides, most non-parametric tests assume only nominal or ordinal data, whereas parametric tests require measurement equivalent to at least an interval scale. As a result, non-parametric tests need more observations than parametric tests to achieve the same size of Type I and Type II errors. We take up in the present chapter some of the important parametric tests, whereas non-parametric tests will be dealt with in a separate chapter later in the book.

IMPORTANT PARAMETRIC TESTS

The important parametric tests are:

1. z-test;
2. t-test;
3. χ^2-test, and
4. F-test.

All these tests are based on the assumption of normality i.e., the source of data is considered to be normally distributed. In some cases the population may not be normally distributed, yet the tests will be applicable on account of the fact that we mostly deal with samples and the sampling distributions closely approach normal distributions.

Z-test is based on the normal probability distribution and is used for judging the significance of several statistical measures, particularly the mean. The relevant test statistic, Z, is worked out and compared with its probable value (to be read from table showing area under normal curve) at a specified level of significance for judging the significance of the measure concerned. This is a most frequently used test in research studies. This test is used even when binomial distribution or t-distribution is applicable on the presumption that such a distribution tends to approximate normal distribution as 'n' becomes larger. Z-test is generally used for comparing the mean of a sample to some hypothesised mean for the population in case of large sample, or when population variance is known. Z-test is also used for judging the significance of difference between means of two independent samples in case of large samples, or when population variance is known. Z-test is also used for comparing the sample proportion to a theoretical value of population proportion or for judging the difference in proportions of two independent samples when n happens to be large. Besides, this test may be used for judging the significance of median, mode, coefficient of correlation and several other measures. t-test is based on t-distribution and is considered an appropriate test for judging the significance of a sample mean or for judging the significance of difference between the means of two samples in case of small sample(s) when population variance is not known (in which case we use variance of the sample as an estimate of the population variance). In case two samples are related, we use paired t-test (or what is known as difference test) for judging the significance of the mean of difference between the two related samples. It can also be used for judging the significance of the coefficients of simple and partial correlations. The relevant test statistic, t, is calculated from the sample data and then compared with its probable value based on t-distribution (to be read from the table that gives probable values of t for different levels of significance for different degrees of freedom) at a specified level of significance for concerning degrees of freedom for accepting or rejecting the null hypothesis. It may be noted that t-test applies only in case of small sample(s) when population variance is unknown.

χ^2- test is based on chi-square distribution and as a parametric test is used for comparing a sample variance to a theoretical population variance.

F-test is based on F-distribution and is used to compare the variance of the two-independent samples. This test is also used in the context of analysis of variance (ANOVA) for judging the significance of more than two sample means at one and the same time. It is also used for judging the significance of multiple correlation coefficients. Test statistic, F, is calculated and compared with its probable value (to be seen in the F-ratio tables for different degrees of freedom for greater and smaller variances at specified level of significance) for accepting or rejecting the null hypothesis.

Review of Questions

1. What is the meaning of hypothesis and what are their importances?
2. What are the criteria for selection of hypothesis?
3. What are the rules for constructing hypothesis?
4. What are the types of hypothesis?
5. What are the measurements of variables and what are its levels?
6. What are the criteria for determining good measurement?
7. What are null hypothesis and alternative hypothesis?

9

Analysis and Interpretation of Data

Introduction

After processing of data the next step is the analysis of data. Analysis of data means studying the tabulated material in order to determine inherent facts or meanings. In other words the analysis means the computation of certain indices or measure or coefficients along with searching for pattern of relationships that exist among data groups. In case of survey and experimental data, analysis involves estimating the values of unknown parameters of the population and testing of hypotheses for drawing inferences.

Analysis can be classified into two.

1. Descriptive analysis
2. Inferential analysis.

Descriptive Analysis

It is the study of distributions of variables. In descriptive analysis we tries to workout various measures that illusion, the size and shape of distribution along with the study in measuring relationships between two or more variables. It consists of three types of analysis.

I. Unidimensional analysis

If the study is related one variable it is called uni-dimensional analysis. It includes average dispersion, skewness and kurtosis.

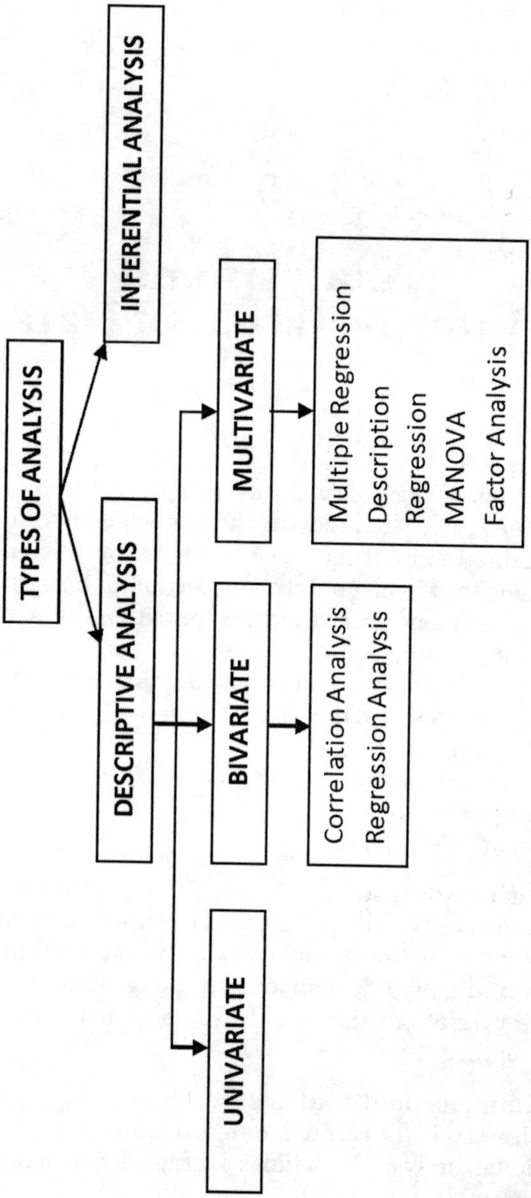
TYPES OF ANALYSIS
DESCRIPTIVE ANALYSIS
INFERENTIAL ANALYSIS
UNIVARIATE
BIVARIATE
MULTIVARIATE
Correlation Analysis
Regression Analysis
Multiple Regression
Description
Regression
MANOVA
Factor Analysis

II. Bivariate analysis

If the study is related with two variables it is called bivariate analysis.

(a) Correlation analysis

It studies the joint variation of two or more variables. Correlation measures the degree of relationship between the variables under study. A.M. Tuttle defines correlation as an analysis of the covariation of two or more variables; it is more related to social and business researches.

(b) Casual analysis or regression analysis

It is concerned with the study of how one or more variable effect changes in another variable. It is the study of the functional relationship existing between two or more variables. It is a statistical tool with the help of which we are in a position to estimate or predict the unknown values of one variable from known values of another variable. This analysis is more important in experimental researches.

III. Multivariate analysis

When the study is related with more than two variables it is termed as multivariate analysis. Multivariate analysis may be defined as all statistical methods which simultaneously analyse more than two variables on a sample of observations. The following analyses are included in multivariate analysis.

(a) Multiple regression analysis

This analysis is suitable when the researcher has one independent variable which is to be assumed as the function of the two or more independent variables. The aim of this analysis is to predict the dependent variable on the basis of its covariance with the all concerned independent variables.

(b) Multiple discriminate analyses

This analysis is adopted when the researcher has one independent variable that cannot be measured, but can be classified into two or more groups on the basis of some attribute. The object of this analysis is to predict an entity's possibility of belonging to a particular group based on numerous predictable variables.

(c) Multivariate analysis of variance

This analysis is an extension of two way analysis of variance. This analysis is mainly used by a researcher to test the hypothesis related with multivariate differences in group responses to experimental manipulations. In this, ratio among group variance to, within the group variance is calculated on a set of variables. This analysis is useful for a study involving a number of metric dependent variables along with many non-metric explanatory variables.

IV. Factor Analysis

Factor analysis is another multivariate analysis technique. It is particularly a powerful and useful analytical approach to psychological, behavioural, financial and other types of data. It is a method for extracting common factor variances from a set of observations. It groups the number of variables into a smaller set of uncorrelated factors potentially conveying an enormous deal of information.

V. Canonical analysis

This analysis may be used in both measurable and non-measurable variables for predicting a set of dependent variables from their joint covariance with a set of independent variables. It studies the relationship between two sets of data with several independent and dependent variables. It is a regression analysis of data.

Other Methods

There are other methods like ratios, proportions and percentages are also used for comparing distributions or sub-groups. Ratio is a figure which is expressed in terms of other. These are relative measures and allow the comparison of groups of unequal size. The aim of using percentages is to simplify the problem of comparison.

INFERENTIAL ANALYSIS

It is concerned with testing of hypothesis and significance. It is also related with estimation of unknown population parameters.

Tools for Statistical Analysis

There are two major areas of statistics related with research, Descriptive statistics and other is inferential statistics.

Descriptive statistics is related with the development of certain indices from the collected data. Inferential statistics or sampling statistics is related with the process of generalisation. The following are the important statistical tools used for summarising the research data:

1. Measures of the central tendency or averages
2. Measures of the dispersion
3. Measures of the skewness
4. Other measures.

1. Measures of the Central Tendency

One of the most basic purposes of statistics is simply to enable us to make sense of large numbers. For example, if you want to know how the students in your college are doing in the state wide achievement test and somebody gives you a list of all 600 of their scores, that's useless. This everyday problem is even more obvious and staggering when you're dealing, let's say, with the population data for the nation. We've got to be able to consolidate and synthesise large numbers to reveal their collective characteristics and interrelationships, and transform them from an incomprehensible mass to a set of useful and enlightening indicators. Measures of the central value are a typical value of the entire group or data. It describes the characteristics of entire mass data. It is the average value of the entire data. In other word it is the single value that describes the characteristics of the entire group. There are five types of averages namely, mean, median, mode, geometric mean and harmonic mean.

Mean

One of the most useful and widely used techniques for doing this—one which you already know—is the *average*, or, as it is known in statistics, the *mean*. Mean is known as arithmetic mean. It is the most common measure of central tendency. Its value is obtained by adding all items and by dividing this by the total number of items. You simply add up a set of scores and divide by the number of scores. Thus, we have our first and perhaps the most basic statistical formula:

$$\bar{X} = \frac{\Sigma X}{N}$$

Sample Mean	Population Mean
$\overline{X} = \dfrac{\sum X}{n}$	$\mu = \dfrac{\sum X}{N}$

Where $\sum X$ is sum of all data values

N is number of data items in population

n is number of data items in sample

In short cut method the following formula is to be applied to find out mean.

$\overline{X} = A \pm \sum d/N$

Where:

$\overline{X}$ (Sometimes call the X-bar) is the symbol for the mean.

A is the assumed mean

Σ (The Greek letter *sigma*) is the symbol for summation.

X is the symbol for the scores.

N is the symbol for the number of scores.

$\sum d$ is the sum of deviations

Mean is the simplest measurement of tendency and it is widely used. It is relatively stable measure of tendency. It is also relatively reliable in the sense that it does vary too much the repeated samples are from one and the same population. It has some limitations also. It is unduly affected by extreme items. That is very large and small items.

Median

Median is the middle value in the distribution when it is arranged in descending or ascending order. It may be defined the value of that item which divides the series in to equal parts, one half contains values greater than it and the other half contains value less than it. Therefore, the series is to be arranged in ascending or descending order.

$$Median \left(\frac{n+1}{2}\right)^{th} term$$

If the total number of the numbers (n) is an **even number,** then the formula is given below:

$$Median = \frac{\left(\frac{n}{2}\right)^{th} term + \left(\frac{n}{2}\right)^{th} term}{2}$$

Median is not frequently used sampling theory.

Mode

It is the most common item of a series. Mode is the average and it is not affected by the values of extreme-Mode is defined as the value of the variable which is most frequently in distribution. The chief feature of the mode is that it is the size of that item which has the maximum frequency and is also affected by the frequencies of the neighbouring items. It is particularly useful in study of popular sizes.

Geometric Mean

The geometric mean of n positive is the nth root of their products. Thus, the geometric mean is obtained by multiplying together all the values of the series and calculating the root of their product corresponding to number of items in the group i.e. nth root of product of 'n' numbers

$$\text{Geometric mean (GM)} = \sqrt{nX_1 \times X_2 \times X_3 \ldots\ldots\ldots(X_n)}$$

n is number of items

$X_1, X_2 \ldots X_n$ are various values.

It is often used in the preparation of the index numbers or when we deal in ratios. It cannot be computed if any item in the series is negative or zero.

Harmonic Mean

It is a special type measure of central tendency used to solve special type of problems. It is the reciprocal of values of various items in the variable. Harmonic mean is used to calculate the average of a set of numbers. Here the number of elements will be averaged and divided by the sum of the reciprocals of the elements. The Harmonic mean is always the lowest mean.

Harmonic Mean Formula

Harmonic Mean = $N/(1/a_1+1/a_2+1/a_3+1/a_4+\ldots\ldots+1/a_N)$

where

X = Individual score

N = Sample size (Number of scores)

$a_1, a_2, a_3 \ldots a_n$ = the various values in the observations.

Harmonic Mean Example: To find the Harmonic Mean of 1, 2, 3, 4, 5.

Step 1: Calculate the total number of values.

N = 5

Step 2: Now find Harmonic Mean using the above formula.

$N/(1/a_1+1/a_2+1/a_3+1/a_4+.......+1/a_N)$

= 5/(1/1+1/2+1/3+1/4+1/5)

= 5/(1+0.5+0.33+0.25+0.2)

= 5/2.28

So, Harmonic Mean = 2.19

It has limited application. It gives largest weight to the smallest item and smallest item to the largest item.

From the above, it is clear that there are large numbers of averages. The selection of the particular statistical average depends upon the nature, type and objectivity of the research. All averages are not suitable for all studies.

2. Measures of Dispersion

The measures of central tendency indicate the central tendency of a frequency distribution in the form of an average. These averages tell something about the general level of magnitude of the distribution, but it does not show anything further about the distribution. Especially it fails to find an idea about the dispersion of variables. In order to measure dispersion statistical devise names measures of dispersion is to be calculated.

According to Spiegel, the degree to which numerical data tend to spread about an average value is called the variation or dispersion of data. The variation measure is used to test the representative character of an average. The following are the important measures of dispersion.

(a) Range

(b) Mean deviation

(c) Standard deviation

Range

It is the simplest measure of dispersion. Its measure depends upon the extreme items and not on all items. It is defined to the difference between the highest value and the lowest value in a series. It gives an idea about the variability very quick. The limitation is that the range is affected greatly in fluctuation of sampling. It is not suitable for mathematical treatment. It is not considered as an appropriate measure in research studies.

Mean deviation

The mean deviation is a measure of dispersion based on all items of in a distribution. It is the arithmetic mean of the deviation of series computed from any measure of central tendency. It is the average of the absolute difference of values of items from an average. It is worked out as under:

$$\text{Mean deviation} = \frac{\sum|D|}{N}$$

$\sum | D |$ = sum of deviations

N = number of items.

Mean deviation is calculated by any measure of central tendency. It is an absolute figure. To compare variation among different series which are expressed in the same in different units a relative mean deviation is required. This relative mean deviation is known as coefficient of mean deviation. The coefficient of mean deviation can be obtained by dividing mean by the average used for calculating mean deviation.

$$\text{Coefficient of mean deviation} = \frac{\text{Mean Deviation}}{\text{Mean or Median or Mode}}$$

Standard Deviation

Karl Pearson introduced the concept of standard deviation in 1983. It is the most important measure of dispersion and it is Widely used in many statistical formulae. It is commonly denoted by the symbol σ (sigma). It is defined as the positive square root of the arithmetic mean of the squares of the deviation of the given observation from their arithmetic mean. The following formula is to be applied to find standard deviation.

Standard deviation or in the case of raw data

$$\sigma = \sqrt{\frac{\sum x^2}{N}} = \text{total of the squared deviations,}$$

$\sum x^2$ = total of the squared deviations.

N = Number of observations.

Standard deviation when deviation taken from assumed

$$\text{mean } \sqrt{\frac{\sum d^2}{N} - \left(\frac{\sum d}{N}\right)^2}$$

Where d stands of deviation from assumed mean

Coefficient of standard deviation

If we divide the standard deviation by the arithmetic average of the series we will get coefficient of standard deviation. It is relative measure which is used to compare it with similar measure of other series.

Coefficient of variation

If we multiply the coefficient of standard deviation with 100, we will get coefficient variation. The square of the standard deviation is known as *variance*. It is considered as the best appropriate method in comparing the variability of two or more distribution.

The standard deviation along with several other related measure like variance, coefficient variation etc are used mostly in research studies. It is a very satisfactory measure dispersion in a series. It is possible for further algebraic treatment. It is less effected by the fluctuations of sampling is the basis for measuring the coefficient of correlation sampling and statistical inferences. The main limitation on the method is that, it is an absolute measure of variability, so it cannot be used for the purpose of comparison.

3. Measures of Skewness

The measures of dispersion give an idea about the spread of the observation about the central tendency of items. The measures of dispersion and measures of central tendency do not indicate whether the distribution is symmetric or not. We know that frequency distribution differ widely in their nature and composition. Even then they may have central tendencies and the dispersions same.

When the items in a series are dispersed in even fashion, the frequency curve representing the distribution will be symmetrical. If the distribution of the items in a series happen to be symmetrical, curve of the distribution will be normal it is known as normal curve. In a symmetrical distribution the items show a perfect balance on either side of the central tendency. In this case the mean, median and mode will be the same. There is no skewness. If the distribution asymmetrical, it shows that it has skewness. So, skewness is measure of asymmetry.

It shows the manner in which the items are clustered around the average. The measure of skewness helps us to determine the nature and extent of concentration of the observations towards higher or lower values lies of the variables. It also helps to measure direction. The following formula can be used to find measure of skewness.

$$\text{Karl Pearson coefficient of skewness} = \frac{3\,(Mean - Median)}{\sigma}$$

4. Measures of Correlation and Regression

Measures of central tendency, measures of dispersion, skewness etc are used in the context of univariate population. If we have bivariate population it is used for finding out the relationship and cause and effect relationship between variables. Correlation technique is used to know the correlating between the two or more variables. Regression techniques are used to know the cause and effect relationship between the two variables.

If there is multivariate population coefficient of partial coefficient of multiple variations, multiple regressions etc are used for study. Correlation between variable can be studied in the following ways:

1. Scatter diagram method: It is the simplest device for ascertaining the relationship between two variables. Under this method, the values are plotted simply in a graph paper in dots. By looking the scatter of dots, we can form an idea as to whether the variables are related or not. The greater the scatter of the plotted points, lesser is the relationship between the variables. The more closely points come to a straight line, and then it indicates that there is high degree of relationship. If all the points lie on a straight line from the lower left hand corner to the upper right hand corner, the correlation is said perfectly positive correlation, ($r = +1$). If all the points on a straight line rising from the upper hand left corner to the lower right hand corner, it indicate that there is perfect negative correlation, ($r = -1$).

2. Graphic method: Under this method the individual values of the two variables are plotted on a graph paper. The points are then joined together. It will provide two curves. That is one for '*x*' variable and other for '*y*' variable. If both are running parallel, we can conclude that there is perfect positive correlation. If they are running in opposite direction we can conclude that there is a perfect negative correlation. This method does not give the idea about the degree of correlation between them. Hence this method is treated as rough method for studying correlation.

3. Coefficient of correlation: Karl Pearson's coefficient correlation is the most popular method used to find out the coefficient of correlation. It is also known as rank correlations. Under short cut method the coefficient correlation can be found out by using the following where the assumed mean is taken.

$$r^* = \frac{\Sigma xy}{\sqrt{\Sigma x^2 \; x \; \Sigma y^2}}$$, where

$$x = \left(X - \overline{X}\right) and \;\; y = \left(Y - \overline{Y}\right)$$

$$r* = \frac{\Sigma xy}{N\sigma_x\sigma_y}, \; \sigma_x = \sqrt{\frac{\Sigma x^2}{N}}, \quad \Sigma\sigma_y = \sqrt{\frac{\Sigma y^2}{N}},$$

When deviations are taken from an assumed mean

$$r = \frac{N\Sigma d_x d_y - (\Sigma d_x) \; x \; (\Sigma d_y)}{\sqrt{N\Sigma d_x^2 - (\Sigma d_x)^2} \quad \sqrt{N\Sigma d_y^2 - (\Sigma d_y)^2}}$$

Here r stands for coefficient of correlation, d_x refers to deviations of X series from the assumed mean- that is (X-A)

In the same way d_y refers to deviations of Y series from their assumed means. (Y-A)

The value of '*r*' lies between ± 1. Positive values of '*r*' indicate positive correlation between two variables and negative values '*r*' indicates negative correlation. When '*r*' indicates 0 there is no relationship between the two variables, this method gives a numerical measure of correlation. Great care must be taken while interpreting the value of this because it is very often misinterpreted.

Regression Analysis

Correlation analysis helps to determine the relationship between two variables. Regression technique is used to estimate or predict the value of one variable (dependent variable) with the help of another variable (independent variable). Regression is the measure which indicates the average relationship between two or more variables in terms of original units of data. The line describing the average relationship between two variables is known as line of regression or estimating line or regression line. The direction of the line indicates the nature of correlation. If the lines are sloping upwards from left to right, it is positive and if they are sloping downwards it is negative. If the lines coincide, there is perfect correlation. This technique is useful for prediction in business. Regression analysis is used where two or more relative variables are having the tendency to go back to the average. It is widely used in social sciences. It is used to estimate the relationship between two economic variables such as income and expenditure.

Regression equations

As there are two regression lines, there are two regression equations. For the two variables X and Y there are two regression equations namely regression equation of X on Y and regression equation Y on X. where there is positive or negative ($\pm$) correlation between variables, the regression lines will coincide. That means it is one line. If regression lines are farther, the lesser is the degree of correlation and nearer the regression lines, correlation is greater.

Regression Equation of Y on X:

$Y_c = a + bX$, Y= Dependent variable and X = independent variable.

To calculate 'a' and 'b' the following normal equation is to be used.

$$\Sigma Y = Na + b \Sigma X$$

$$\Sigma XY = a \Sigma X + b \Sigma X^2$$

Regression equation X on Y

$$X_c = a + bY$$

$$\Sigma X = \Sigma a + b \Sigma X$$

$$\Sigma XY = \Sigma a + b \Sigma X^2$$

Multiple Correlations and Multiple Regressions

When there are more than two independent variables, multiple correlation technique is used to describe relationship. The coefficient of multiple correlations serves as a measure of the degree of correlation between one variable taken as the dependent variable and a group of other variables taken as dependent variables. It has many limitations. It is based on assumption that the relationship between the variables is linear and the effects of independent variable on the dependent variables are separate, additive and distinct. The fundamental equation of the multiple regression analysis is

$R^2 = c'R_{xx}^{*1}\, c.$

The regression analysis which uses two or more independent variables is called multiple regressions. The equation relating correlationship is expressed through multiple regression equation.

Partial Correlation

It is the correlation between one dependent variable with other indipendent variable putting all other variables constant. It helps to measure the relationship between two variables in such a way that the effects of other related variables are eliminated. That means the relationship between a dependent variable and a particular independent variable is studied by taking the other variable as constant.

For example

$$r_{12..3} = \frac{r_{12} - r_{13}r_{23}}{\sqrt{(1 - r_{13}^2)\,(1 - r_{23}^2)}}$$

$$r_{13..2} = \frac{r_{13} - r_{12}r_{23}}{\sqrt{(1 - r_{12}^2)\,(1 - r_{23}^2)}}$$

$$r_{23..1} = \frac{r_{23} - r_{12}r_{13}}{\sqrt{(1 - r_{12}^2)\,(1 - r_{13}^2)}}$$

$$\hat{B} = \frac{\Sigma\, yt - \dfrac{(\Sigma Y)(\Sigma t)}{n}}{\Sigma\, t^2 - \left(\dfrac{\Sigma\, t^2}{n}\right)}$$

5. Other Measurement Tools

Following are the other measuring tools available for data analysis.

Index numbers

When series of data are expressed in different units, we cannot use averages to compare them. In such cases we want to depend certain other measures through which the figures are reduced to a common base. One such method is to convert series into a series of index numbers. An index number may be described as a specialised average designed to measure the change in a group of related variables over a period of time. So these are devices for measuring the differences in the magnitude of a group of related variables.

Changes in the various economic and business phenomena can be measured and compared with the help of index numbers. It may used to find out the change in price level over a period of time. Price movements can be studied to know its cause or effect on the economy. Index numbers may measure cost of living index of different classes of people. Index numbers have limitations. It is often difficult to take into account of the changes in the quality of products. Chances of error may remain at one point or the other while constructing an index number.

Time Series Analysis

It is an arrangement of statistical data in accordance with the time of occurrence or in a chronological order. The numerical data which are collected from different points of time is known as time series. This technique has an important role in economics, statistics and commerce. For example, daily sales in a shop, population growth of ten years etc.

There are four types of variations which are the components of the time series.

1. Secular trend or long term movement.

2. Seasonal variation
3. Cyclical fluctuation
4. Random fluctuation

Secular trend is the long-term trend which requires 15 to 20 years. There are upward trend and downward trend. Seasonal variation is the variation which occurs with some degree of regularity within a specified period of time of one year or shorter. The seasonal variations occur due to change in climate and custom, habits of the people, etc. Cyclical fluctuations are the fluctuation occurs over a long period of time. It is up and down movement. For example, depression period, then boom period. Random variation is the irregular movements of the data over a period of time. Irregular variations occur due to unforeseen and unpredictable events like flood, draught, lock outs etc. Generally four methods are used to measure these trends namely, graphic method, semi-average method, moving average method and method of least squares.

The analysis of time series is done to understand the dynamic conditions to achieve short-term and long-term goals of business enterprises. The management can predict the future patterns on the basis of the past figures. The knowledge of the personal variations is very much useful to take decisions related with production, inventory, purchase etc. by studying clinical fluctuations; the policy of the business can be emulated. So it is a power tool in the hands of business searchers and analysts.

Growth Rates

Estimates of trend are required for almost research studies. It is a considerable significance relate to academicians and policy-makers. For example, trend in deposits. Computation of worth rate is the most important method used for this purpose. The entire series of observation is used for the purpose of finding growth rate. There are two common functional forms used for computation of growth rates with the help of least square method.

Linear growth rate

The following equation is used $Y_t = A+Bt$

Y_t = the value of the variables in the period t for which the growth rate is to be estimated.

That $t = l, 2..........n$

A and *B* are constants to be estimated.

This formula assumes that the change in *Y* is a constant linear rate of *B* units per year and this rate does not depend on the value of *Y* in the previous year or any other factor.

$$\hat{B} = \frac{\Sigma yt - \frac{(\Sigma Y)(\Sigma t)}{n}}{\Sigma t^2 - \left(\frac{\Sigma t^2}{n}\right)}$$

A can be estimated by using the following formula:

$$\hat{A} = \overline{Y} - \hat{B}\,\overline{X}$$

In this case is the linear growth in the units of the variable.

$$\text{Linear Growth rate} = \frac{\hat{B}}{Y_0} \times 100$$

Compound growth rate

Linear rate of growth is not applicable when the growth in any period is not independent of the value of the variable in the precious period. In this case the compound growth rate is applied.

Compound growth rate in percentage =

$$\hat{g} = \left[\text{Antilog } \hat{B}. - 1\right] \times 100$$

$$\hat{B}^* = \frac{\Sigma Y^* t - \frac{(\Sigma Y^*)(\Sigma t)}{n}}{\Sigma t^2 - \frac{(\Sigma t)^2}{n}}$$

2. INFERENTIAL ANALYSIS

The purpose of sampling is to estimate some characteristics of the population from which the sample is selected. In almost all fields the statistical enquiry deals with drawing of conclusions related with a population from a sample selected from it.

Statistical inference is the process by which we draw a conclusion about some measure of population on the basis of a sample value.

The statistical inference can be classified into two.

1. Test of hypothesis
2. Estimation of population parameters.

Parameter and Statistic

Parameters include the statistical constants of population like an (μ.), variance (ό^2), coefficient correlation (r) etc. the statistical constants for the sample drawn from the population like mean (), variance (ό^2), correlation coefficient (r), portion (p) etc are known as statistic. In other terms ammeters are the functions of the population values and statistic are the functions of sample observations. A sampling estimation produces a result which has to be compared with one expected with on the basis of population parameter.

Testing of Hypothesis

Hypothesis is considered as the most important instrument in research. Hypothesis is a tentative conclusion logically drawn discerning any parameter of the population. In other words a hypothesis is an assumption or some assumption to be proved disapproved. For example, the mean height of students is 65 inches.

Features of Hypothesis

Hypothesis posses the following features:

1. It should be clear and precise.
2. It should be capable of being tested.
3. It should be stated in simple terms.
4. It should state the relationship between variables.
5. It must be specific.
6. It should be consistent with known facts.

Steps in Testing Hypothesis

The following steps are to be taken to test the hypothesis:

1. State the problem.
2. Set up a hypothesis.
3. Decide a test statistic.
4. Select a level of significance

5. Calculate the value of the test statistic.
6. Obtain the table value
7. Make a decision to accept or reject hypothesis.

1. Statement of the problem

The problem should be stated in the clear terms. It is the first step in testing a hypothesis. The problem may be whether the hypothesis is to be accepted or rejected. Is the difference between the parameter and statistic has significant difference.

2. Set up a hypothesis

Generally we formulate a null hypothesis for study. The common way of stating a hypothesis is that there is no difference between two values, when population mean is compared with a sample mean. In other words we presume that there is no significant difference between population parameter and statistic. The term 'no difference' means that the difference if any is merely due to sampling fluctuations. The process of accepting or rejecting a null hypothesis on the basis of a sample is called testing of hypothesis. If the statistical test shows that the difference is significant, the hypothesis is rejected. If the difference is very small, then our hypothesis is correct. Generally two hypotheses must be constructed. If one hypothesis is correct the other is to be rejected.

Null hypothesis

A statistical hypothesis which is stated for the purpose of possible acceptance is called null hypothesis.

$$H_0 = \mu$$

The following points must be kept in mind while selecting a null hypothesis.

(a) If we want to test the significance of the difference between a statistic and the parameter or between two sample statistics then we set up the null hypothesis that the difference is not significant. That means the significance is due to difference due to fluctuation in sapling.

(b) If we want to test any statement about the population, we would set up the null hypothesis that it is true.

As against null hypothesis the researcher may start with alternative analysis. Any hypothesis which is complementary to null hypothesis is termed as alterative hypothesis. (H_1)

3. Selection of the test statistic

Acceptance or rejection of null hypothesis is done on the basis of statistic computed from the sample. Such a statistic is called the test statistic based on an appropriate probability distribution. Some common probability distributions which are used for testing are Z-test, t-test, F-test or X^2-test.

4. Select level of significance

I. Types of errors

We will take decision whether to accept or reject null hypothesis is done on the basis of the information supplied by the sample data. There is always a possibility of making error while taking decision. There are two possible errors which may occur in testing of hypothesis.

(a) Type I error

(b) Type II error.

When a statistical hypothesis is tested there is a possibility for obtaining four possible types of results. They are as follows:

(a) The hypothesis is true but our tests reject it (type I error).

(b) The hypothesis is false, but our test accepts it (Type II error).

(c) The hypothesis is true and our test accepts it.

(d) The hypothesis is false and our test reject it.

In other words, type I error is made when we reject a null hypothesis which is true by making a difference significant although no difference exists. On the other hand suppose there is true difference between the two population, and our test of significance leads to a judgement that not significant. In this case we commit a type II error.

II. Level of significance

The maximum probability of making type I error mentioned in a test of hypothesis is called level of significance. In general 5% level of significance or 1% level of significance fixed in statistical tests.

i.e., $\sigma = .05$ or $\sigma = 0.01$

If we adopt 5% level of significance it implies that in 5 out of 100 we are likely to reject a correct hypothesis.

III. Critical region or rejection region

The critical or rejection region is one which corresponds to a predetermined level of significance.

IV. Computation of the standard error

After determining the level of significance the next step is determination of the standard error. The standard deviation of the sampling distribution of a statistic is known as its standard error. Standard error for a well known statistic is given below.

For random samples of size n

Standard error of sample mean $\overline{X} = \sqrt{\frac{\sigma}{n}}$

V. Calculation the value of the test stastic

The significant ratio is determined on the basis of test statistic applied.

VI. Derive the inference (make a decision)

Critical value: It is the value of a test statistic which separates the critical region or acceptance region. By referring the appropriate statistical table in the appendix of the statistics text books, the critical value is to be ascertained. The significant ratio is compared with the critical value. If the ratio is less than critical value at 5% level of significance, the difference is considered insignificant.

Test of significance of difference between sample mean and population mean

Test procedure to be adopted to test the significance

1. Sct up a null hypothesis that there is no significant difference between sample mean and population mean.
2. Decide the test criteria t or Z. When sample is large or standard deviation of population is known, apply Z test. Otherwise use t test.
3. Calculate the test statistic by applying the following formula

$$\frac{\overline{X} - \mu}{SE}$$

SE =when population standard deviation is known $\frac{\sigma}{\sqrt{n}}$

$= \frac{s}{\sqrt{n}}$ (when population standard deviation is not known and sample size is large)

$\frac{s}{\sqrt{n-1}}$ (When population standard deviation is not known and sample is small).

4. Decide the level of significance at 5% or 1% level of significance and the degree of freedom. The degree of freedom is n-1 for small samples and infinity for large samples.
5. Find out the table value.
6. Make a decision either to accept or reject the null hypothesis. If the calculated value of Z or t is numerically less than the table value, it falls in acceptance region. So we can accept the null hypothesis. Otherwise we can reject it.

Problem 1

A company market bus tyres. Their lives are normally distributed with a mean of 80,000 kms and standard deviation 6000 kms. A change in the production process is believed to result in a better product. A test samples of 64 new tyres has a mean life of 82,400 kms can you conclude that the new product is significantly better than the current one?

Answer

Null hypothesis (H_0) = there is no significant difference between population mean and sample mean.

i.e., $\mu = 80{,}000$

H_1 = m ¹ 80,000

Test statistic

$$Z = \frac{\overline{X} - \mu}{SE} \quad \text{where } SE = \frac{\sigma}{\sqrt{n}}$$

$$SE = \frac{6000}{\sqrt{64}} = \frac{6000}{8} = 750$$

$$Z = \frac{41200 - 40{,}000}{750} = +1.6$$

At 0.05 level of significance, the critical (table) value of Z is ± 1.96. The computed value of Z is +1.6 which falls in the acceptance region. Thus, we accept the null hypothesis. The difference is not significant. Hence we conclude that the new tyres are not better than the currently one.

Problem 2

Samples of 121 wooden rods are drawn from a large number of wooden rods, whose length are normally distributed with mean 6 ft. The standard deviation is 1.2 ft, if the sample mean is 6.4 ft. Can the sample be regarded as a truly random sample?

Answer

Sample is large so use *Z* test

Apply *Z* test $Z = \frac{\overline{X-1}\,\mu}{SE}$ $SE = \frac{\sigma}{\sqrt{n}}$ where *n* = number of sample.

Null hypothesis (H_0) = there is no significant difference between population mean and sample mean = 6 ft.

$$H_1 = \mu \neq 6ft \quad SE = \frac{1.2}{\sqrt{121}} = 0.109$$

$$Z = \frac{6.4 \quad -6}{0.109} = +3.67$$

At 0.05 level of significance the critical value as per table value of *Z* = ±1.96. The computed value is + 3.67. It falls in the rejection region. Thus, we reject the null hypothesis that there is no difference between population means and sample mean. The difference is significant. Hence the sample cannot be regarded as truly random sample.

Problem 3

A talcum manufacturing company was distributing a particular brand of talcum powder through a large number of retail shops. Before a heavy advertisement campaign, the mean sales per week per shop were 70 dozens. After the campaign, a sample of 10 shops was taken and the mean sales were found to be 74 dozens with standard deviation of 8. Can you consider the advertisement effective?

Answer

No. of sample size is less than 30, so apply *t* test.

(H_0) = 70 dozens (the deviation between X *and* μ. is due to sampling fluctuations)

For 9 degree of freedom at 5% level of significance the table value of t is 2.26. The calculated value of t is less than the table value. So it falls in acceptance region. Hence the increase in sales can be attributed to fluctuations of sampling. We conclude that the advertisement is not effective in increasing sales.

Comparison of Two Means

It frequently happens that samples are from two different sources and it is required to know whether there is any significant difference in their means. We also want to know when the difference is due to chance, whether the samples belong to the same population. Hence the problem is (i) to test the equality of the population and (ii) to test the significance of the difference between two independent samples.

The following steps are required to solve the above problems.

1. Fix null hypothesis:

1. The population means are equal. That is $\mu_1 - \mu_2$
2. There is no significant difference between the sample means. The difference is due to fluctuation of sampling. In other words the samples are drawn from the same population.

2. Sampling distribution of the differences

$$\text{Standard error} = \overline{X}_1 - \overline{X}_2 = \sqrt{\frac{\sigma_1^2}{n_1} + \frac{\sigma_2^2}{n_2}}$$

$SE(\overline{X}_1 - \overline{X}_2)$ is the standard error of the difference and $SE(\overline{X}_1)$ and $SE(\overline{X}_2)$ are the standard error of the sampling distribution of means.

n_1 = number of observations in sample

Decision with regard to Test statistic

1. When the sample size is large

$$Z = \frac{\overline{X}_1 - \overline{X}_2}{SE} = \frac{\overline{X}_1 - \overline{X}_2}{\sqrt{\frac{\sigma_1^2}{n_1} + \frac{\sigma_2^2}{n_2}}}$$

If are unknown, then their estimates provided by the corresponding sample vacancies respectively are used.

Hence in this case the test statistic becomes.

$$Z = \frac{\overline{X_1} - \overline{X_2}}{\sqrt{\frac{S_1^2}{n_1} + \frac{S_2^2}{n_2}}}$$

When the sample size are small use *t* test

Under this case the assumption is that $\sigma_1^2 = \omega_2^2 = \sigma^2$, that is population variance are equal but unknown the test statistic under H_0 is

$$t = \frac{\overline{X_1} - \overline{X_2}}{\sqrt{S^2\left(\frac{1}{n_1} + \frac{1}{n_2}\right)}}$$

Degree of freedom = $(n_1 + n_2 - 2)$

$$S = \sqrt{\frac{\Sigma\left(X_1 - \overline{X_1}\right)^2 + \Sigma\left(X_2 - \overline{X_2}\right)^2}{n_1 = n_2 - 2}}$$

Make a decision

Compare the computed value of *t* with the tabulated value of *t* for $(n_1 + n_2 - 2)$ Degree of freedom.

The desired level of significance is usually 1% or 5%, we reject or accept null hypothesis.

Problem 4

A and B companies manufacture electronic bulbs gave the following results:

	A company	B company
No. of bulbs used	100	100
Mean life in hours	1300	1248
Standard deviation in hours	82	93

Using the standard error of the difference between mean state whether there is any significant difference in the mean life of the two makes.

Answer

Let μ_1 = mean of the population of bulbs of A company.

μ_2 = mean population of the bulbs manufactured by Company B.

Null hypothesis -$H_0 = \mu_1 = \mu_2$

(The two population means are same)

$H_1 = \mu_1 \mu_2$

Test statistic for large samples

$$Z = Z = \frac{\overline{X_1} - \overline{X_2}}{SE} = \frac{\overline{X} - \overline{X_2}}{\sqrt{\frac{\sigma_1^2}{n_1} + \frac{\sigma_2^2}{n_2}}}$$

$$= Z = \frac{\overline{X_1} - \overline{X_2}}{SE} = \frac{1300 - 1248}{\sqrt{\frac{82^2}{100} + \frac{93^2}{100}}} = 4.19$$

At 0.05 level of significance the difference is significant for a two tailed test of Z falls outside the range ± 1.96. The calculated Z value is 4.19 which are outside of the range. Thus, we conclude that the two population means are not same. In other words there is a significant difference in the mean life of the two makers.

T-Test:

Analysis of Variance and Covariance

T-test is used to test the hypothesis of equality between two sample means. F-test is used to verify the hypothesis of equality between two variances. The same test is extended towards the test of hypothesis of equality amongst several means.

Analysis of variance (ANOVA) is an important statistical tool related with researches in the field of economics, biology, education, psychology, sociology, business and industries, and several other disciplines. If there are only two groups, the researcher can apply 't' test to determine the significance. Even if there are three groups of sample results, they can be compared pair by pair by employing 't' test. But there are several groups; it is difficult to compare the sample statistics pair by pair. In these cases analysis of variance is only the tool that can be employed to test the null hypothesis that the samples are drawn from the same population. This technique is used when multiple sample cases are involved in our studies. It can be used to draw inferences about whether the samples have been drawn from populations having the same mean.

This technique is based on three important assumptions.

1. The distribution of individual values in each group is assumed to have normal shape curve.
2. The variance of individual values within each group is assumed to be the same.
3. That the individuals (samples) being observed have been selected randomly from the population.

Classifications of data are done according to two different criteria or factors. There are two techniques of analysis of variance such as one way classification and two way classifications.

One way classification

In one way classification data are classified on the basis of one criterion. The following are the important steps.

B. *Calculate variance within samples.*

Steps

1. Calculate mean of each sample.
2. Calculate the grand average.
3. Take the difference between the means of the various samples and the grand average.
4. Square these deviations and find the sum of squares between the samples (SSC).
5. Divide SSC by degree of freedom. We will get mean square between samples (MSC)

$$\text{Grand average} = \overline{\overline{X}} = \frac{\overline{X_1} + \overline{X_2} + \overline{X_3} + \ldots\ldots}{N_1 + N_2 + N_3 + \ldots\ldots}$$

Degree of freedom = k-1 (k = number of samples)

B. Calculate variance with in samples

Steps

1. Calculate mean value of each sample.
2. Take the deviations of the various items in a sample from the mean values of the respective samples.

3. Square these deviations. Then we will get the sum of Squares with in the Samples. (SSE)
4. Divide the sum of squares with the degree of freedom. That will give Mean Square with in Samples. (MSE).
   Degree of freedom = N-k
   N = total number of all observations.
   K = number of samples.
   C. Calculate the value of 'F'
   It can be find out by using the following formula.

$$F = \frac{\text{Mean square between groups}}{\text{Mean square within groups}}$$

'F' indicates the variance ratio. F value is compared with the critical value or table value (F distribution). If the computed value is greater than the critical value, we shall reject the hypothesis that all the groups are drawn from the common population.

Analysis of variance - two way classification

In this case the data is classified according to two different criteria or factors. The procedure for calculation of F under two way classifications is summarised in the table given below.

ANOVA TABLE

Source of variations	*Sum of squares*	*df*	*Mean square*
Between columns	SSC	(c-1)	MSC= SSC/ (c-1)
Between rows	SSR	(r-1)	MSR = SSR/ (r-1)
Residual	SSE	(c-l) (r-l)	MSE =SSE/ (r-1)(c-1)
Total	**SST**	**(N-l)**	

(Source - Gupta S. P., Statistical methods)

SSC indicates the sum of squares between columns.
MSC indicates mean square between columns.
SSR denotes sum of squares between rows.
MSR indicates mean square between rows.
SSE indicates the sum of Squares for the residual.
MSE denotes the Mean Square with in residuals.
SST is the total sum of squares.

The problem which involves two way classification', 'residual' is the measuring rod to test significance. It represents the extent of variation due to forces called 'chance'.

Residual = total sum of squares - sum of squared between columns - sum of squares between rows.

Problem 5

The Cuttack Traders' Ltd wishes to test whether its three salesmen named Sushil, Avinash and Bijaya tend to make sales of the same size or whether they differ in their selling ability as measured by the average size of their sales. During the last week, there have been 14 sales calls. Sushil made 5 calls, Avinash made 4 calls and the Bijaya have made 5 calls. The following is the weekly sales record of the three salesmen.

Sushil (Rs)	*Avinash (Rs)*	*Bijaya (Rs)*
300	600	700
400	300	300
300	300	400
500	400	600
0	-	500

Perform the analysis of variance test and draw your conclusions.

Answer

Hypothesis- there is no difference between the selling ability of three salesmen, measures in terms of sales.

That is $(H_0) = \mu_1 = \mu_2 = \mu_3 H_1 = \mu_1{}^1\mu_2{}^1\mu_3$

Sushil (Rs)		*Avinash (Rs.)*		*Bijaya (Rs.)*	
X_1	X_1^2	X_2	X_2^2	X_3	X_3^2
3	9	6	36	7	49
4	16	3	9	3	9
3	9	3	9	4	16
5	25	4	16	6	36
0	0	-	-	5	25
15	59	16	70	25	135
ΣX_1	ΣX_1^2	ΣX_2	ΣX_2^2	ΣX_3	ΣX_3^2

$$F = \frac{\text{Mean square between groups}}{\text{Mean square within groups}}$$

Coding method is applied to simplify data. '100' is taken as common factor.

1. Total sum of squares

Sum of all items of various samples = 1500 + 1600+ 2500 = 5600

$$= \Sigma X_1^2 - \frac{(\Sigma X_1)^2}{N}$$

$$\Sigma X_1^2 = \Sigma X_1^2 + \Sigma X_2^2 + \Sigma X_3^2$$

$$= 59 + 70 + 135 = 264$$

$$\Sigma X_1 = \Sigma X_1 + \Sigma X_2 + \Sigma X_3 = 15+16 + 25 = 56$$

$$N = 14$$

$$\text{Total sum of squares} = 264 - \frac{(56)^2}{14} = 40$$

2. Sum of squares between samples

$$\frac{(\Sigma X_1)^2}{n_1} + \frac{(\Sigma X_2)^2}{n_2} + \frac{(\Sigma X_3)^2}{n_3} - \frac{(\Sigma X_1)^2}{N}$$

$$= \frac{(15)^2}{5} + \frac{(16)^2}{5} + \frac{(25)^2}{5} - 224 = 234 - 223 = 10$$

Degree of freedom between samples = k - 1 = 3 - 1 = 2
Mean square between samples = 10/2 =5

3. Sum of squares with in the samples

Total sum of squares - sum of squares between samples
= 40 - 10 = 30
Degree of freedom with in samples = N - 1 = 14 - 3 =11
Mean square with in samples = 30/11 = 2.73

$$F = \frac{\text{Mean square between groups}}{\text{Mean square within groups}}$$

= 5/2.73= 1.83

The table value of F at 5% level of significance for 2, 11 degree of freedom is 3.98. The calculated is less than the table value. So we accept the null hypotheses. So we conclude that there is no significant difference among salesmen in their ability measured in terms of mean sales per week.

Non-parametric tests

While applying the parametric test like 't', F and Z test, it is assumed that samples are drawn from normally distributed population. It is also assumed that mean; standard deviation or proportion can be derived from sample data and can be used for estimating the corresponding population parameter. In certain situations it is not possible to make any rigid assumption about the distribution of the population from which samples are being drawn. This limitation has led to the development of non-parametric tests. It is also known as distribution free methods. So while applying non-parametric tests no assumption about population parameter of the populations or populations from which samples are drawn is made. Chi-square test is the most widely used test under this category. A large variety of non-parametric tests are developed by different statisticians. It includes sign tests, Fisher Irwin tests, Wilcoxon-Mann Whitney Test (or U test), Kruskal-Wallis Test (or H test) and Spearman's Correlation.

Chi-square test

Chi-square test is one of the important tests developed to test hypothesis. It is a non-parametric test. This test is first used by Karl Pearson in the year 1900. We want to ascertain the frequency of events falling in specified categories in a number of business problems. For example, in marketing research we count the number of people who prefer a particular brand of talcum powder. Chi-square test is applied to such frequencies of occurrence as against the expected ones without referring the population parameters. It is frequently used for testing hypothesis concerning the difference between a set of observed frequencies of a sample and corresponding set of expected or theoretical frequencies. In other words, it is a test statistic which measures the discrepancy between observed in actual frequencies and their corresponding expected frequencies is called the chi-square *test*-X^2.

$$X^2 = \Sigma \frac{(O - E)^2}{E} \text{ Where}$$

O = observed frequencies
E = expected frequencies
Degree of freedom (v) = $n - k$
n = number of frequency classes
k = number of independent constraints or restrictions. For a contingency table with 'r' number of rows and 'c' number of columns the degree of freedom is
v = (r - 1) (c - 1)

The following steps are required to determine the value of the chi-square test.

1. Calculate the expected frequencies
2. Take the difference between observed and expected frequencies.
3. Obtain the square of the difference.
4. Divide $(O — E)^2$ with the expected frequency.
5. Obtain $X^2 = \Sigma \frac{(O - E)^2}{E}$

If X^2 is 0, it means that the expected and observed frequencies are completely coinciding. The greater the discrepancy between observed and expected frequencies, the greater shall be the value of X^2. The calculated value of X^2 is compared with the table value of X^2 for a given degree of freedom at a certain specified level of significance. At 5% level of significance, the calculated value of X^2 is more than the table value of X^2, the difference between theory and observation is considered as significant. That means it could not have arisen due fluctuation of simple sampling. The value of X^2 is always positive.

Problem 6

The table given below depicts the data obtained during an epidemic of cholera.

	Attacked	Not attacked	Total
Inoculated	21	479	500
Not inoculated	175	1325	1500
Total	**196**	**1804**	**2000**

Test the effectiveness of inoculation in preventing the attack of cholera.

Answer

(Ho) = the inoculation is not effective in preventing the attack of cholera

That is inoculation and attack is independent. On the basis this hypothesis the expected frequency corresponding to the number of persons inoculated and attached would be:

$$\text{Expectation of } (AB) = \frac{(A) \times (B)}{N}$$

Here A = Attacked

B = inoculated.

Therefore A = 196, B = 500, N = 2000

$$AB = \frac{196 \times 500}{2000} = 49.$$

On the basis of the above value we can find other values.

	Attacked	*Not attacked*	*Total*
Inoculated	49	451	500
Not inoculated	147	1353	1500
Total	**196**	**1804**	**2000**

Now put the observed frequencies and expected frequencies togcthcr.

O		E	O-E	(O-E)2	$\frac{(O-E)^2}{E}$
21		49	25	784	16
175		147	28	784	5.33
479		451	28	784	1.74
1325		1353	28	784	0.58 23.65

$V = (r - 1)(c - 1)$

$= (2 - 1)(2 - 1) = 1$

When v = 1, X_2 at 5% level of significance = 3.84.

The calculated value of X^2 is higher than the table value and hence the result of the experiment does not support the hypothesis. We therefore conclude that the inoculation is effective in preventing the attack of cholera.

Fisher Irwin test

This test is used to test the hypothesis relating to the difference between two sets of data.

Mann Whitney U test or Wilcoxon test

It is a most useful test to see whether the values in two samples differ in size. It resembles the Median-Test in scope, but it is much more sensitive. In fact, for large numbers it is almost as sensitive as the Two Sample Student t-tests. For small numbers with unknown distributions this test is even more sensitive than the Student t-test. As it is only on rare occasions that we do know that values are Normal distributed, (his test is to be preferred over the Student t-test. In this test data are ranked. If I is used when only populations are involved. All the observations in the two samples are to be ranked. A null hypothesis is fixed that there is no difference between the qualities of two samples. The statistic U is calculated from the sum of the rank in sample one and sample two.

McNemar's Test

McNemar's Test is generally used when the data consist of paired observations of labels. This non-parametric test uses matched-pairs of labels *(A, B)*. It determines whether the proportion of *A*- and /Mabel's is equal for both members. It is very good test when only nominal data are available.

The Sign Test

The Sign Test is a nonparametric test that may be of use when it is only necessary (or possible) to know if observed differences between two conditions are significant. Thai r, to say, with appropriate use of the sign test, it would be possible to determine if *X* is really "more" than *Y*, or however the conditions are arranged.

The sign test is structured so that plus (+) and minus (-) "signs" are used to denote change in magnitude, as opposed to any attempt at quantitative measurement.

Interpretation of Data

Analysis and interpretation are the integral parts of research. The important objective of analysis of data is to provide answers to the questions activated in research. Interpretation refers drawing inferences from the collected facts of the analytical study.

According to C. William Emory, interpretation has two major aspects namely, establishing continuity in research through linking the results of a given study with those of another and the establishment of some relationship with the collected data. Analysis is not complete without interpretation. So, both are inter-dependent.

In the words of Jahada and Cook, scientific interpretation seeks for relationship between the data of study and between the study findings and other scientific knowledge. It helps the researcher to understand the conceptual principles that work. underneath his findings. He can connect his findings will those of other studies having relationship with other established concepts.

It is also a critical examination of the results one own analyses of data in the light of all limitations of data collection. It is through the interpretation the researcher is able to understand the real significance of his findings.

Techniques of Interpretation

Interpretation is not an easy job. Technical skills are required to interpret data. A number of methods are used to interpret data. The following are some of the methods.

1. **Relationship:** It is one of the most fundamental bases for interpretation of analysed data. There may be three types of relationship such as symmetrical relationship, reciprocal relationship and asymmetrical relationship. The data can be interpreted on the basis of these relationships.
2. **Proportion:** It is another method used of interpretation of data. It is generally ascertained to determine the nature and form of absolute changes in the subject of study.
3. **Percentages:** It is used to make a comparison between two or more series of data. Percentages are also used to describe the relationship between variables.
4. **Average:** The average or other measures of comparison are used for interpretations of analysed data. There are three forms of averages such mean, median and mode. For analysing and interpreting of long statistical table we will

use averages or other measures to interpret the results. Averages or other measures of comparison are considered as the most appropriate one for the purpose of interpretation.

Pre Requisites of Interpretation

A researcher can interpret all collected data and information. The following essentials of interpretations may be considered to interpret the data in a desirable and perfect manner.

1. Adequate data

The data may be large enough and it is unbiased. Then only the results will represented the whole population. The entire collected are not suitable for statistical study. The data collected may be such that it is suitable for statistical treatment.

2. Accurate Data

The collected data may be reliable and accurate. The accuracy of data helps the researcher to arrive at a true conclusion. If the data collected are not accurate it is very difficult to interpret it and get a true conclusion.

3. Appropriate type of classification and tabulation

The researcher depends on classified, tabulated and properly calculated data for analysis and interpretation. If the classification and tabulation done is not in proper way, it will make errors or will help to reach wrong conclusions about the study. So data collected should be systematically classified and properly tabulated.

4. Requirement of homogeneous data

When we want to get a uniform and accurate result the data should be homogeneous. The use of heterogeneous data will not give the desired result.

5. Data consistency

If data collected are inconsistent, it will not be useful to provider accurate results. For applying statistical tools, the data should be consistent.

6. Use of statistical tools

If the researcher use in appropriate statistical tools, inadequate sample size and faulty calculations, it will make fake results.

Conclusions and generalisations

As a last step the researcher comes with his conclusions of his study. He should review carefully the evidence for and against each hypothesis while deriving conclusions. The generalisations put forward by him should be agreed with the facts revealed by the study. He should also check the generalisations with the facts and experiences of other researchers.

Review Questions

1. What is meant by primary data and secondary data?
2. What are the factors which are to be taken into consideration while selecting data source?
3. What are the important sources of data?
4. Explain different documentary source.
5. What are the merits and demerits of Secondary Data?
6. What are the precautions to be taken by the research in while using secondary data?
7. What are the Sources or Methods of Collecting Primary Data?
8. Define interview. What are the Types of interview used for data collection?
9. What is Observation? Explain the process of observation?
10. What the merits and demerits of observation?
11. Define experimental method.
12. What is Simulation?
13. Write short notes on:
    (a) Projective techniques and b. Content analysis.
14. What are the important projective techniques?
15. What are focus groups? For what purpose focus groups are used ?
16. What are in-depth interviews? What are the guidelines to effectively operate an in-depth interview?
17. Write a note on the Delphi technique.
18. What do you mean by mail surveys? Explain its different types.
19. Write notes on:
    (a) Sociometry
    (b) Content analysis
20. Explain what the different tools used for data collections?
21. What is a questionnaire? What are the different forms of questionnaires which are used for statistical investigation?

22. What are the points to be noted while developing questionnaires?
23. Explain the Guidelines for the Preparation of the Questionnaire.
24. What are the important Contents of Questionnaire?
25. What is a schedule? Explain the steps involved in Schedule Preparation Types of schedules.
26. What is Pre Testing? Explain the steps involved in it.
27. Explain Types of Measurement Scales
28. What are the possible types or errors which are occurring while measurement?
29. What are the essentials of a sound measurement scale?
30. What are the approaches Related with Construction of Scale?
31. What are the frequently used scaling techniques?
32. What are the Steps involved in construction of a Likert scale?
33. Explain the merits and limitation of Likert's scale.
34. What is pilot study? Explain advantages and limitations of the pilot study.
35. What is meant by field work? What are the objectives of the field work?
36. Explain the steps in processing operations.
37. What are the principles of classifying data?
38. What are the Principles of Tabulation?
39. What are the common methods used for Tabulation?
40. What is Analysis? Classify it.
41. Explain the tools for statistical analysis inferential analysis.
42. What is meant by Test of hypothesis? What are the features?
43. What are the Steps required to test the Hypothesis?
44. What are the steps involved in determine the value of the chi-square test?
45. What is the different parametric test used for analysis of data?
46. Explain different Non parametric tests used for statistical analysis.
47. Explain the Test procedure to be adopted to test the significance.
48. Explain different types of errors involved in while testing hypothesis.
49. What is interpretation? What are the Techniques of Interpretation.
50. Explain the Pre Requisites of Interpretation.

10

Report Writing

Introduction

Research is genuine exploration of the unknown that leads to new knowledge which often warrants publication. But whether or not the results of a research project are publishable, the project should be communicated in the form of a research report written by the student. It is important to realise that science depends on precise transmission of facts and ideas. Preparation of a comprehensive written research report is an essential part of a valid research experience, and the student should be aware of this requirement at the outset of the project. Interim reports may also be required, usually at the termination of the quarter or semester. Sufficient time should be allowed for satisfactory completion of reports, taking into account that initial drafts should be critiqued by the faculty advisor and corrected by the student at each stage.

Report writing is considered as a major component of the research study. The research task will be incomplete, if the report has not been presented about the study conducted by the researcher. That means the generalisations or findings and conclusions made by the researcher must be communicated to others. Then only the purpose of the research should be complete. The report should be well written. A lot of skills are required to design the format of the report.

A research report is a presentation of the research findings in the form of a report and it is necessary part of the research process. Reporting is the end product of the research work.

Functions of Research Report

The research report serves three functions.

(a) It serves as a means to place the problem, data analysis, findings and conclusions in an organised and permanent form. A systematic record of research will serve as an essential reference for future research along the related lines.

(b) The research report helps to know the quality of the work done by the researcher. The report is the manifestation of the researcher's skill and presentation.

(c) The report helps the policy-makers to take appropriate action and policy. It can be done only if the report is presented in an organised and systematic manner.

Importance of Reporting

The research findings can be presented either orally or in written form. The results of the study should be communicated to the interested parties and to the public. So communication of results becomes part of the general stores of knowledge.

- The report helps the researcher to communicate the problem, the method, facts, the conclusions and their interrelationship.
- It helps the researcher to evaluate the success of his research effort.
- The report reveals the research ability of the researcher.
- The report is very much useful to the policy-makers and administrators for taking decisions and policies.

Types of Report

The type or report to be prepared depends upon the background of the potential audience, their total research situation and their technical background and knowledge. A report directed to a fellow researcher will be different from a report addressed to administrators or executives. While planning the report the researcher should consider the following questions.

- What does the reader wants to know about the study?
- How can this information be presented most excellent?

In general there are three types or readers of the report.

- General public.
- The administrator or executive and the project sponsor.

- The fellow researcher or the technical expert. The report can be classified as follows.

1. Oral report

Reporting may be done to an administrator either orally or in written form. Oral report has an important place in USA while reporting to government or industries. But it is not developed in India. The oral report is helpful to communicate continuously to fellow workers. It is also effective when policy recommendations are important.

2. The written report

The written report may be three types

(a) Popular report

It is a report prepared for a layman. It is prepared to those persons who are not interested in technical aspects of the study. It is intended to explain the broad facts, findings of the recommendations. It is prepared in a lucid and simple style.

(b) Report submitted to an administrator

This report is prepared for the use of administrator in executive or for fellow researcher. It is intended for taking decisions. The Administrators require only the essence of the research study. So in this type of report, some technical details and supporting data are included. It will follow the summary and important recommendations of the study.

(c) Technical Report

It is a report prepared for specialists who are interested in understanding the technical aspects of research methodology and research findings. They are interested in hypothesis for the study, logical and statistical details that led to the conclusions. The report is prepared in technical language. While presenting conclusions, the whole development of the underlying data and reasoning is to be given to the technical expert. These reports also include the complicated technical appendices of on the methodology and complete bibliographies. It will be helpful the reader to refer them further. The technical report may be detailed report or an article published in a journal or a full technical report. It should contain the following four aspects.

- The nature of the problem.
- The research methodology adopted for study.
- Analysis of data and the results.
- The inference drawn from the results.

All the above facts have to be presented logically and sequentially with simplicity, intelligibility and brevity.

Format of a Research Report

The research report may be presented either in the form of dissertation or in the form of thesis. It all these cases there are a number of format specifications to be followed by the research report writer. These specifications allows the writer to include his own contribution within a conventional frame work which is both chronological and reasonable.

The mechanical format of a research report consists of three parts:

I. The preliminaries
II. The text
III. The reference materials.

I. The Preliminaries: It includes the following which is written in as sequential order:

1. Title page
2. Preface, including acknowledgements.
3. Table of contents
4. List of tables.
5. List of figures or illustrations.

II. The Text

(i) Abstract
(ii) Introduction
(iii) Research procedure
(iv) Results
(v) Discussions
(vi) Conclusion and summary

III. The Reference Material

(i) Bibliography.
(ii) Appendix/Appendices.
(iii) Index (if any).

The Preliminaries

The title should reflect the content and emphasis of the project described in the report. It should be as short as possible may include essential key words.

Title Page

It should show the following details

1. Title of the thesis.
2. Name of the candidate or researcher.
3. Name and designation of the supervisor or guide.
4. Degree for which the thesis is presented.
5. Name of the institution to which the thesis is being submitted.
6. Month and year the thesis is being presented.

Specimen Title page of a thesis

TITLE OF THE THESIS

THESIS SUBMITTED TO THE XYZ UNIVERSITY
FOR THE AWARD OF THE DEGREE OF DOCTOR OF PHILOSOPHY
IN
BUSINESS MANAGEMENT

By

Mr. Abc Xxxxx

Registration No: ######

Under the Guidance of

Dr.Name of the Guide	**Prof. Name of the Co-Guide**
P.G. Department of	P.G. Department of
Business Administration	Business Management
Xyz University	Xyz University,
Address	Address

LOGO OF THE
UNIVERSITY

DEPARTMENT OF BUSINESS MANAGEMENT
XYZ UNIVERSITY
DISTRICT, STATE, COUNTRY

(YEAR OF SUBMISSION OF THE THESIS)

All of the above could appear on a single cover page. Acknowledgements and a table of contents can be added as preface pages if desired.

Preface (Often Used Synonymously with Foreword)

The preface may include the purpose of conducting study by the researcher, a brief resume of background, scope and general nature of the research upon which the report is being based and acknowledgements.

The acknowledgement recognise the persons to whom the writer is indebted for guidance and assistance during the study and credit institutions for providing funds to implement the study or the use of personnel, facilities and other resources.

Table of Contents

The table of contents is prepared to shoe an analytical view of the material included in the study together with the sequence of presentation. It includes the major divisions of the thesis such as introduction, chapters with their sub-sections, bibliography and appendix.

List of Tables

List of Tables

Table No.		Description	Page No.
2.1	:	IDBI Nifty Junior Index Fund	23
2.2	:	IDBI Nifty Index Fund	25
2.3	:	IDBI Short Term Bond Fu	26
2.4	:	IDBI Fixed Maturity Plan	29
3.1	:	IDBI Monthly Income Plan	32
3.2	:	IDBI Ultra Short Term Fund	33
3.3	:	IDBI Liquid Fund	35
3.4	:	Categories of Client	37
4.1	:	Key ratios IDBI Capital Market Services Ltd. Descriptive Statistics	40
4.2	:	Linear trend of Key ratios	

After the preparation of the table of contents the writer is required to prepare a list of tables. The list of tables is to be centred on a separate page. A specimen of the list of tables is given below.

Different numbers are to be assigned to each table.

LIST OF FIGURES

The list of figures appears in the same form as the list of tables.

List of Figures

List of Figures

THE TEXT

The text is the most important part of a thesis. In this section the researcher presents his arguments. He should devote full attention for as careful organisation and presentation of his findings or general argument. This section explains everything related to the study. It consists of the following.

(i) Abstract

The abstract should, in the briefest terms possible, describe the topic, the scope, the principal findings, and the conclusions. It should be written last to reflect accurately the content of the report. The length of abstracts varies but seldom exceeds 200 words. It is given at the beginning of the report.

A primary objective of an abstract is to communicate to the reader the essence of the paper. The reader will then be the judge of whether to read the full report or not. If the report is to appear in the primary literature, the abstract would serve as a key source of indexing terms and key words to be used in information retrieval.

(ii) Introduction

The nature of the problem and why it is of interest should be conveyed in the opening paragraphs. This section should describe clearly but briefly the background information on the problem, what has been done before (with proper literature citations), and the objectives of the current project. A clear relationship between the current project and the scope and limitations of earlier work should be made so that the reasons for the project and the approach used will be understood.

The introduction should be written with due care. Usually the introductory part contains the following.

- A lucid, complete and concise statement of the problem being investigated.
- A description of the scope of study.

- An explanation of the need for study and importance.
- A resume of the historical background and present importance of the problem.
- A brief statement with regard to the source of data, the technique used for analysing data, the assumptions used in the analysis and the technical terminologies used in the study.
- The reference which we made to other books and other articles, if relevant for our study should also be given.

(iii) Research Procedure

The methodology describes what was actually done. The reader is interested to know how the study was carried out. The means he wants to know, the basic design, experimental manipulations, methods of data collection, asked questions, experience of interviewer, etc. The researcher should also give the accounts of the sample used. The researcher also gives information about the statistical tools used for study.

(iv) Results

In this section, relevant data, observations, and findings are summarized. Tabulation of data, equations, charts, and figures can be used effectively to present results clearly and concisely. Schemes to show reaction sequences may be used here or elsewhere in the report.

(v) Discussion

The crux of the report is the analysis and interpretation of the results. What do the results mean? How do they relate to the objectives of the project? To what extent have they resolved the problem? Because the "Results" and "Discussion" sections are interrelated, they can often be combined as one section.

(vi) Conclusions and Summary

A separate section outlining the main conclusions of the project is appropriate if conclusions have not already been stated in the "Discussion" section. Directions for future work are also suitably expressed here. The writer may also list out the unanswered questions which require further research.

A lengthy report, or one in which the findings are complex, usually benefits from a paragraph summarising the main features of the report - the objectives, the findings, and the conclusions.

References

Following are the popular types of referencing in research thesis

1. **APA** (American Psychological Association): used in psychology, education, and other social sciences.
   Format of APA style
   Author(s) (Date). Title of Book/Title of Article/Title of Periodical, Volume(issue), Pages, Place of Publication, Publisher, Other Information

Books

Okuda, M., and Okuda, D.(1993). Star trek chronology: The history of the future. New York, NY: Pocket Books.

Journal Article

Devine, P. G., and Sherman, S. J. (1992). Intuitive versus rational judgment and the role of stereotyping in the human condition: Kirk or Spock? Psychological Inquiry, 3(2), 153-159. http://dx.doi.org/10.1207/s15327965pli0302_13

2. **MLA** (Modern Language Association): used in literature, arts, and humanities.

Format of MLA style

Author(s) Title of Book or Website Title of Article Title of Periodical Volume Place of Publication Publisher or Database Date Other Information Pages.

Book

Okuda, Michael, and Denise Okuda. Star Trek Chronology: The History of the Future. New York: Pocket, 1993. Print.

Journal Article

Devine, Patricia G., and Steven J. Sherman. "Intuitive Versus Rational Judgment and the Role of Stereotyping in the Human Condition: Kirk or Spock?" Psychological Inquiry 3.2 (1992): 153-59. Print.

3. **Chicago:** used in history and many other subjects in scholarly and non-scholarly publications.

Format of Chicago Style:

Author(s). Date. "Title of Book" Title of Article: Title of Periodical, Volume(issue): Place of Publication: Publisher, Other Information

Book

Okuda, Michael, and Denise Okuda. 1993. "Star Trek" Chronology: The History of the Future. New York: Pocket Books.

Journal Article

Cantor, Paul A. 2000. "Shakespeare in the Original Klingon: Star Trek and the End of History." Perspectives on Political Science 29 (3): 158-66.

4. **Turabian:** adaptation of the Chicago style is designed for college students to use with all subjects called Turabian.
5. **AMA** (American Medical Association style): used in medicine, health, and biological sciences.

Format of AMA Style:

Author(s). Title of Book or Website: Title of Article. Title of Periodical, Volume, Place of Publication, Publisher or Database; Date, Other Information; Pages

Book

Okuda M, Okuda D. Star Trek Chronology: The History of the Future. New York: Pocket Books; 1993.

Journal or Magazine Article (with volume numbers)

Wilcox RV. Shifting roles and synthetic women in Star trek: the next generation. Stud Pop Culture. 1991; 13:53-65.

Literature references should be collated at the end of the report. All references should be checked against the original literature.

General Guide to Formatting a Bibliography/Reference

Basic Format

Lastname, Firstname. *Title of Book*. Place of Publication: Publisher, Year of Publication. Medium of Publication.

One author:

Nabokov, Vladimir. *Lolita*. New York: Putnam, 1955. Print.

Another work, same author:

—. *Speak, Memory: An Autobiography Revisited*. New York: Knopf, 1999. Print.

Two authors:

Cross, Susan, and Christine Hoffman. *Bruce Nauman: Theaters of Experience*. New York: Guggenheim Museum; London: Thames & Hudson, 2004. Print.

Three authors:

Lowi, Theodore, Benjamin Ginsberg, and Steve Jackson. *Analyzing American Government: American*

Government, Freedom and Power. 3rd ed. New York: Norton, 1994. Print.

More than three authors:

Gilman, Sander, et al. *Hysteria beyond Freud*. Berkeley: U of California P, 1993. Print.

Corporate author:

Herbert F. Johnson Museum of Art. *A Guide to the Herbert F. Johnson Museum of Art, Cornell University*. Ithaca: Cornell U, 1973. Print.

Multivolume work:

Morison, Samuel Eliot, Henry Steele Commager, and William E. Leuchtenburg. *The Growth of the American Republic*. 2 vols. New York: Oxford UP, 1980. Print.

No author or editor:

Peterson's Annual Guides to Graduate Study. 33rd ed. Princeton, NJ: Peterson's, 1999. Print.

Editor (anthology or collection of essays):

Hill, Charles A., and Marguerite Helmers, eds. *Defining Visual Rhetorics*. Mahwah, NJ: Lawrence Erlbaum Associates, 2004. Print.

Essay or Chapter in Edited Books or Anthologies:

References to an essay or chapter in an edited book or compilation must include the following elements:

- essay or chapter author(s)
- essay or chapter title
- book title
- book editor(s) or compilers
- place of publication
- the shortened name of the publisher
- date of publication
- inclusive page numbers of the cited piece
- medium of publication

Article in a book:

Ahmedi, Fauzia Erfan. "Welcoming Courtyards: Hospitality, Spirituality, and Gender." *Feminism and Hospitality: Gender in the Host/Guest Relationship*. Ed. Maurice Hamington. Lanham: Lexington Books, 2010. 109-24. Print.

Reprinted article:

Hunt, Tim. "The Misreading of Kerouac." *Review of Contemporary Fiction* 3.2 (1983): 29-33. Rpt.

in *Contemporary Literary Criticism*. Ed. Carl Riley. Vol. 61. Detroit: Gale, 1990. 308-10. Print.

Articles or entries from reference books:

If the article or entry is signed, place the author's name first; if it is unsigned, give the title first. For well-known reference works, it is not necessary to include full publication information. Include only the title of the reference source, edition, and date of publication.

Dictionary entry:

"Hospitality." Def. 1a. *Webster's Third New World Dictionary*. 1993. Print.

Encyclopedia entry:

Mercuri, Becky. "Cookies." *The Oxford Encyclopedia of Food and Drink in America*. Ed. Andrew F. Smith. Vol. 1. 2004. Print.

Article from a less familiar reference book:

For articles from less familiar reference sources, include the full publication information.

Bernheisel, J. Frank. "Setting Recycling Goals and Priorities." *McGraw-Hill Recycling Handbook*. Ed. Herbert F. Lund. 2nd ed. New York: McGraw-Hill, 2001. Print.

Article in Journals, Magazines, and Newspapers:

References to periodical articles must include the following elements:

- author(s)
- article title
- publication title (journal, magazine, etc.)
- volume number
- publication date (abbreviate months, if used)
- the inclusive page numbers
- medium of publication

Issue numbers should be stated as decimals to a given volume number. In the example below, the number 25.4 reads as Volume 25, issue 4. When citing newspapers, it is important to specify the edition used (e.g. late ed.) because different editions of a newspaper may contain different material.

Journal article, one author:

Matarrita-Cascante, David. "Beyond Growth: Reaching Tourism-Led Development." *Annals of Tourism Research* 37.4 (2010): 1141-63. Print.

Journal article, two authors:

Laing, Jennifer, and Warwick Frost. "How Green Was My Festival: Exploring Challenges and Opportunities Associated With Staging Green Events." *International Journal of Hospitality Management* 29.2 (2010): 261-7. Print.

Magazine article:

Kaplan, David A. "Corporate America's No. 1 Gun For Hire." *Fortune* 1 Nov. 2010: 81-95. Print.

Newspaper article, no author:

"Africa Day Celebrated in Havana." *Granma International* 31 May 2009, English ed.: 16. Print.

Newspaper article, one author, discontinuous pages:

Bajaj, Vikas. "The Double-Edged Rupee." *New York Times* 27 Oct. 2010: B1+. Print.

Government Documents:

References to government documents vary in their required elements. In general, if you do not know the writer of the document, cite the government agency that issued the document as author.

State document:

New York State. Commission on Capital Punishment. *Report of the Commission to Investigate and Report the Most Humane and Practical Method of Carrying Into Effect the Sentence of Death in Capital Cases.* Albany: Troy, 1888. Print.

Federal document:

United States. Cong. Senate. Committee on Governmental Affairs. *The Future of the Independent Counsel Act.* Hearings 106th Cong., 1st sess. Washington: GPO, 1999. Print.

International document:

United Nations. General Assembly. *Convention on the Elimination of All Forms of Discrimination Against Women.* New York: United Nations, 1979. Print.

Audio Visual

Film or video recording:

Annie Hall. Dir. Woody Allen. 1977. Videocassette. MGM/UA Home Video, 1991.

Sound recording:

Counting Crows. *August and Everything After.* DGC, 1993. CD.

Sound recording, specific song:

Counting Crows. "Mr. Jones." *August and Everything After*. DGC, 1993. CD.

CD-ROM

Citations should include the medium of the electronic publication (CD-ROM), the name of the vendor that made the material available on CD-ROM, and publications dates for the version used, if relevant.

"Marriage." *Encyclopedia Judaica*. CD-ROM. Vers. 1.0. Jerusalem: Judaica Multimedia, 1997.

Citing Materials from Online Sources

Online Sources:

Citations for online sources, like those for print sources, should provide information that both identifies a source and allows that source to be located and retrieved again. All citations should include the medium of publication (Web) and the date the content was accessed. If the source is difficult to locate or your instructor requires a URL, list the complete address within angle brackets after the date. In many cases, it is also necessary to identify the Web site or database that has made the material available online. Because there are currently few standards that govern the organisation and presentation of online publications, the information that is available to fulfill these objectives can vary widely from resource to resource. In general, references to online works require more information than references to print sources.

Web page:

This example includes the optional URL. All other examples below use the shorter citation format.

Cornell University Library. "Introduction to Research." *Cornell University Library*. Cornell University, 2009. Web. 19 June 2009 <http://www.library.cornell.edu/resrch/intro>.

Personal Web site:

If a work is untitled, you may use a genre label such as Home page, Introduction, etc.

Rule, Greg. Home page. Web. 16 Nov. 2008.

Entry in an online encyclopedia:

"Einstein, Albert." *Encyclopaedia Britannica Online*. Encyclopedia Britannica, 1999. Web. 27 Apr. 2009.

Article from a less familiar online reference book:

Nielsen, Jorgen S. "European Culture and Islam." *Encyclopedia of Islam and the Muslim World*. Ed. Richard C. Martin. New York: Macmillan Reference-Thomson/Gale, 2004. Web. 4 July 2009.

Article in an online periodical:

If pagination is unavailable or is not continuous, use n. pag. in place of the page numbers.

Chaplin, Heather. "Epidemic of Extravagance." *Salon* 19 Feb. 1999: n. pag. Web. 12 July 1999.

Article in a full-text journal accessed from a database:

Vargas, Jose Antonio. "The Face of Facebook." *New Yorker* 86.28 (2010): 54-63. *Academic Search Premier*. Web. 25 Jan. 2011.

Online book with print information:

Frost, Robert. *North of Boston*. 2nd ed. New York: Henry Holt and Co., 1915. *Google Books*. Web. 30 June 2009.

PLANNING OF REPORT WRITING

There are mainly three stages in preparing a research report.

1. Organisations/structure
2. Write up
3. Documentation

1. Organisation or Structure of a Research Report

The first phase in a research report is ordering the parts and planning in writing. It is done after collecting the data and analysis. The organisation or structure of the research report forms the base for preparing the research report. The researcher is required to plan how to arrange his ideas in a logical and sequential order. A well created form will help to overcome wrong emphasis. This helps the work to be more attractive. So the organisation or planning of the report is the essential prerequisite for easy communication of research results. The research report as a whole and in parts should have unity, uniformity and flow. That means the facts mentioned in part should have continuity in other parts.

The organisation or plan does not constitute itself the style. But it is the foundation. The organisation of report can be classified into three such as the horizontal, sequential and mixed.

These forms are not applicable in all research communications. The horizontal organisation indicates the topics and subtopics in the research report. The topics and sub topics are the basic to the writing and they are interrelated with the other. It is appropriate to research on current problems. It is found that majority of research reporting belongs to this category. The sequential form of organisation gives emphasis on the time and developmental aspects. It looks back over a period. In the mixed organisation both aspects are considered. That means it is mixture of horizontal and sequential organisation. It can be adopted wherever it is feasible. The organisation or plan adopted depends upon the research problem, nature, the purpose of study, the availability of time for investigation etc.

Whatever may be the form of report, transition should be provided even before writing begins. Transition is a part of the form of research report. Transition demands unity, sequence and coherence of facts and ideas in the whole report.

2. Write Up

Writing of the report precisely requires a careful choice of the words which will serve to convey exact meaning. Proper presentation of the report is an integral part of the whole project. Colloquial, conversational or other modes of expressions (as in short stories) are not suitable in a thesis. The personal pronouns such as I, we, you, me, my, our and us should not be used except in quotations. It should be written in past tense. Exaggerated statements should be avoided. Quotations must be accurately cited and suitably acknowledged. The report should be clear. The clarity of the report depends upon the language command of the writer, his knowledge about facts and techniques, and the data and documentation.

(a) Contents of the research report

The research report presented to the fellow researcher or to business administrators should reveal enough facts by which they can judge the adequacy of the methods adopted for study. They can form opinion about the seriousness of the findings. So to provide necessary information to the reader, the research report should contain the detail of the method and the general theoretical approach followed in the study. Therefore the technical report should include the following points.

I. Introduction. It deals with the statement of the problem to be studied and the scope of the study.

II. Methodology, the study design, the nature of the sample, data and data collection methods, and the statistical tools used for analysis.

III. The results of the study.

IV. The inference drawn from the results.

I. Introduction

Generally a research report begins with an introduction. A good introduction is a clear statement of the problem or project and why you are studying it. The introduction leads into the main subject matter by giving the necessary background of the report, its aims, premises, scope, limitations, approach intended audience, possible benefits and any instructions that may be useful for the reader. In introductory part, the researcher deals

- the nature of the problem.
- The scope of the enquiry.
- The reasons for study and its place within the theoretical context.

All this has to be indicated in introductory part clearly. It will enable the reader to follow the course of the report and to appreciate the materials, methods and results. There is no need of explaining the above aspects in this part, because it is to be explained in the succeeding pages of the report.

The importance of tho study of the problem should be explained in introduction. It is also better to mention the major finding of the study also. It will act as a guide to the reader. The length of the introduction varies according to the nature of the report. Introduction should be written with din-care to fulfill the dual objectives.

- To introduce the problem in a suitable context.
- To arouse the readers interest.

If the introductory part is dull, lacks precision, direction and specificity and creates confusion, then it will prevent the reader for further reading of the report.

The introductory chapter contains the followings:

- The general purpose of the study or a logical, complete and brief statement of the problem.
- Justification for the study. It helps to establish the importance of the study.

- A preview of the organisation of the rest of the report.
- A concise statement of the sources of data, the experimental procedure, and the proposed statistical treatment of the findings. If the research is a major one, a separate chapter named methodology is enclosed in this respect. Thus, the introduction leads into the main subject matter by giving the necessary background of the report, its aims, premises, scope, limitations, approach intended readers, possible benefits and any instructions that may be useful for the reader.

II. Statement of the problem

The research report starts with the statement of the problem on which study is focused. The first step in every research report is the formulation and development of a research problem. The researcher should give enough evidence to the reader why he has selected such a problem for study. The statement of the problem should mention the hypothesis of study if any were formulated and the definitions of the major concepts employed.

If it is presented as a chapter, then the researcher should explain the scope of the study and point out the limits or limitations in study in clear terms in this. The limitations may be the finance, time and restrictions of length in reporting etc. certain assumptions are required for study. If assumptions are made that may be stated in clear terms.

III. Research methodology

The technical personnel or reader needs to know technical aspects of the study in detail. They want to know how the study was carried out. The researcher should give elaborate details of this in his research report. So this chapter is an important part of the research report. If the used technique is well known and commonly used, the researcher should avoid elaborating the technique and to avoid irrelevant details. This chapter should mention the following details.

(i) The basic design of the study.

(ii) The nature of the sample.

(iii) The data collection techniques.

(iv) Statistical tools for analysis.

(i) Basic design of the study

If study is an experimental one, the experimental treatments are to be mentioned in the report. But if the study is done by using questionnaire, the questions, nature and kind of interview etc should be stated.

(ii) Nature of the sample

If samples are used for study, the class of the sample, in selection procedure of the sample, the number of samples selected for study etc should be stated. That means whether samples are selected at random from universe or not what is the size of the sample, choice etc. are to be stated.

(iii) Data collection techniques

The type of data employed for study is to be explained. Its source and feature is also explained. If a field survey is conducted to collect data, the manner of conducting, repose rates, validation and representativeness of the sample etc are to be explained in detail. If the researcher uses secondary data for study, he should explain how far original sources are checked for suitability of the data for study.

(iv) Statistical tools

Technical experts or scientific readers are interested to know the statistical tools used for study the problem. In general, the techniques used are mentioned simply in the report. But if the technique is a new one, the formulas are to be givon.

IV. Facts presentation

The next step is the presentation of data and its analysis. In the case of fields work, the findings should be continued by supporting statistical tables, charts, diagrams and so on. If it is a bibliographical research, the findings should be followed by sufficient referencc of the source. It is better to avoid many tables, charts, too much of statistics, or too much referencos. The supporting data should be abridged at the minimum possible in the text.

V. The findings

The findings are the important part of the research report. The findings may be positive or negative. Whatever may be the findings, the basic rule in presenting it is that to give all the evidence relevant to the research problem, whether the results are in accordance with the investigator's views or not. It is the prime rule of scientific reporting.

While presenting the findings the followings points are to be considered.

- The findings presented should simple and understandable.
- It should be written in a sequence order.
- It should be clear and precise.
- Simple language should be used to present findings.

The researcher is required to explain how the findings are arrived from the preceding data and how already known facts are pertinent to the current study. If the table and charts used in the text are simple, the written explanation of that is to be avoided. It is essential to indicate how far the investigation agrees with other findings, how far it differentiates, and to what extent such differences suggest for further study.

There is no need of making a demarcation between findings and conclusions. Findings are derived from the facts and conclusions are derived from findings.

VI. The inference

A mere presentation of findings is not enough to convey its meaning to its readers. The reader is interested to know the implications of the study. The implications locate the real significance of the facts and findings of the study. Explanation of these implications are done either with the presentation of data or placed in a separate section. In general, it includes the following aspects.

- A statement which shows the inferences drawn from the findings which can be applied for similar circumstances.
- The researcher should remind the reader of the features of the sample he selected for study and the possibility of its difference with the population from which it is selected.
- It also includes the unanswered questions or the new questions or problems which arise from the study.

VII. The conclusions

The conclusion is the researcher's final assessment about the data and findings. Conclusions are drawn from evidence, analysis, interpretation and evaluation presented in the report. The researcher has to look back the work done with the facts, findings and implications and look forward to the application of the findings and implications. While writing conclusions the researcher should suppress his personal prejudices so as to prevent possible alternative conclusions.

VIII. Recommendations

These are the suggestions put forward by the researcher on the basis of the study. It may be acceptable or not. Sometimes it may not be correct.

IX. Summary or abstract

It is better to include a brief summary of the outline problem, the procedures, the major findings and the major conclusions drawn from them. The abstract (also known as the Summary) is a concise summary presentation of the essential elements of the report, from the introduction through to and including the recommendations. It should be independent (can be read on its own), comprehensive (covers all the main points), clear and concise. As a general rule it should be short, only 10-15 per cent of the length of the report, and should be written in full sentences and paragraphs. It should include a summary of details such as Purpose, Scope, Achievements, Main points, Conclusions and Recommendations. It will enable the leader to get an overall view of the work within a few seconds. New idea or facts should not be indicated in the summary.

Drafting of the Report

Various defects may occur while writing the research report. Sometimes the language and the ideas may not be clear. In certain cases crucial data and statistics are omitted. So to make the research scientific and attractive, the report has to be written in three times. After finalising the outline of the research report, the next step is to draft report. There are three steps involved in the actual write up of the report such as the first, second and final drafts.

First Draft

In the first draft, the researcher's main concentration is for substances. That means the report should be full of facts. In addition to this, accuracy of facts should also be taken into consideration. Apart from this there should be balance, transition and development in facts. Importance should be given to the comprehensiveness of the report. Less importance is to be given to language and form in the first draft report. He should have control over his notes so as to achieve balance, development and overall unity in the report. The first draft should be re-written a number of times. The first draft should be written for the following purposes.

1. To avoid blank paper fright.
2. To attain overall balance of the report.
3. To knit the material together for clearing the connections between facts.

The first draft can be written in two ways.

1. ***Write from one's own head:*** In this case the researcher should read the notes and get familiar with facts. Then he should close the notes and write the report from his own memory. It is a tedious task. The researcher requires a photographic memory. All the researchers should not have such capacity.
2. ***Write up from the notes:*** In this case the researcher writes the report on the basis of slips-notes. For this purpose he has to arrange all the notes-slips in sequence under each topic and omit the useless notes. It is done after considering the basic outline of the report.

By expanding and correcting notes, the researcher is able to write the rough draft. The first draft will progress gradually both in terms of number of pages and content.

There are certain difficulties while making the first draft.

- There would be gaps in facts, ideas and presentation.
- There should be repetition of notes.
- Clearness and consciousness may be absent.

To avoid these obstacles in the first draft itself, the researcher has to put the facts comprehensibly as possible. The researcher should not spend time for correction in this stage. The researcher should write the 'body' first. The introduction is to be written at last. The statistical tables, charts and diagrams should be kept separate from the text to avoid avoiding recopying them at every revision. That it should not be written at every draft. The following are the steps in writing the first draft.

- Shamble the notes and put them in order.
- Expand the notes and outline. The ideas including new which are occurring at the time of expansion is put into document.

- To mention the fundamental points in each chapter, section and paragraph.
- To read the notes-slips repeatedly to depict its full significance and to unite facts and ideas.

Second Draft

After completing the first draft, the researcher should start the revision of first draft. Then he can proceed to prepare second draft. In second draft stage the researcher is required to concentrate on form and language in report. He can start editing the first draft to make it precise, concise and brief. Proper emphasis should be given to the facts. So in this stage the researcher should make a critical evaluation of the facts, findings, conclusion and suggestions. In this stage he should try to improve the language used in the report. The following tips must be kept in mind while making second draft of the report.

- Make the research design simple. That means it should be simple to the reader.
- Expand the condensed writing.
- Give emphasis on points in method, facts and findings.
- Use simple words especially common words. Avoid complex sentences.
- Eliminate repetition of ideas.
- Slash wrong uses and superfluous words.
- Make the report as clear as possible.
- Read and re-read the draft.

The Third Draft

The third draft is the final report. It concentrates mainly on final touch. That is documentation and polishes the report as far as possible to make the report attractive and reliable.

Editing of the final Draft

After preparing final draft it is to be printed or typed, but before typing, it should be edited thoroughly. It is the responsibility of the writer to see that the final draft is free from spelling mistakes and grammatical errors. There should be proper punctuation, capitalisation, hyphenation and abbreviations.

Specifications to be observed

The researcher is required to consider the following specifications while typing and submission of original thesis.

- All headings should be in captions.
- The headings given should be concise and informative.
- The body of the text should be double spaced.
- Numbering should be done in each page.
- The preliminaries are to be numbered in Roman numerals such as i, ii, iii etc.
- All other pages are numbered with Arabic numerals.
- The margin to be maintained at the left of the page is 1.5 inches.
- Put one inch margin on right hand side of the page.
- Maintain a margin of 1.5 inches at the top and bottom of the page.

Documentation

It is the third stage in report writing. The documentations are done for the following purposes.

- It supports the facts presented by the researcher.
- It enables the researcher to acknowledge to others who have helped them for investigation.
- It is helpful to indicate the differences in views, facts and findings.
- It helps the reader to get additional information. The documentation includes
  - (a) Footnotes
  - (b) Bibliography
  - (c) Tables, charts and graph
  - (d) Quotations
  - (e) Appendices

Footnotes

It is the most important part of the documentation. They are intended to refer readers to the exact pages of the works listed in the *Works Cited, References,* or *Bibliography* section. The footnotes are generally used in research reports to

1. Authenticate an argument or point.

2. Supplement the materials which are included in the main body.

The main purposes of the documentation in a research report are as follows:

(i) To acknowledge facts and ideas borrowed: All the information which are presented in the report is not the view of the researcher. He has taken it from the findings and investigations of the previous researcher. That information is represented through footnotes. So the footnotes are the mark of the honesty of the researcher. It helps to identify materials used in quotations in the report. The footnotes help the reader to verify the references made by the researcher for his study.

(ii) To provide a reference to the source: The footnote indicates the references made by the researcher while investigating the subject. All the points cannot be explained in detail in the report. So it acts as a reference for further readings to the reader related with the particular subject.

(iii) To identify the quotation: It helps to identify whose quotations are done used by the researcher in his research report.

The following information is included in footnotes.

- Name of the author/source
- Title of the source
- Page of the source of reference
- Date of publication
- Name of the publisher and the date of the publication

The following points are kept in view while writing footnotes:

- The footnotes are to be inserted in the first draft stage itself.
- Footnotes are placed at the bottom of the page on which the reference or quotation which they identify.
- Foot notes are normally separated by from the textual material by a space of half an inch and a line about one and half inches long.
- Footnotes should be numbered consecutively, usually beginning with ' 1' in each chapter separately.
- Footnotes should be brief, clear and concise.
- All foot notes should be terminated by a full stop.
- The same bottom Margin should be maintained on each page of the typescript, regardless of the number of footnotes.
- Mention the source correctly and fully.
- Avoid too many or few footnotes. Over documentation is bad and under documentation is worse.

Tables, Charts and Diagrams

If the research is statistically based one, the tables, charts and diagrams are useful. A large volume of numerical data can be presented by using tables and charts. Table is the basic form which brings out the fumbling of the investigations more brightly and quickly. It facilitates comparison. By using tables a lot of space can be saved. It makes report more attractive and readable.

The following points are to be noted while inserting charts, diagrams and tables in the report.

- A large volume of data is collected for research project. Unnecessary data may be eliminated. The selected data is to be reduced to a managed size.
- Each table is to be limited to one page. It helps easy interpretation of the table.
- If the table is a long one, it is better to give it in appendix and brief table is used in text.
- Each table should be self-explanatory. A clear, brief and complete title should be given for the table. Each table also possesses column headings.
- It is better not to repeat the table. Repetition will make the reader to be tired. It also shows the researcher's inability to explain analytically the content of the table.
- The number and form of the table depends upon the nature of the research problem and the technique of presenting the report.
- If tables and figures occupy more than half a page, they should be presented in a new page without accompanying text.
- All tables should be numbered consecutively with Arabic numerals such as 1, 2, 3....
- If tables are included in the appendix, the numbering sequence continuing from the last number of the table in the text.
- Abbreviations are not normally used in the body of the thesis or assignment. They can be frequently used in tables and charts. If the researcher used abbreviations, it should be indicated by defining it either from heading or footnotes.

Bibliography

A bibliography is a list of the sources used by the researcher to get information for research report. It is included at the end of the report, on the last page (or last few pages). It is an essential part of the report. It contains information about books, reports, articles and other sources relevant t < the investigation. The main purpose of the bibliography is to guide the reader. The researcher should list all the literature which considered relevant to the problem even though it not noted in footnotes.

Kinds of bibliography

1. Working bibliography
2. Final bibliography

Working bibliography

Generally it is formed at the starting stage of the enquiry, it may be prepared even before the selection of the research problem. It helps the researcher to understand the problem. It also helps to start investigation and to determine the hypothesis.

Final Bibliography

It is prepared after the completion of the investigation or research report. It helps the researchers who are interested to further study of the problem. It also helps to verify the facts and statements in the report.

Forms of bibliography

1. *Works cited:* It includes a list of sources, which have been mentioned in the test part and footnotes of the thesis.

2. *Consulted sources:* It includes a comprehensive list of books and papers which are consulted for the work.

3. *Selected bibliography:* It includes the resources cited in the work together with the more relevant of the works which have been consulted.

4. *Brief annotated bibliography:* It is a list of references. Out of this some of them are followed with a note on the content and usefulness of the references.

The form of bibliography used in research work depends upon the problem and technique of investigation employed by the investigator. The form of bibliography is finalised at the stage of second draft of the report.

The following points are to be kept in mind while presenting the bibliography.

(a) It is easier to prepare a final bibliography if the researcher keeps track of each book, encyclopedia, or article which has used for reading and taking notes.

(b) It is better to start a preliminary, or draft, bibliography by listing on a separate sheet of paper all sources. The full title, author, and place of publication, publisher, and date of publication for each source are to be noted.

(c) Every time a fact gets recorded on a note card, its source should be noted in the top right corner. (For example, noted as, *The World Book,* Volume 2, page 21, has been shortened to: WB, 2, p. 133. in a note card.) After completing the report the researcher can use the information on note cards to double-check the bibliography.

(d) When assembling a final bibliography, list the sources (texts, articles, interviews, and so on) in alphabetical order by authors' last names.

(e) Sources that do not have authors (encyclopedias, movies) should be alphabetised by title.

(f) For each book, the author's name, the title of the book and details relating with the imprint (date, place of publication and publisher) has to be given.

(g) If a journal article is to be shown, the place of publication and the publishers are not included. But the volume, number and inclusive pages which contain the articles are given.

(h) If the author is a women or one of the author is a women, her first name is given in full.

(i) Put the surname of the author first and then the personal and other names.

(j) Underline the title of the books or journal. Underlining is not required in the case of unpublished work.

(k) All key words in the title of the books and journals are to be capitalized. But in the case of articles, manuscripts, thesis, unpublished papers, capital is used only to begin pronoun and the first word of the title.

(l) If the researcher list more than one book by the same author, they are arranged chronologically, with the oldest book listed first.

(m) There are different formats for bibliographies. So it is better to use the one the researcher's guide prefers. There are two places where the bibliography is to be used.
   (i) At the end of the each chapter or part
   (ii) At the end of the completed report.

When it is entered at the end of each chapter, it draws attention of the references shown in that chapter or part.

While taking note the researcher may copy the extracts from source verbatim, with the intension of incorporating it in final report. The copy of extract is known as quotations. A quotation serves the following purposes.

The following points are to be kept in mind while incorporating quotation in the report.

- The research report should not be stuffed with quotations. Over quoting indicates poor integrated argumentation.
- Quotation should be brief as possible. It should not exceed one or two lines.
- Quotation number, frequency and volume should be minimum in a research report.
- If too many quotations are used in the research report, it will indicate the inability of the researcher to do own thinking.
- Mention the sources at every respect.
- Always use quotation marks, double (“.....”) for the direct quotation and single (‘....’) when the extract itself quotes.
- Retain the original spelling, words, punctuation etc even though it incorrect.
- If the researcher used his own comments, use square brackets.
- If the researcher thinks certain words or continuation in quotations is not necessary, it should be indicated by notes.

Appendices

In research reports, some relevant evidence or explanation in the body of the text should only serve to clutter it up, rendering the text more difficult to read. Such explanations or evidences can be put to an appendix, by which the thesis remain uncluttered. By doing so, the interested reader can be directed to refer particular pages of an appendix for further details. Thus, the appendices are useful for placing cumbersome materials breaking the continuity of the main text. Each appendix should be referred to in the body of the thesis. Usually the copy of the questionnaire and the interview schedule used for collecting primary data are included in the appendix.

Review Questions

1. What is a research report? Explain the important Functions of Research Report.
2. Explain the Importance of Reporting.
3. What are the Types of Report used for reporting research?
4. What are the aspects to be included in a full technical report?
5. What are the stages in preparing a research report?
6. What are the steps involved in the actual write up of the report?
7. What are the specifications to be considered by the researcher while typing and submission of original thesis?
8. For what purpose the documentations are done?
9. Write a short note on Footnotes.
10. What are the purposes of the documentation in a research?
11. What are the points to be noted while inserting charts, diagrams and tables in the report.
12. Explain different Kinds of bibliography.
13. What are the Forms of bibliography.
14. What are the points to be kept in mind while presenting the bibliography?
15. What are the points to be kept in mind while incorporating quotation in the report?
16. Describe the layout of a research report covering all relevant points.
17. Write a short note on:
    (a) Focus Group Discussion
    (b) Bibliography
    (c) Diagnostic Research

11

SPSS Software Application in Research

Role of Computers in Research:

The computer has become an indispensable tool in research. A question arises what makes it so? It is because it has the following charactoristics, which matches the requirement for research purpose. These are:

Speed: Computers can outperform human calculations in fraction of seconds. So many impossible scientific surveys and social research which were otherwise thought became reality.

Accuracy: The degree of accuracy can be defined to our requirement and the machinery error can be overcome with the error-detecting techniques, leading to accurate results. Error if any is not due to computer but the way data is fed or used.

Automation: Once machine language instructions are clear, then unless there is a technical failure, the computer functions automatically.

Storage and Retrieval: A large amount of data can not only be stored but also can be retrieved as and when required. Of course, the storage capacity can be adjusted as desired.

Diligence: As it is a machine, it can perform any number of computations for any number of times at any time exactly the same way. Question of human exertion does not arise at all.

Thus, computers facilitate the research. Voluminous data can be processed and analysed with accuracy and speed. The data and calculations can easily be represented in the form of diagrams, graphs, charts and such other pictorial modes. Thus, knowledge of usage of computers is essential for research work. The major limitation of computers in research is that, computer can follow only what has been programmed. The entire research process can go wrong if the data is not fed properly and statistical tools are not selected properly or proper tools of representation is not used.

SPSS Use in Research

Statistical Package for the Social Science (SPSS) it stands for Statistical Product and Service Solutions. **SPSS Statistics application** is a *software package* used for *statistical analysis* was originally produced by *SPSS Inc.*, and later it was acquired by *IBM* in 2009. But, as it further led to confusion in the minds of the user about IBM and SPSS as to know the applicability for the social science research, from the very next year it was relaunched with the combination of IBM and SPSS to reinforce that this is a statistical product and used for service solutions. The current versions (2015) are officially named **IBM SPSS Statistics.** It is a Windows based program that can be used to perform data entry and analysis and to create tables and graphs. SPSS is capable of handling large amounts of data and can perform all of the analyses covered in the text and much more. SPSS is commonly used in the Social Sciences and in the business world. IBM SPSS Statistics is the world's leading statistical software used to solve business and research problems. The latest version of this have been released in March 2015 under the name IBM SPSS Statistics 23.0.

How to use SPSS Software

The trial version of SPSS can be obtained from the IBM SPSS company. Filling up Data View and Variable view is the most crucial step while using SPSS. All statistical functions can be performed on just a mouse click. But it has to be remembered very clearly that, SPSS is a tool only and it does not take decisions nor it suggests also. Further, using the SPSS for research is an art and science while interpreting the results.

Essential Tools for Statistical Analysis through IBM-SPSS

1. IBM® SPSS® **Statistics Base** is statistical analysis software that delivers the core capabilities one need to take

the analytical process from start to finish. It is easy to use and includes a broad range of procedures and techniques to assist increase revenue, outperform competitors, conduct research and make better decisions.

SPSS Statistics Base provides essential statistical analysis tools for every step of the analytical process.

- A comprehensive range of statistical procedures for conducting accurate analysis.
- Built-in techniques to prepare data for analysis quickly and easily.
- Sophisticated reporting functionality for highly effective chart creation.
- Powerful visualisation capabilities that clearly show the significance of your findings.
- Support for all types of data including very large data sets.

2. The IBM SPSS Statistics **Standard Edition** offers the core statistical procedures business managers and analysts need to address fundamental business and research questions. This software provides tools that allow users to quickly view data, formulate hypotheses for additional testing, and carry out procedures to clarify relationships between variables, create clusters, identify trends and make predictions. The IBM SPSS Statistics Standard edition includes the following key capabilities:

- Linear models offer a variety of regression and advanced statistical procedures designed to fit the inherent characteristics of data describing complex relationships.
- Nonlinear models provide the ability to apply more sophisticated models to data.
- Geospatial analytics techniques enable users to integrate, explore and model location and time data.
- Simulation capabilities help analysts automatically model many possible outcomes when inputs are uncertain, improving risk analysis and decision making.
- Customised tables enable users to easily understand their data and quickly summarise results in different styles for different audiences.

3. The IBM SPSS **Statistics Professional Edition** goes beyond the core statistical capabilities offered in the Standard Edition to address issues of data quality, data complexity, automation and forecasting. It is designed for users who perform many types of in-depth and non-standard analyses and who need

to save time by automating data preparation tasks. The IBM SPSS Statistics Professional edition includes the following key capabilities:

- Linear models offer a variety of regression and advanced statistical procedures designed to fit the inherent characteristics of data describing complex relationships.
- Nonlinear models provide the ability to apply more sophisticated models to data.
- Geospatial analytics enables users to integrate, explore and model location and time data.
- Simulation capabilities help analysts automatically model many possible outcomes when inputs are uncertain, improving risk analysis and decision making.
- Customised tables enable users to easily understand their data and quickly summarise results in different styles for different audiences.
- Data preparation streamlines the data preparation stage of the analytical process.
- Data validity and missing values increase the chance of receiving statistically significant results.
- Decision trees make it easier to identify groups, discover relationships between groups and predict future events.
- Forecasting features enable you to analyse historical data and predict trends faster.

4. The IBM SPSS Statistics **Premium Edition** helps data analysts, planners, forecasters, survey researchers, program evaluators and database marketers – among others – to easily accomplish tasks at every phase of the analytical process. It includes a broad array of fully integrated Statistics capabilities and related products for specialised analytical tasks across the enterprise. The software will improve productivity significantly and help achieve superior results for specific projects and business goals. The IBM SPSS Statistics Premium Edition includes the following capabilities:

- Linear models offer a variety of regression and advanced statistical procedures designed to fit the inherent characteristics of data describing complex relationships.
- Nonlinear models provide the ability to apply more sophisticated models to data.
- Geospatial analytics enables users to integrate, explore and model location and time data.

- Simulation capabilities help analysts automatically model many possible outcomes when inputs are uncertain, improving risk analysis and decision making.
- Customised tables enable users to easily understand their data and quickly summarise results in different styles for different audiences.
- Data preparation streamlines the data preparation stage of the analytical process.
- Data validity and missing values increase the chance of receiving statistically significant results.
- Categorical and numeric data can be used to predict outcomes and reveal relationships graphically.
- Decision trees make it easier to identify groups, discover relationships between groups and predict future events.
- Forecasting features enable you to analyse historical data and predict trends faster.
- Structural equation modeling tools let you build structural equation models with more accuracy than standard multivariate statistics models using intuitive drag-and-drop functionality.
- Bootstrapping makes it simple to test the stability and reliability of models so that they produce accurate, reliable results.
- Advanced sampling assessment and testing helps make more statistically valid inferences by incorporating the sample design into survey analysis.
- Direct marketing and product decision-making tools help marketers identify the right customers easily and improve campaign results.
- High-end charts and graphs make it easy to create and share and interact with compelling visualisations results on a range of platforms and smart devices.

5. IBM® SPSS® **Modeler** is a predictive analytics platform that is designed to bring predictive intelligence to decisions made by individuals, groups, systems and the enterprise. It provides a range of advanced algorithms and techniques, including text analytics, entity analytics, decision management and optimisation, to help you select the actions that result in better outcomes. Available in several editions, including a cloud-based version, SPSS Modeler can scale from desktop deployments to integration within operational systems.

SPSS Modeler is designed to:

- Improve decisions and outcomes.
- Help you extract value from data.
- More easily integrate into your existing systems.

6. The IBM® SPSS® Data Collection **has the following features:**

Authoring: Streamline the process of creating surveys using familiar, intuitive interfaces and incorporate sophisticated logic to increase completion rates and ensure high-quality data.

Interviewing: Advanced, easy-to-use technology for deploying and managing compelling surveys by phone, over the web, or face-to-face. Keep up with trends such as SMS messaging.

Reporting: Easily and efficiently develop professional, interactive reports in online or desktop environments, and deliver the right information to the right people at the right time. Management centralise the management of surveys and data with tools for all stages of the research lifecycle, increase efficiency and staff utilisation, and automate processes.

Following are the Operating System requirements and configuration:

1. **Operating System:** Microsoft Windows XP (32-bit version), Windows Vista (32-bit and 64-bit versions), or Windows· 7 (32-bit and 64-bit versions).
2. **Configuration** Intel or AMD processor running at 1 gigahertz (GHz) or higher.· 1 gigabyte (GB) of RAM or more.· 800 megabytes (MB) of available hard-disk space. If using physical installation media, DVD/CD drive.· XGA (1024x768) or a higher-resolution monitor.

Disadvantages of SPSS Software

Though it has the greatest advantage of user friendliness, still SPSS has the following limitations:

1. Does not support Structural Equation Modelling.
2. Does not allow for simultaneous estimation of regression parameters and associations between independent variables.
3. Does not check content validity and construct validity.
4. Does not provide model fit indices to evaluate how well data is represented.
5. Does not allow including latent traits without building composite scores or extracting factor regression scores.

(*Source*: IBM SPSS website)

Research Methodology Glossary

Research: It refers to search for knowledge. It is a scientific and systematic search if information on a particular topic or issue. It also known as the art of scientific investigation.

Research Methods: It includes all those techniques/ methods that are adopted for conducting research. Thus, research techniques or methods are the methods that are the researchers adopt for conducting the research studies.

Research Methodology: It is the way in which research problems are solved systematically. Under this, the researcher acquaints himself / herself with the various steps generally adopted to study a research problem, along with the underlying logic behind them.

Descriptive Research: It consists of surveys and fact-finding enquiries of different types. The main objective of descriptive research is describing the state of affairs as it prevails at the tie of study.

Analytical Research: Under this research, the researcher has to use the already available facts or information, and analysis them to make a critical evaluation of the subject.

Applied Research: If an attempt has made to find a solution to an immediate problem encountered by a firm, an industry, a business organisation, or the society is known as applied research.

Fundamental Research: It is mainly concerns generalisations and formulation of a theory. Researches relating to pure mathematics or concerning some natural phenomenon are instances of fundamental research.

Quantitative Research: It relates to aspects that can be quantified or can be expressed in terms of quantity. It involves the measurement of quantity or amount.

Qualitative Research: It is concerned with qualitative phenomena, or more specifically, the aspects related to or involving quality or kind.

Conceptual Research: If any research related to some abstract idea or theory is known as conceptual research. Normally, philosophers and thinkers use it for developing new concepts or for interpreting the existing ones.

Empirical Research: This is also known as experimental types of research, in which it is important to first collect the facts and their sources, and actively take steps to stimulate the production of desired information.

Exploratory Research: It is designed to provide a background, to familiarise and as the word implies, just "Explore", the general subject. A part of exploratory research is the investigation of relationships among variables without knowing why they are studied.

Conclusive Research: It is used for the purpose of testing the hypothesis generated by exploratory research.

Case study Research: The objective of case study method is to examine the factors that cause the behavioural patterns of a given unit and its relationship with the environment.

Research Process: It consists of a series of steps or actions required for effectively conducting research.

Hypothesis: It is an unproven statement or proposition about factor or phenomenon that is of interest to the researcher. Hypothesis can be tested by using suitable statistical procedure.

Research Design: It helps to decide upon issues like what, when, where, how much, by what means etc. with regard to an enquiry or a research study.

Sample: It is the selection of part of the population, on the basis of which a decision concerning the population is made.

Sample Size: The number of individuals in a sample is called sample size.

Primary data: It is one, which is collected by the investigator himself for the purpose of a specific inquiry or study. Such data is original in character and is generated by surveys conducted by individuals or research institutions.

Secondary Data: Any data which has already been collected by others, such data is called secondary data.

Research Proposal: The research proposal presents a problem, discusses related research efforts, outlines the data needed and shows the research design.

Executive Summary: It is essentially an informative abstract, giving executives the chance to grasp the essentials of the proposal without having to read the details.

Literature Review: The review of literature is a list of relevant books and other sources, each followed by a description and comment on its relevance. The literature review should demonstrate that the researcher have read and analysed the literature relevant to the topic.

Observation Method: It involves human or mechanical observation of what people actually do or what events take place during a buying or consumption situation.

Direct Personal Interview Method: Under this method data can be collected through face-to-face contact with the informant.

Indirect Oral Interview: Under this method of data collection, the investigator contacts third parties generally called 'Witness' who are capable of supplying necessary information.

Mailed Questionnaire Method: Under this method, a list of questions pertaining to the survey which is known as Questionnaire is prepared and sent to the various informants by post.

Sample Questions for UGC NET Examination

01. To test null hypothesis, a researcher uses
  a. T-test
  b. ANOVA
  c. Chi-square
  d. Factor analysis

02. A research problem is feasible only when
  a. It has utility and relevance
  b. It is researchable
  c. It is new and adds something to knowledge
  d. All the above

03. Bibliography given in a research report:
  a. Shows vast knowledge of the researcher
  b. Helps those interested in further research
  c. Has no relevance to research
  d. All the above

04. Fundamental research reflects the ability to
  a. Synthesise new ideas
  b. Expound new principles
  c. Evaluate the existing material concerning research
  d. Study the existing literature regarding various topics

05. A study in which the investigators attempts to trace an effect is known as
  a. Survey research
  b. Ex-post facto research
  c. Historical research
  d. Summative research

06. One of the essential characteristics of research is
   a. Replicability
   b. Generalisability
   c. Usability
   d. Objectivity

07. An investigator studied the census date for a given area and prepared a write-up based on them. Such a write-up is called
   a. Research paper
   b. Article
   c. Thesis
   d. Research report

08. Research can be conducted by a person who:
   a. has studied research methodology
   b. holds a postgraduate degree
   c. possesses thinking and reasoning ability
   d. is a hard worker

09. Which of the following statements is correct?
   a Objectives of research are stated in first chapter of the thesis
   b. Researcher must possess analytical ability
   c. Variability is the source of problem
   d. All the above

10. Which of the following is not the Method of Research?
   a. Observation
   b. Historical
   c. Survey
   d. Philosophical

11. Research can be classified as:
   a. Basic, Applied and Action Research
   b. Quantitative and Qualitative Research
   c. Philosophical, Historical, Survey and Experimental Research
   d. All the above

12. The first step of research is :
   a. Selecting a problem
   b. Searching a problem
   c. Finding a problem
   d. Identifying a problem

13. The research is always-
   a. Verifying the old knowledge
   b. Exploring new knowledge
   c. Filling the gap between knowledge
   d. All of the above

14. The research that applies the laws at the time of field study to draw more and more clear ideas about the problem is
   a. Applied research
   b. Experimental research
   c. Action research
   d. None of these

15. When a research problem is related to heterogeneous population, the most suitable sampling method is
   a. Cluster sampling
   b. Stratified sampling
   c. Convenient sampling
   d. Lottery method

16. The process not needed in experimental research is
   a. Observation
   b. Manipulation and replication
   c. Controlling
   d. Reference collection

17. A research problem is not feasible only when:
   a. It is researchable
   b. It is new and adds something to knowledge
   c. It consists of independent and dependent variable
   d. It has utility and relevance

18. Action research means
   a. A longitudinal research
   b. An applied research
   c. A research initiated to solve an immediate problem
   d. A research with socio-economic objective

19. Research is
   a. Searching again and again
   b. Finding solution to any problem
   c. Working in a scientific way to search for truth of any problem
   d. None of the above

20. A common test in research demands much priority on
   a. Reliability
   b. Useability
   c. Objectivity
   d. All of the above

21. Which of the following is the first step in starting the research process?
   a. Searching sources of information to locate problem
   b. Survey of related literature
   c. Identification of problem
   d. Searching for solutions to the problem

22. If a researcher conducts a research on finding out which administrative style contributes more to institutional effectiveness? This will be an example of
   a. Basic Research
   b. Action Research
   c. Applied Research
   d. None of the above

23. Which of the following phrases is not relevant to describe the meaning of research as a process?
   a. Systematic Activity
   b. Objective Observation
   c. Trial and Error
   d. Problem Solving

24. Which of the following is not an example of a continuous variable?
   a. Family size
   b. Intelligence
   c. Height
   d. Attitude

25. How can the objectivity of the research be enhanced?
   a. Through its impartiality
   b. Through its reliability
   c. Through its validity
   d. All of these

26. Action-research is:
   a. An applied research
   b. A research carried out to solve immediate problems
   c. A longitudinal research
   d. All the above

27. The basis on which assumptions are formulated:
   a. Cultural background of the country
   b. Universities
   c. Specific characteristics of the castes
   d. All of these

28. Which of the following is classified in the category of the developmental research?
   a. Philosophical research
   b. Action research
   c. Descriptive research
   d. All the above

29. We use Factorial Analysis:
   a. To know the relationship between two variables
   b. To test the Hypothesis
   c. To know the difference between two variables
   d. To know the difference among the many variables

30. The term *'phenomenology'* is associated with the process of
   a. Qualitative Research
   b. Analysis of Variance
   c. Correlational Study
   d. Probability Sampling

31. A null hypothesis is
   a. when there is no difference between the variables
   b. the same as research hypothesis
   c. subjective in nature
   d. when there is difference between the variables

32. The research which is exploring new facts through the study of the past is called
   a. Philosophical research
   b. Historical research
   c. Mythological research
   d. Content analysis

33. The process <u>not</u> needed in Experimental Researches is
   a. Observation
   b. Manipulation
   c. Controlling
   d. Content Analysis

34. Manipulation is always a part of
   a. Historical research
   b. Descriptive research
   c. Fundamental research
   d. Experimental research

35. Which correlation co-efficient best explains the relationship between creativity and intelligence?
   a. 1.00
   b. 0.6
   c. 0.5
   d. 0.3

36. A group of experts in a specific area of knowledge assembled at a place and prepared a syllabus for a new course. The process may be termed as
   a. Seminar
   b. Workshop
   c. Conference
   d. Symposium

37. In the process of conducting research "Formulation of Hypothesis" is followed by
   a. Statement of Objectives
   b. Analysis of Data
   c. Selection of Research Tools
   d. Collection of Data

38. Which one of the following does not come under the methods of data classification?
   a. Qualitative
   b. Normative
   c. Spatial
   d. Quantitative

39. The essential qualities of a researcher are
   a. Spirit of free enquiry
   b. reliance on observation and evidence
   c. systematisation or theorising of knowledge
   d. all the above

40. Research is conducted to

I. Generate new knowledge II. Not to develop a theory
III. Obtain research degree IV. Reinterpret existing knowledge

Which of the above are correct?

I, III & II   III, II & IV   II, I & III
I, III & IV

41. Which of the following variables cannot be expressed in quantitative terms?
   a. Socio-economic Status
   b. Marital Status
   c. Numerical Aptitude
   d. Professional Attitude

42. A doctor studies the relative effectiveness of two drugs of dengue fever. His research would be classified as
   a. Descriptive Survey
   b. Experimental Research
   c. Case Study
   d. Ethnography

43. Generalised conclusion on the basis of a sample is technically known as:
   a. Data analysis and interpretation
   b. Parameter inference
   c. Statistical inference
   d. All of the above

44. The experimental study is based on :
   a. The manipulation of variables
   b. Conceptual parameters
   c. Replication of research
   d. Survey of literature

45. The main characteristic of scientific research is :
   a. empirical
   b. Theoretical
   c. experimental
   d. all of the above

46. Authenticity of a research finding is its :
   a. Originality
   b. Validity
   c. Objectivity
   d. All of the above

47. Which technique is generally followed when the population is finite?
   a. Area Sampling Technique
   b. Purposive Sampling Technique
   c. Systematic Sampling Technique
   d. None of the above

48. Which of the following options are the main tasks of research in modern society?

I. To keep pace with the advancement in knowledge.
II. To discover new things.
III. To write a critique on the earlier writings.
IV. To systematically examine and critically analyse the investigations sources with objectivity.

IV, II and I I, II and III I and III
II, III and IV

49. Match List-I (Interviews) with List-II (Meaning) and select the correct answer from the code given below :

List - I (Interviews)	**List - II (Meaning)**
Structured interviews	(i) greater flexibility approach
Unstructured interviews	(ii) attention on the questions to be answered
Focussed interviews	(iii) individual life experience
Clinical interviews	(iv) Predetermined question
	(v) non-directive

Code :

(iv)	(i)	(ii)	(iii)
(ii)	(iv)	(i)	(iii)
(v)	(ii)	(iv)	(i)
(i)	(iii)	(v)	(iv)

50. What do you consider as the main aim of inter disciplinary research?

a. To bring out holistic approach to research.
b. To reduce the emphasis of single subject in research domain.
c. To over simplify the problem of research.
d. To create a new trend in research methodology.

51. One of the aims of the scientific method in research is to :

a. Improve data interpretation
b. Eliminate spurious relations
c. Confirm triangulation
d. Introduce new variables

52. The depth of any research can be judged by :

a. Title of the research.
b. Objectives of the research.
c. Total expenditure on the research.
d. Duration of the research.

53. Which one of the following is not a non-parametric test?
   a. t-test
   b. Sign test
   c. Chi-square test
   d. Run test

54. Identify the correct sequence of research steps :
   a. Selection of topic, review of literature, data collection, interpretation of findings
   b. Review of literature, selection of topic, data collection, interpretation of findings
   c. Selection of topic, data collection, review of literature, interpretation of findings
   d. Selection of topic, review of literature, interpretation of findings, data collection

55. Deconstruction is a popular method of research in
   a. Basic Science
   b. Applied Science
   c. Social Science
   d. Literature

56. With which one of the following techniques communality is associated?
   a. Univariate analysis
   b. Factor analysis
   c. Case studies
   d. SWOT analysis

57. The variable which impacts the relationship between an independent variable and a dependent variable is known as
   a. antecedent variable
   b. precedent variable
   c. predictor variable
   d. control variable

58. Which one of the following is a nonprobability sampling method?
   a. Simple Random Sampling
   b. Stratified Sampling
   c. Cluster Sampling
   d. Quota Sampling

59. In a thesis, figures and tables are included in
   a. the appendix
   b. a separate chapter
   c. the concluding chapter
   d. the text itself

60. A thesis statement is
  a. an observation
  b. a fact
  c. an assertion
  d. a discussion

61. The research approach of Max Weber to understand how people create meanings in natural settings is identified as
  a. positive paradigm
  b. critical paradigm
  c. natural paradigm
  d. interpretative paradigm

62. Which one of the following is a non-probability sampling?
  a. Simple random
  b. Purposive
  c. Systematic
  d. Stratified

63. The research stream of immediate application is
  a. Conceptual research
  b. Action research
  c. Fundamental research
  d. Empirical research

64. Which is the main objective of research?
  a. To review the literature
  b. To summarise what is already known
  c. To get an academic degree
  d. To discover new facts or to make fresh interpretation of known facts

65. Sampling error decreases with the
  a. decrease in sample size
  b. increase in sample size
  c. process of randomisation
  d. process of analysis

66. The principles of fundamental research are used in
  a. action research
  b. applied research
  c. philosophical research
  d. historical research

67. The sequential operations in scientific research are
  a. Co-variation, Elimination of Spurious Relations, Generalisation, Theorisation

b. Generalisation, Co-variation, Theorisation, Elimination of Spurious Relations
c. Theorisation, Generalisation, Elimination of Spurious Relations, Co-variation
d. Elimination of Spurious Relations, Theorisation, Generalisation, Co-variation.

68. In sampling, the lottery method is used for
a. Interpretation
b. Theorisation
c. Conceptualisation
d. Randomisation

69. A research paper
a. Is a compilation of information on a topic.
b. Contains original research as deemed by the author.
c. Contains peer-reviewed original research or evaluation of research conducted by others.
d. Can be published in more than one journal.

70. Which one of the following belongs to the category of good 'research ethics'?
a. Publishing the same paper in two research journals without telling the editors.
b. Conducting a review of the literature that acknowledges the contributions of other people in the relevant field or relevant prior work.
c. Trimming outliers from a data set without discussing your reasons in a research paper.
d. Including a colleague as an author on a research paper in return for a favour even though the colleague did not make a serious contribution to the paper.

71. Which of the following sampling methods is not based on probability?
a. Simple Random Sampling
b. Stratified Sampling
c. Quota Sampling
d. Cluster Sampling

72. A workshop is
a. A conference for discussion on a topic.
b. A meeting for discussion on a topic.
c. A class at a college or a university in which a teacher and the students discuss a topic.

d. A brief intensive course for a small group emphasising the development of a skill or technique for solving a specific problem.

73. A working hypothesis is
a. A proven hypothesis for an argument.
b. Not required to be tested.
c. A provisionally accepted hypothesis for further research.
d. A scientific theory.

74. Which one of the following is an indication of the quality of a research journal?
a. Impact factor
b. h-index
c. g-index
d. i10-index

75. Good 'research ethics' means
a. Not disclosing the holdings of shares/stocks in a company that sponsors your research.
b. Assigning a particular research problem to one Ph.D./ research student only.
c. Discussing with your colleagues confidential data from a research paper that you are reviewing for an academic journal.
d. Submitting the same research manuscript for publishing in more than one journal.

76. Which of the following sampling methods is based on probability?
a. Convenience sampling
b. Quota sampling
c. Judgement sampling
d. Stratified sampling

77. Which one of the following references is written according to American Psychological Association (APA) format?
a. Sharma, V. (2010). Fundamentals of Computer Science. New Delhi : Tata McGraw Hill
b. Sharma, V. 2010. Fundamentals of Computer Science. New Delhi : Tata McGraw Hill
c. Sharma, V. 2010. Fundamentals of Computer Science, New Delhi : Tata McGraw Hill
d. Sharma, V. (2010), Fundamentals of Computer Science, New Delhi : Tata McGraw Hill

78. Arrange the following steps of research in correct sequence :

(1) Identification of research problem
(2) Listing of research objectives
(3) Collection of data
(4) Methodology
(5) Data analysis
(6) Results and discussion

a. 1 – 2 – 3 – 4 – 5 – 6
b. 1 – 2 – 4 – 3 – 5 – 6
c. 2 – 1 – 3 – 4 – 5 – 6
d. 2 – 1 – 4 – 3 – 5 – 6

79. Identify the incorrect statement :

a. A hypothesis is made on the basis of limited evidence as a starting point for further investigations.
b. A hypothesis is a basis for reasoning without any assumption of its truth.
c. Hypothesis is a proposed explanation for a phenomenon.
d. Scientific hypothesis is a scientific theory.

80. Which is a â-error

a. Accepting a hypothesis when it is true
b. Accepting a hypothesis when it is false
c. Rejecting a hypothesis when it is true
d. Rejecting a hypothesis when it is false

81. When planning to do as social research, it is better to

a. approach the topic with an open mind
b. do a pilot study before getting stuck into it
c. be familiar with literature on the topic
d. forget about theory because this is a very practical

82. When academicians are called to deliver lecture or presentation to an audience on certain topics or a set of topics of educational nature, it is called

a. Training Programme
b. Seminar
c. Workshop
d. Symposium

83. The core elements of a dissertation are

a. Introduction; Data Collection; Data Analysis; Conclusions and Recommendations

b. Executive Summary; Literature review; Data gathered; Conclusions; Bibliography
c. Research Plan; Research Data; Analysis; References
d. Introduction; Literature Review; Research Methodology; Results; Discussion and Conclusion

84. What is a Research Design ?
a. A way of conducting research that is not grounded in theory.
b. The choice between using qualitative or quantitative methods.
c. The style in which you present your research findings e.g a graph.
d. A framework for every stage of the collection and analysis of data.

85. '*Sampling Cases*' means
a. Sampling using a sampling frame
b. Identifying people who are suitable for research
c. Literally the researcher's brief case
d. Sampling of people, newspapers, television programmes etc.

86. The frequency distribution of a research data which is symmetrical in shape similar to a normal distribution but center peak is much higher, is
a Skewed
b. Mesokurtic
c. Leptokurtic
d. Platykurtic

87. If á = 0.05 and â = 0.10, the power of that hypothesis test is
a. 0.15
b. 0.90
c. 0.85
d. 0.95

88. A researcher should
a. Be constrained by the research of others
b. Use even anonymous sources if they appear relevant
c. Use only sources that appear credible
d. None of the above

89. Triangulation involves
a. Collecting data from variety of different sources
b. Consulting the works of three other researchers

c. Consulting the works of authors with the same perspective as the researcher

d. The use of three different research tools in one study.

90. Qualitative research is

a. Not as rigorous as quantitative research

b. Primarily concerned with in-depth exploration of phenomena

c. Primarily concerned with the collection and analysis of numerical data

d. Primarily concerned with the quality of the research.

91. Which of the following is not an essential element of report writing?

a. Research methodology

b. Reference

c. Conclusion

d. None of these

92. Testing hypothesis is a ________

a. Inferential statistics

b. Descriptive statistics

c. Data preparation

d. Data analysis

93. What is the purpose of doing research

a. To identify problem

b. To find the solution

c. Both a and b

d. None of the above

94. In group interview there are ______

a. One interviewer and one interviewee

b. More than One interviewer and one interviewee

c. One interviewer and more than one interviewee

d. More than One interviewer and more than one interviewee

95. Which of the following are associated with behavioural observation?

a. Non-verbal analysis

b. Linguistic analysis

c. Spatial analysis

d. All of these

96. Uniting various qualitative methods with quantitative methods can be called as
   a. Coalesce
   b. Triangulation
   c. Bipartite
   d. Impassive

97. Which method can be applicable for collecting qualitative data
   a. Artifacts (Visual)
   b. People
   c. Media products (textual, visual and sensory)
   d. All of these

98. The non-random sampling type that involves selecting a convenience sample from a population with a specific set of characteristics for your research study is called _____.
   a. Convenience sampling
   b. Quota sampling
   c. Purposive sampling
   d. Snowball sampling

99. A number calculated with complete population data and quantifies a characteristic of the population is called which of the following?
   a. A datum
   b. A statistic
   c. A parameter
   d. A population

100. When each member of a population has an equally likely chance of being selected, this is called:
   a. A non-random sampling method
   b. A quota sample
   c. A snowball sample
   d. An Equal probability selection method

Answers: Try to Solve Yourself.

01:	02:	03:	04:	05:	06:	07:	08:	09:	10:
11:	12:	13:	14:	15:	16:	17:	18:	19:	20:
21:	22:	23:	24:	25:	26:	27:	28:	29:	30:
31:	32:	33:	34:	35:	36:	37:	38:	39:	40:
41:	42:	43:	44:	45:	46:	47:	48:	49:	50:
51:	52:	53:	54:	55:	56:	57:	58:	59:	60:

61:	62:	63:	64:	65:	66:	67:	68:	69:	70:
71:	72:	73:	74:	75:	76:	77:	78:	79:	80:
81:	82:	83:	84:	85:	86:	87:	88:	89:	90:
91:	92:	93:	94:	95:	96:	97:	98:	99:	100:

Research Support Provided by Government of India (ICSSR)

Indian Council of Social Science Research (ICSSR), New Delhi

Indian Council of Social Science Research (ICSSR) was established in the year of 1969 by the Government of India to promote research in social sciences in the country. With the following functions:

1. Reviewing the progress of social science research and give advice to its users;
2. Sponsoring social science research programmes and projects and administer grants to institutions and individuals for research in social sciences;
3. Institutionalising and administering scholarships and fellowships for research in social sciences;
4. Indicating areas in which social science research is to be promoted and adopt special measures for development of research in neglected or new areas;
5. Giving financial support to institutions, associations, and journals engaged in social science research;
6. Arranging for technical training in research methodology and to provide guidance for research;
7. Coordinating research activities and encourage programmes for interdisciplinary research;
8. Developing and supporting centers for documentation services and supply of data;
9. Organising, sponsor, and finance seminars, workshops and study groups;
10. Undertaking publication and assist publication of journals and books in social sciences;

11. Advising the Government of India on all matters pertaining to social science research as may be referred to it from time to time;
12. Taking such measures generally as may be necessary from time to time to promote social science research and its utilisation.

NASSDOC

National Social Science Documentation Centre is India's premier information centre for research and innovations in social sciences was established in 1969 as a Division of the ICSSR with the objective to provide library and information support services to researchers in social sciences; those working in academic institutions, autonomous research organisations, policy making, planning and research units of government departments, business and industry etc. NASSDOC also provides guidance to libraries of ICSSR Regional Centres and ICSSR supported Research Institutes.

Facilities Available at NASSDOC

The following facilities are available at the NASSDOC located throughout the country.

1. Documentation Library and Reference Service;
2. Collection of unpublished doctoral dissertations, research project reports, current and old volumes of social science journals of Indian and foreign origin;
3. Literature Search Service from printed and digital databases, i.e. CD-ROMS, floppies, Online database etc;
4. Compilation of short bibliographies on request;
5. Study grant to doctoral students for collection of research material from various libraries located in different parts of India;
6. Financial assistance is provided for taking up bibliographical and documentation projects;
7. Document Delivery Service is provided by procuring books and journals on Inter-library loan or by photocopying the documents;
8. Short-term training courses are organised for the research scholars, social scientists, librarians and IT professionals to acquaint them with the latest information and communication technology; and
9. Cyber Cafe, to facilitate access to internet resources on social sciences.

Research Institute Funded by Indian Council of Social Science Research (ICSSR)

Following are the oranisations which are designated as research institute and funded by the Indian Council of Social Science Research (ICSSR).

1. Institute for Social and Economic Change (ISEC), Bangalore
2. Centre for Development Studies (CDS), Thiruvananthapuram
3. Centre for Studies in Social Sciences (CSSS), Kolkata
4. Gandhian Institute of Studies (GIS), Varanasi
5. A.N. Sinha Institute of Social Studies (ANSISS), Patna
6. Institute of Public Enterprise (IPE), Hyderabad
7. Institute of Economic Growth (IEG), Delhi
8. Centre for the Study of Developing Societies (CSDS), Delhi
9. Centre for Social Studies (CSS), Surat
10. Madras Institute of Development Studies (MIDS), Chennai
11. Indian Institute of Education (IIE), Pune
12. Giri Institute of Development Studies (GIDS), Lucknow
13. Centre for Policy Research (CPR), Delhi
14. Sardar Patel Institute of Economic and Social Research (SPIESR), Ahmedabad
15. G.B. Pant Social Science Institute (GBPSSI), Allahabad
16. Council for Social Development (CSD), Hyderabad
17. Institute of Development Studies (IDS), Jaipur
18. Centre for Research in Rural and Industrial Development (CRRID), Chandigarh
19. Centre for Women's Development Studies (CWDS), Delhi
20. Centre for Economic and Social Studies (CESS), Hyderabad

21. NKC Centre for Development Studies (NKCCDS), Bhubaneswar
22. Gujarat Institute of Development Research (GIDR), Ahmedabad
23. Institute for Studies in Industrial Development (ISID), Delhi
24. O.K.D. Institute of Social Change and Development (OKDISCD), Guwahati
25. Centre for Multi-Disciplinary Development Research (CMDR), Dharwad
26. Dr. Babasaheb Ambedkar National Institute of Social Sciences (BANISS), Mhow
27. Madhya Pradesh Institute of Social Science Research (MPISSR), Ujjain

Regional Centers under ICSSR

- Eastern Regional Centre, Kolkata
- North-Eastern Regional Centre, Shillong
- North-Western Regional Centre, Chandigarh
- Northern Regional Centre, New Delhi
- Southern Regional Centre, Hyderabad
- Western Regional Centre, Mumbai

Bibliography

1. Gopal, M.H, *An introduction 10 research procedure in social sciences,* Mumbai: Asian Publishing House, New Delhi, 1970.
2. Gupta, S.P., *Statistical Methods,* * New Delhi: Sultan Chand & Sons, 2002.
3. Kothari, C. R., *Research Methodology- Methods and Techniques.* Mumbai: Wishwa Prakashan, 2003.
4. Paul., E.Green, Donald S. Tull, and Gerald Albaum, *Research for marketing decisions*, New Delhi: Prentice, Hall of India, 2003.
5. Sadhu, A.N. and Amarjith Singh, *Research Methodology in Social Sciences,* New Delhi, Himalaya Publishing House, 1980.
6. Saravanavel, P., *Research Methodology,* Allahabad: Kitab Mahal, 2003.
7. Sharma, S.P. and Mukahrjee, S.P., *Research in Economics, Commerce, Methodology and sources,* Indian Bibliographical centre: Varanasi, 1976.
8. Thanulingam, N., *Research Methodology,* Mumbai: Himalaya Publishing House, 2000.
9. Venugopalan, K., *Research Methodology,* Calicut university press, 2008.
10. Wilkinson, T.S. and Bhandarkar, P.L., *Methodology and Techniques of Social Research, Bombay:* Himalaya Publishing House, 1979.
11. Young, Pauline V., *Scientific Social Surveys and Research,* 3rd ed., New York: Prentice Hall, 1960.
12. Study Material, "Research Methodology" Sikkim Manipal University.
13. Wisdomjobs.com/research methodology.
14. www.icssr.org.
15. www.ibm.com.

Table 1
Area Under Normal Curve

An entry in the table is the proportion under the entire curve which is between z=0 and a positive value of z. Areas for negative values for z are obtained by symmetry

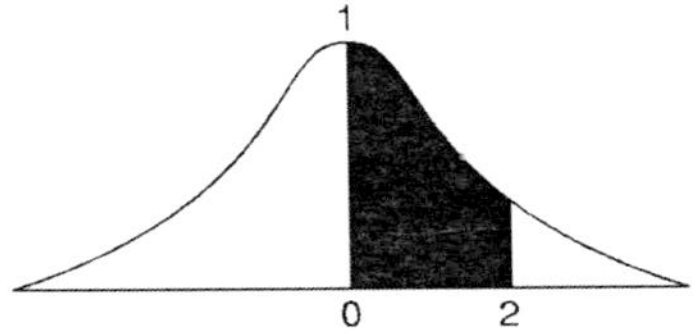

z	.0	0.01	.02	.03	.04	.05	.06	.07	.08	.09
.0	.0000	.0040	.0080	.0120	.0160	.0199	.0239	.0279	.0319	.0359
.1	.0398	.0438	.0478	.0517	.0557	.0596	.0636	.0675	.0714	.0753
.2	.0793	.0832	.0871	.0910	.0948	.0987	.1026	.1061	.1103	.1141
.3	.1179	.1217	.1255	.1293	.1331	.1368	.1406	.1443	.1480	.1517
.4	.1554	.1591	.1628	.1664	.1700	.1736	.1772	.1808	.1844	.1879
.5	.1915	.1950	.1985	.2019	.2051	.2088	.2123	.2157	.2190	.2221
.6	.2257	.2291	.2324	.2357	.2389	.2422	.2454	.2486	.2517	.2549
.7	.2580	.2611	.2642	.2673	.2903	.2734	.2764	.2794	.2823	.2852
.8	.2881	.2910	.2939	.2967	.2995	.3023	.3051	.3078	.3106	.3133
.9	.3159	.3186	.3212	.3238	.3261	.3289	.3315	.3340	.3365	.3389
1.0	.3413	.3438	.3461	.3485	.3508	.3531	.3554	.3577	.3599	.3621

(Contd.)

(Contd.Table 1)

1.1	.3643	.3665	.3686	.3708	.3729	.3749	.3770	.3790	.3810	.3830
1.2	.3849	.3869	.3888	.3907	.3925	.3944	.3962	.3980	.3997	.4015
1.3	.4032	.4049	.4066	.4082	.4099	.4115	.4131	.4147	.4162	.4177
1.4	.4192	.4207	.4222	.4236	.4251	.4265	.4279	.4292	.4306	.4319
1.5	.4332	.4345	.4357	.4370	.4382	.4394	.4406	.4418	.4429	.4441
1.6	.4452	.4463	.4474	.4484	.4495	.4505	.4515	.4525	.4535	.4545
1.7	.4554	.4564	.4573	.4582	.4591	.4599	.4608	.4616	.4625	.4633
1.8	.4641	.4649	.4656	.4664	.4671	.4678	.4686	.4693	.4699	.4706
1.9	.4713	.4719	.4726	.4732	.4738	.4744	.4750	.4756	.4761	.4767
2.0	.4772	.4778	.4783	.4788	.4793	.4798	.4803	.4808	.4812	.4817
2.1	.4821	.4826	.4830	.4834	.4838	.4842	.4846	.4850	.4854	.4857
2.2	.4861	.4864	.4868	.4871	.4875	.4878	.4881	.4884	.4887	.4890
2.3	.4893	.4896	.4898	.4901	.4901	.4906	.4909	.4911	.4913	.4916
2.4	.4918	.4920	.4922	.4925	.4927	.4929	.4931	.4932	.4934	.4936
2.5	.4938	.4940	.4941	.4943	.4945	.4946	.4948	.4949	.4951	.4952
2.6	.4953	.4955	.4956	.4957	.4959	.4960	.4961	.4962	.4963	.4964
2.7	.4965	.4966	.4967	.4968	.4969	.4970	.4971	.4972	.4973	.4974
2.8	.4974	.4975	.4976	.4977	.4977	.4978	.4979	.4979	.4980	.4981
2.9	.4981	.4982	.4982	.4983	.4984	.4984	.4985	.4985	.4986	.4986
3.0	.4987	.4987	.4987	.4988	.4988	.4989	.4989	.4989	.4990	.4990

Table 2: Critical Values of Student's t-Distribution

d.f.	Level of significance for two-tailed test					d.f.
	0.20	0.10	0.05	0.02	0.01	
	Level of significance for two-tailed test					
	0.10	0.05	0.025	0.01	0.005	
1	3.078	6.314	12.706	31.821	63.657	1
2	1.886	2.920	4.303	6.965	9.925	2
3	1.638	2.353	3.182	4.541	5.841	3
4	1.533	2.132	2.776	3.747	4.604	4
5	1.476	2.015	2.571	3.365	4.032	5
6	1.440	1.943	2.447	3.143	3.707	6
7	1.415	1.895	2.365	2.998	3.499	7
8	1.397	1.860	2.306	2.896	3.355	8
9	1.383	1.833	2.262	2.821	3.250	9
10	1.372	1.812	2.228	2.764	3.169	10

(Contd.)

(Contd. Table 2)

11	1.363	1.796	2.201	2.718	3.106	11
12	1.356	1.782	2.179	2.681	3.055	12
13	1.350	1.771	2.160	2.650	3.012	13
14	1.345	1.761	2.145	2.624	2.977	14
15	1.341	1.753	2.731	2.602	2.947	15
16	1.337	1.746	2.120	2.583	2.921	16
17	1.333	1.740	2.110	2.567	2.898	17
18	1.330	1.734	2.101	2.552	2.878	18
19	1.328	1.729	2.093	2.539	2.861	19
20	1.325	1.725	2.086	2.528	2.845	20
21	1.323	1.721	2.080	2.518	2.831	21
22	1.321	1.717	2.074	2.508	2.819	22
23	1.319	1.714	2.069	2.500	2.807	23
24	1.318	1.711	2.064	2.492	2.797	24
25	1.316	1.708	2.060	2.485	2.787	25
26	1.315	1.706	2.056	2.479	2.779	26
27	1.314	1.703	2.052	2.473	2.771	27
28	1.313	1.701	2.048	2.467	2.763	28
29	1.311	1.699	2.045	2.462	2.756	29
Infinity	1.282	1.645	1.960	2.326	2.576	Infinity

Table 3: Critical Values of χ^2

Degrees of freedom	Probability under H_0 that of χ^2 > Chi square						
	.99	.95	.50	.10	.05	.02	.01
1	.000157	.00393	.455	2.706	3.841	5.412	6.635
2	.0201	.103	1.386	4.605	5.991	7.824	9.210
3	.115	.352	2.366	6.251	7.815	9.837	11.341
4	.297	.711	3.357	7.779	9.488	11.668	13.277
5	.554	.1145	4.351	9.236	11.070	13.388	15.086
6	.872	1.635	5.348	10.645	12.592	15.033	16.812
7	1.239	2.167	6.346	12.017	14.067	16.622	18.475
8	1.646	2.733	7.344	13.362	15.507	18.168	20.090
9	2.088	3.325	8.343	14.684	16.919	19.679	21.666
10	2.558	3.940	9.342	15.987	18.307	21.161	23.209
11	3.053	4.575	10.341	17.275	19.675	22.618	24.725
12	3.571	5.226	11.340	18.549	21.026	24.054	26.217
13	4.107	5.892	12.340	19.812	22.362	25.472	72.688
14	4.660	6.571	13.339	21.064	23.685	26.873	29.141
15	4.229	7.261	14.339	22.307	24.996	28.259	30.578

(Contd.)

(Contd. Table 3)

16	5.812	7.962	15.338	23.542	26.296	29.633	32.000
17	6.408	8.672	16.338	24.769	27.587	30.995	33.409
18	7.015	9.390	17.338	25.989	28.869	32.346	34.805
19	7.633	10.117	18.338	27.204	30.144	33.687	36.191
20	8.260	10.851	19.337	28.412	31.410	35.020	37.566
21	8.897	11.591	20.337	29.615	32.671	36.343	38.932
22	9.542	12.338	21.337	30.813	33.924	37.659	40.289
23	10.196	13.091	22.337	32.007	35.172	38.968	41.638
24	10.856	13.848	23.337	32.196	36.415	40.270	42.980
25	11.524	14.611	24.337	34.382	37.652	41.566	44.314
26	12.198	15.379	25.336	35.363	38.885	41.856	45.642
27	12.879	16.151	26.336	36.741	40.113	44.140	46.963
28	13.565	16.928	27.336	37.916	41.337	45.419	48.278
29	14.256	17.708	28.336	39.087	42.557	46.693	49.588
30	14.953	18.493	29.336	40.256	43.773	47.962	50.892

Table 4(a): Critical Values of F-Distribution (at 5 per cent)

v_2 \ v_1	1	2	3	4	5	6	8	12	24	∞
1	161.4	199.5	215.7	224.6	230.2	234.0	238.9	243.9	249.1	243.3
2	18.51	19.00	19.16	19.25	19.30	19.33	19.37	19.41	19.45	19.50
3	10.13	9.55	9.28	9.12	9.01	8.94	8.85	8.74	8.64	8.53
4	7.71	6.94	6.59	6.39	6.26	6.16	6.04	5.91	5.77	5.63
5	6.61	5.79	5.41	5.19	5.05	4.95	4.82	4.68	4.53	4.36
6	5.99	5.14	4.76	4.53	4.39	4.28	4.15	4.00	3.84	3.67
7	5.59	4.74	4.35	4.12	3.97	3.87	3.73	3.57	3.41	3.23
8	5.32	4.46	4.07	3.84	3.69	3.58	3.44	3.28	3.12	2.93
9	5.12	4.26	3.86	3.63	3.48	3.37	3.23	3.07	2.90	2.71
10	4.96	4.10	3.71	3.48	3.33	3.22	3.07	2.91	2.74	2.54
11	4.84	3.98	3.59	3.36	3.20	3.09	2.95	2.79	2.61	2.40
12	4.75	3.88	3.49	3.26	3.11	3.00	2.85	2.69	2.51	2.30
13	4.67	3.80	3.41	3.18	3.02	2.92	2.77	2.60	2.42	2.21
14	4.60	3.74	3.34	3.11	2.96	2.85	2.70	2.53	2.35	2.13
15	4.54	3.68	3.29	3.06	2.90	2.79	2.64	2.48	2.29	2.07
16	4.49	3.63	3.24	3.01	2.85	2.74	2.59	2.42	2.24	2.01

(Contd.)

(*Contd. Table 4a*)

17	4.45	3.59	3.20	2.96	2.81	2.70	2.55	2.38	2.19	1.96
18	4.41	3.55	3.16	2.93	2.77	2.66	2.51	2.34	2.15	1.92
19	4.38	3.52	3.13	2.90	2.74	2.63	2.48	2.31	2.11	1.88
20	4.35	3.49	3.10	2.87	2.71	2.60	2.45	2.28	2.08	1.84
21	4.32	3.47	3.07	2.84	2.68	2.57	2.42	2.25	2.05	1.81
22	4.30	3.44	3.05	2.82	2.66	2.55	2.40	2.23	2.03	1.78
23	4.28	3.42	3.03	2.80	2.64	2.53	2.38	2.20	2.01	1.76
24	4.26	3.40	3.01	2.78	2.62	2.51	2.36	2.18	1.98	1.73
25	4.24	3.38	2.99	2.76	2.60	2.49	2.34	2.16	1.96	1.71
26	4.22	3.37	2.98	2.74	2.59	2.47	2.32	2.15	1.95	1.69
27	4.21	3.35	2.96	2.73	2.57	2.46	2.31	2.13	1.93	1.67
28	4.20	3.34	2.95	2.71	2.56	2.45	2.29	2.12	1.91	1.65
29	4.18	3.33	2.93	2.70	2.54	2.43	2.28	2.10	1.90	1.64
30	4.17	3.32	2.92	2.69	2.53	2.42	2.27	2.09	1.89	1.62
40	4.08	3.23	2.84	2.61	2.45	2.34	2.18	2.00	1.79	1.51
60	4.00	3.15	2.76	2.52	2.37	2.25	2.10	1.92	1.70	1.39
120	3.92	3.07	2.68	2.45	2.29	2.17	2.02	1.83	1.61	1.25
∞	3.84	2.99	2.60	2.37	2.21	2.10	1.94	1.75	1.52	1.00

Table 4(b): Critical Values of F-Distribution (at 1 per cent)

v_2 \ v_1	1	2	3	4	5	6	8	12	24	∞
1	4052	4999.5	5403	5625	5764	5859	5982	6106	6235	6366
2	98.50	99.00	99.17	99.25	99.30	99.33	99.37	99.42	99.46	99.50
3	34.12	30.82	29.46	28.71	28.24	27.91	27.49	27.05	26.60	26.13
4	21.20	18.00	16.69	15.98	15.52	15.21	14.80	14.37	13.93	13.45
5	16.26	13.27	12.06	11.39	10.97	10.67	10.29	9.89	9.47	9.02
6	13.75	10.92	9.78	9.15	8.75	8.47	8.10	7.72	7.31	6.88
7	12.25	9.55	8.45	7.85	7.46	7.19	6.84	6.47	6.07	5.65
8	11.26	8.65	7.59	7.01	6.63	6.37	6.03	5.67	5.28	4.86
9	10.56	8.02	6.99	6.42	6.06	5.80	5.47	5.11	4.73	4.31
10	10.04	7.56	6.55	5.99	5.64	5.39	5.06	4.71	4.33	3.91
11	9.65	7.21	6.22	5.87	5.32	5.07	4.74	4.40	4.02	3.60
12	9.33	6.93	5.95	5.41	5.06	4.82	4.50	4.16	3.78	3.36
13	9.07	6.70	5.74	5.21	4.86	4.62	4.30	3.96	3.59	3.17
14	8.86	6.51	5.56	5.04	4.69	4.46	4.14	3.80	3.43	3.00
15	8.68	6.36	5.42	4.89	4.56	4.32	4.00	3.67	3.29	2.87
16	8.53	6.23	5.29	4.77	4.44	4.20	3.89	3.55	3.18	2.75

(Contd. Table 4b)

17	8.40	6.11	5.18	4.67	4.34	4.10	3.79	3.46	3.08	2.65
18	8.29	6.01	5.09	4.58	4.25	4.01	3.71	3.37	3.00	2.57
19	8.18	5.93	5.01	4.50	4.17	3.94	3.63	3.30	3.92	2.49
20	8.10	5.85	4.94	4.43	4.10	3.87	3.56	3.23	2.86	2.42
21	8.02	5.78	4.87	4.37	4.04	3.81	3.51	3.17	2.80	2.36
22	7.95	5.72	4.82	4.31	3.99	3.76	3.45	3.12	2.75	2.31
23	7.88	5.66	4.76	4.26	3.94	3.71	3.41	3.07	2.70	2.26
24	7.82	5.61	4.72	4.22	3.90	3.67	3.36	3.03	2.66	2.21
25	7.77	5.57	4.68	4.18	3.85	3.63	3.32	2.99	2.62	2.17
26	7.72	5.53	4.64	4.14	3.82	3.59	3.20	2.96	2.58	2.10
27	7.68	5.49	4.60	4.11	3.78	3.56	3.26	2.93	2.45	2.13
28	7.64	5.45	4.57	4.07	3.75	3.53	3.23	2.90	2.52	2.06
29	7.60	5.42	4.54	4.04	3.73	3.50	3.20	2.87	2.49	2.03
30	7.56	5.39	4.51	4.02	3.70	3.47	3.17	2.84	2.47	2.01
40	7.31	5.18	4.31	3.83	3.51	3.29	2.99	2.66	2.29	1.80
60	7.08	4.98	4.13	3.65	3.34	3.12	2.82	2.50	2.12	1.60
120	6.85	4.79	3.95	3.48	3.17	2.96	2.66	2.34	1.95	1.38
∞	6.64	4.60	3.78	3.32	3.02	2.80	2.51	2.18	1.79	1.00

(Contd.)

Table 5: Value for Spearman's Rank Correlation (r) for Combined Areas in Both Ta

n	.20	.10	.05	.02	.01	.002
4	.8000	.8000	—	—	—	—
5	.7000	.8000	.9000	.9000	—	—
6	.6000	.7714	.8236	.8857	.9429	—
7	.5357	.6786	.7450	.8571	.8929	.9643
8	.5000	.6190	.7143	.8095	.8571	.9286
9	.4667	.5833	.6833	.7667	.8167	.9000
10	.4424	.5515	.6364	.7333	.7818	.8667
11	.4182	.5273	.6091	.7000	.7455	.8364
12	.3986	.4965	.5804	.6713	.7273	.8182
13	.3791	.4780	.5549	.6429	.6978	.7912
14	.3626	.4593	.5341	.6220	.6747	.7670
15	.3500	.4429	.5179	.6000	.6536	.7464
16	.3382	.4265	.5000	.5824	.6324	.7265
17	.3260	.4118	.4853	.5637	.6152	.7083
18	.3148	.3994	.4716	.5480	.5975	.6904
19	.3070	.3895	.4579	.5333	.5825	.6737
20	.2977	.3789	.4451	.5203	.5684	.6586

(Contd.)

(Contd. Table 5)

21	.2909	.3688	.4351	.5078	.5545	.6455
22	.2829	.3597	.4241	.4963	.5426	.6318
23	.2767	.3518	.4150	.4852	.5306	.6186
24	.2704	.3435	.4061	.4748	.5200	.6070
25	.2646	.3362	.3977	.4654	.5100	.5962
26	.2588	.3299	.3894	.4564	.5002	.5856
27	.2540	.3236	.3822	.4481	.4915	.5757
28	.2480	.3175	.3749	.4401	.4828	.5660
29	.2443	.3113	.3685	.4320	.4744	.5567
30	.2400	.3059	.3620	.4251	.4665	.5479

Table 6: Selected Values of Wilcoxon's (Unpaired) Distribution [W-Min W,] or [Max. W_1-W_1]

s	l	Min W_s	Max W_l	0	1	2	3	4	5	6	7	8	9	10	11	12	13	14	15	16	17	18	19	20
2	2	3	7																					
	3	3	12	.100																				
	4	3	18	.067	.134																			
	5	3	25	.048	.095	.190																		
	6	3	33	.036	.071	.143																		
	7	3	42	.028	.056	.111																		
	8	3	52	.022	.044	.089	.133																	
3	2	6	9	.100																				
	3	6	15	.050	.100																			
	4	6	22	.029	.067	.114																		
	5	6	30	.018	.048	.071	.125																	
	6	6	39	.012	.086	.048	.083	.121																
	7	6	49	.008	.028	.033	.058	.092	.133															
	8	6	60	.006	.022	.024	.042	.067	.097	.139														

(*Contd.*)

(Contd. Table 6)

4	2	10	11	.007	*										
	3	10	18	.029	.057	.114									
	4	10	26	.014	.067	.057	.100								
	5	10	35	.008	.048	.032	.056	.095	.143						
	6	10	45	.005	.086	.019	.033	.057	.086	.129					
	7	10	56	.003	.028	.012	.021	.036	.055	.082	.115				
	8	10	68	.002	.022	.008	.014	.024	.036	.055	.077	.107			
5	3	15	21	.018	.036	.071	.125	*							
	4	15	30	.008	.016	.032	.056	.095	.143						
	5	15	40	.004	.008	.016	.028	.048	.075	.111					
	6	15	51	.002	.004	.009	.015	.026	.041	.063	.089	.123			
	7	15	63	.001	.003	.005	.009	.015	.024	.037	.053	.074	.101		
	8	15	76	.001	.002	.003	.005	.009	.015	.023	.033	.047	.064	.085	.111

(Contd.)

(Contd. Table 6)

s	l	Min W_s	Max W_l	0	1	2	3	4	5	6	7	8	9	10	11	12	13	14	15	16	17	18	19	20
6	3	21	24	.012	.024	*																		
	4	21	34	.005	.010	.019	.033	.067	.086	.129	*													
	5	21	45	.002	.004	.009	.015	.048	.041	.063	.089	.123												
	6	21	57	.001	.002	.004	.008	.086	.021	.032	.047	.066	.090	.120										
	7	21	70	.001	.001	.002	.004	.028	.011	.017	.026	.037	.051	.069	.090	.117								
	8	21	84	.000	.001	.001	.002	.022	.006	.010	.015	.021	.030	.041	.054	.071	.091	.114						
7	4	28	38	.003	.006	.012	.021	.036	.055*															
	5	28	50	.001	.003	.005	.009	.015	.024	.037	.053	.074	.101											
	6	28	63	.001	.001	.002	.004	.007	.011	.017	.026	.037	.051	.069	.090	.117								
	7	28	77	.000	.001	.001	.002	.003	.006	.009	.013	.019	.027	.036	.049	.064	.082	.104						
	8	28	92	.000	.000	.001	.001	.002	.003	.005	.007	.010	.014	.020	.027	.036	.047	.060	.076	.095	.116			
8	4	36	42	.002	.004	.008	.014	*																
	5	36	55	.001	.002	.003	.005	.009	.015	.023	.033	.047	.064	*										
	6	36	69	.000	.001	.001	.002	.004	.006	.010	.015	.021	.030	.041	.054	.071	.091	.114						
	7	36	84	.000	.000	.001	.001	.002	.003	.005	.007	.010	.014	.020	.027	.036	.047	.060	.076	.095	.116			
	8	36	100	.000	.000	.000	.001	.001	.001	.002	.003	.005	.007	.010	.014	.019	.025	.032	.041	.052	.065	.080	.097	.117

Table 7: Critical Values of T in the Wilcoxon Matched Paris Test

	Level of significance for one-tailed test		
	.025	.01	.005
	Level of significance for two-tailed test		
n	.05	.02	.01
6	0	—	—
7	2	0	—
8	4	2	0
9	6	3	2
10	8	5	3
11	11	7	5
12	14	10	7
13	17	13	10
14	21	16	13
15	25	20	16

(Contd.)

(Contd.Table 7)

16	30	24	20
17	35	28	23
18	40	33	28
19	46	38	32
20	52	43	38
21	59	49	43
22	66	56	49
23	73	62	55
24	81	69	61
25	89	77	68

(Contd.)

Table 8: Cumulative Binomial Probabilities P(r <r | n, p)

n	r_0	.10	.25	.40	.50
1	0	.9000	.7500	.6000	.5000
	1	1.0000	1.0000	1.0000	1.0000
2	0	.8100	.5625	.3600	.2500
	1	.9900	.9375	.8400	.7500
	2	1.0000	1.0000	1.0000	1.0000
5	0	.5905	.2373	.0778	.0313
	1	.9185	.6328	.3370	.1875
	2	.9914	.8965	.6826	.5000
	3	.9995	.9844	.9130	.8125
	4	.9999	.9990	.9898	.9687
	5	1.0000	1.0000	1.0000	1.0000
10	0	.3487	.0563	.0060	.0010
	1	.7361	.2440	.0463	.0108
	2	.9298	.5256	.1672	.0547
	3	.9872	.7759	.3822	.1719
	4	.9984	.9219	.6330	.3770
	5	.9999	.9803	.8337	.6230

(Contd.)

(Contd. Table 8)

	6	1.0000	.9965	.9452	.8281
	7	1.0000	.9996	.9877	.9453
	8	1.0000	1.0000	.9983	.9892
	9	1.0000	1.0000	.9999	.9990
	10	1.0000	1.0000	1.0000	1.0000
12	0	.2824	.0317	.0022	.0002
	1	.6590	.1584	.0196	.0031
	2	.8891	.3907	.0835	.0192
	3	.9740	.6488	.2254	.0729
	4	.9963	.8424	.4382	.1937
	5	9999	.9456	.6652	.3871
	6	1.0000	.9857	.8418	.6127
	7	1.0000	.9972	.9427	.8064
	8	1.0000	.9996	.9847	.9269
	9	1.0000	1.0000	.9972	.9806
	10	1.0000	1.0000	9997	.9977
	11	1.0000	1.0000	1.0000	1.0000
	12	1.0000	1.0000	1.0000	1.0000

(Contd.)

(Contd. Table 8)

n	r_0	.10	.25	.40	.50
20	0	.1216	.0032	.0000	.0000
	1	.3917	.0243	.0005	.0000
	2	.6768	.0912	.0036	.0002
	3	.8669	.2251	.0159	.0013
	4	.9567	.4148	.0509	.0059
	5	.9886	.6171	.1255	.0207
	6	.9975	.7857	.2499	.0577
	7	.9995	.8981	.4158	.1316
	8	.9999	.9590	.5955	.2517
	9	1.0000	.9861	.7552	.4119
	10	1.0000	.9960	.8723	.5881
	11	1.0000	.9990	.9433	.7483
	12	1.0000	.9998	.9788	.8684
	13	1.0000	1.0000	.9934	.9423
	14	1.0000	1.0000	.9983	.9793
	15	1.0000	1.0000	.9996	.9941
	16	1.0000	1.0000	1.0000	.9987
	17	1.0000	1.0000	1.0000	.9998
	18	1.0000	1.0000	1.0000	1.0000
	19	1.0000	1.0000	1.0000	1.0000
	20	1.0000	1.0000	1.0000	1.0000

Table 9: Selected Critical Values of S in the Kendall's Coefficient of Concordance

Values at 5% level of significance

k	N					Some additional values for $N = 3$	
	3	4	5	6	7	k	s
3			64.4	103.9	157.3	9	54.0
4		49.5	88.4	143.3	217.0	12	71.9
5		62.6	112.3	182.4	276.2	14	83.8
6		75.7	136.1	221.4	335.2	16	95.8
8	48.1	101.7	183.7	299.0	453.1	18	107.7
10	60.0	127.8	231.2	376.7	571.0		
15	89.8	192.9	349.8	570.5	864.9		
20	119.7	258.0	468.5	764.4	1158.7		

(Contd.)

Values at 1% level of significance

3			75.6	122.8	185.6	9	75.9
4		61.4	109.3	176.2	265.0	12	103.5
5		80.5	142.8	229.4	343.8	14	121.9
6		99.5	176.1	282.4	422.6	16	140.2
8	66.8	137.4	242.7	388.3	579.9	18	158.6
10	85.1	175.3	309.1	494.0	737.0		
15	131.0	269.8	475.2	758.2	1129.5		
20	177.0	364.2	641.2	1022.2	1521.9		

Table 10: Table Showing Critical Values of A-Statistic of any Given Value of n-1, Corresponding to Various Levels of Probability

$n-1^*$	Level of significance for two-tailed test				
	.05	.025	.01	.005	.0005
	Level of significance for two-tailed test				
	.10	.05	.02	.01	.001
1	2	3	4	5	6
1	0.5125	0.5031	0.50049	0.50012	0.5000012
2	0.412	0.369	0.347	0.340	0.334
3	0.385	0.324	0.286	0.272	0.254
4	0.376	0.304	0.257	0.238	0.211
5	0.372	0.293	0.240	0.218	0.184
6	0.370	0.286	0.230	0.205	0.167
7	0.369	0.281	0.222	0.196	0.155
8	0.368	0.278	0.217	0.190	0.146
9	0.368	0.276	0.213	0.185	0.139
10	0.368	0.274	0.210	0.181	0.134

(Contd.)

(Contd. Table 10)

11	0.368	0.273	0.207	0.178	0.130
12	0.368	0.271	0.205	0.176	0.126
13	0.368	0.270	0.204	0.174	0.124
14	0.368	0.270	0.202	0.172	0.121
15	0.368	0.269	0.201	0.170	0.119
16	0.368	0.268	0.200	0.169	0.117
17	0.368	0.268	0.199	0.168	0.116
18	0.368	0.267	0.198	0.167	0.114
19	0.368	0.267	0.197	0.166	0.113
20	0.368	0.266	0.197	0.165	0.112
21	0.368	0.266	0.196	0.165	0.111
22	0.368	0.266	0.196	0.164	0.110
23	0.368	0.266	0.195	0.163	0.109
24	0.368	0.265	0.195	0.163	0.108
25	0.368	0.265	0.194	0.162	0.108

(Contd.)

(Contd.Table 10)

26	0.368	0.265	0.194	0.162	0.107
27	0.368	0.265	0.193	0.161	0.107
28	0.368	0.265	0.193	0.161	0.106
29	0.368	0.264	0.193	0.161	0.106
30	0.368	0.264	0.193	0.150	0.105
1	2	3	4	5	6
40	0.368	0.263	0.191	0.158	0.102
60	0.369	0.262	0.189	0.155	0.099
120	0.369	0.261	0.187	0.153	0.095
∞	0.370	0.260	0.185	0.151	0.092

(Contd.)

Index

M

N

O

P

Q

R

S